STUDY GUIDE FOR
Merriman's
A History of Modern Europe

VOLUME TWO

STUDY GUIDE FOR
Merriman's
A History of
MODERN EUROPE

by **Kathleen Nilan**
Arizona State University West

W. W. NORTON & COMPANY, INC.
New York / London

Cover illustration: *Prague, Nostalgia*, 1938, by Oskar Kokoschka.
Private collection. Photograph courtesy Christie's, London.

ISBN 0-393-97017-5 (pbk.)

W. W. Norton & Company, Inc., 500 Fifth Avenue, New York, N.Y. 10110
http://web.wwnorton.com
W. W. Norton & Company Ltd., 10 Coptic Street, London WC1A 1PU

2 3 4 5 6 7 8 9 0

Contents

Preface

Now, what I want is Facts. Teach these boys and girls nothing but Facts. Facts alone are wanted in life. Plant nothing else, and root out everything else.

—CHARLES DICKENS, *Hard Times*

. . . a collection of facts is no more science than a heap of stones is a house.

—JULES-HENRI POINCARÉ

Too many students, perhaps the victims at some time in their educational careers of a fact-obsessed Mr. Gradgrind, are convinced that history involves nothing more than the memorization of heaps of dry-as-dust facts. However, as Poincaré reminds us, the true study of history, like science, involves much more than collecting facts: it requires using facts to analyze the world of the past.

Of course, learning the basics about a historical event or development—the who, what, where, and when—is important because it allows us to begin to look for answers to the critical questions of how and why something happened in the past. But history only becomes a meaningful and engaging pursuit—a full-blooded story of the past—when the budding historian moves beyond a simple mastery of historical detail to a more sophisticated interpretation of human experience over time.

This Study Guide has been designed to provide you with an opportunity to test your knowledge of the factual information presented in John Merriman's *A History of Modern Europe* and to test your ability to make sense of these facts. Most importantly, the Study Guide is intended to allow you to engage with the text as an active apprentice to the study of history. When used conscientiously, it will help you to build your "historical imagination" on a solid foundation of both fact and analysis.

USING THE STUDY GUIDE

As students of history soon learn, the study of history requires a considerable amount of thoughtful and attentive reading of a variety of texts. In order to make the fullest and most efficient use of your study time, begin by reading each chapter of the textbook carefully, paying attention to the specific historical information it presents. As you read, you may wish to consult the list of "people and terms to identify" (Exercise 3 in the Study Guide), marking each item as it appears in the text. Having read through the text once, return to it for a second, more rapid

reading, this time focusing on the broad themes and general outline of events discussed in that particular chapter. This is a good time to highlight the most important facts and points of historical analysis: Having already familiarized yourself with the contents of the chapter, you will be better able to decide which information is most important and will be most useful to you when you return to the chapter to review for an exam.

Once you feel confident that you have thoroughly assimilated the contents of the chapter, turn to the Study Guide and work through the exercises *without reference to the text*. Try to answer as many questions as possible from memory, rather than simply copying information from the textbook into the Study Guide. This is the only way that you can be sure that you have truly mastered the material. Once you have completed the exercises, correct your work using the textbook and the study-drill answers provided at the end of the Study Guide chapter.

You will derive the maximum benefit from your work if you do it far enough in advance to be able to *review* the text and your Study Guide answers before the class meeting for which they have been assigned. This will further reinforce your knowledge of the chapter contents and will greatly improve your comprehension of classroom lectures, discussion, and other activities.

Each chapter of the Study Guide contains an outline of the corresponding textbook chapter, sets of exercises designed to test your knowledge of geography and history, and short excerpts from documents contemporary to the events narrated in the textbook. The following instructions provide guidelines for the use of these materials.

The CHAPTER OUTLINE consists of a brief summary of the key points made in each chapter. It allows you to review the material quickly and efficiently, whether in preparation for a class meeting or an exam. Have you really understood the information presented in the textbook? Test your comprehension by writing your own outline and then comparing it with the Study Guide outline. Writing a concise summary of a substantial body of information is challenging, but it will help you to understand and to remember what you have learned, and it will also help you to hone your note-taking skills.

Students of history should carry an accurate map of the world inside their head. Every chapter of the Study Guide contains a set of HISTORICAL GEOGRAPHY exercises, including one or more blank maps, a list of places to locate on these maps, and several questions. As you are reading the textbook chapter, refer frequently to the maps provided, focusing

especially on finding the places listed in the Study Guide. When you feel confident about your knowledge of this geography, complete the MAP EXERCISES *without reference to the textbook maps*. Your knowledge of historical geography will be greatly reinforced by frequent review. Every few weeks, try quizzing yourself on all of the map exercises you have completed up to that point.

The MAP QUESTIONS ask you to put your knowledge of geography to use in analyzing historical situations and developments. They refer to specific problems of geography raised by material covered in the textbook.

The names, events, and other items listed under PEOPLE AND TERMS TO IDENTIFY have been selected from among the many others presented in the textbook both for their historical importance and for their representativeness. When you "identify" each item, you should be able to do two things:

1. Briefly but thoroughly *describe* the person or thing, remembering to explain *who* was involved, *what* happened, and *where*, *when*, and *how* it happened.
2. Explain the *significance* of the item with reference to the broad historical trends or developments discussed in the text.

The STUDY QUESTIONS ask you to consider specific problems raised by the historical developments covered in each chapter. Once again, make every effort to answer these questions without reference to the text. You can check the accuracy of your answers after you have responded to the questions.

Illustrations provided in the textbook can help you to develop a sense of both how people in the past saw themselves and what their world looked like. The questions in the ANALYZING ART AND ARTIFACTS section of the Study Guide ask you to "read" visual images as historical documents. As you work your way through the textbook, you should make an effort to become a sophisticated reader of visual documents and to familiarize yourself with the ways in which art and material culture are transformed by changing historical circumstances.

Changes in technology—whether agricultural, industrial, military, medical, or related to communications and transportation—often have a significant impact on history, and are themselves the product of changing human needs and interests. The questions posed in the TECHNOLOGY AND HISTORY section ask you to explore the reasons why technologies change and to reflect on how these changes affect human experience.

The questions posed under the heading of HISTORICAL ANALYSIS: INTERPRETIVE ESSAYS ask you to synthesize the information presented in each chapter and to analyze large-scale historical developments. Your responses should take the form of well-organized essays that demonstrate both your mastery of the historical record and your ability to develop a sustained historical argument. While you will undoubtedly not be able to write a full-length answer to every one of these questions, preparing outlines and thinking through possible responses can be helpful preparation for exams.

When historians write history, they rely on a variety of historical documents to reconstruct the world of the past. In the HISTORICAL VOICES section of each chapter of the Study Guide, you will find two or more excerpts from works written during the historical period under discussion in the textbook chapter. You will be asked to read these documents in light of information presented in the textbook and to answer questions about the documents themselves. These documents may sometimes be challenging to read, but they will allow you to hear the people of the past express themselves in their own words and to become more knowledgeable about the distinctive ideas and perceptions of different historical eras.

Finally, the STUDY DRILLS at the end of each Study Guide chapter allow you to test your knowledge of IMPORTANT HISTORICAL FACTS. These exercises consist of multiple-choice questions, various drills testing your knowledge of historical chronology, "fill-in-the-blank" problems, and identification quizzes. The answers to all of these exercises are provided in the following section.

Throughout the Study Guide you will come across questions labeled *Historical Continuities*. Questions listed under this heading ask you to draw connections between material presented in two or more chapters and to analyze the long-term impact of important historical events. They are intended to provide you with an opportunity to review material you have already covered and to become more aware of broad historical trends.

STUDY GUIDE FOR
Merriman's
A History of Modern Europe

12 *The French Revolution*

1. CHAPTER OUTLINE

I. THE OLD REGIME IN CRISIS: The French Revolution, while not inevitable, was the predictable outcome of a set of inter-related eighteenth-century developments.
  A. LONG-TERM CAUSES OF THE FRENCH REVOLUTION included Enlightenment political thought, which emphasized equality before the law and was critical of monarchical despotism; growing tensions between nobles and bourgeois; and increasing peasant anger over poor harvests, exploitation by noble landowners, and vexing feudal obligations.
  B. THE FINANCIAL CRISIS that precipitated the Revolution was the result of the government's inability to pay off an excessive national debt. When the king's ministers proposed fiscal reforms to an "assembly of notables," these nobles refused to accept any taxation of their property.

II. THE FIRST STAGES OF THE REVOLUTION
  A. Faced with a growing "noble revolt," the king finally submitted to CONVOKING THE ESTATES-GENERAL. After considerable debate over voting procedures, the Estates-General met, but the representatives of the third estate soon broke away to form a National Assembly.
  B. STORMING OF THE BASTILLE: Worried about the security of the National Assembly, the ordinary people of Paris rose up in revolt and assaulted the Bastille in search of weapons.
  C. THE GREAT FEAR AND THE NIGHT OF AUGUST 4: French peasants then joined the Revolution as well, storming seigneurial châteaux and sparking panic in rural regions. The National Assembly responded by abolishing the "feudal regime."

III. CONSOLIDATING THE REVOLUTION: Over the following two years, the National Assembly laid the foundations for a new, constitutional monarchy.
  A. THE DECLARATION OF THE RIGHTS OF MAN AND CITIZEN set forth the general principles of the new order, including equality before the law and the sovereignty of the nation.
  B. When the king resisted the National Assembly's proposals, Parisian women marched to Versailles and forced the royal family—"THE BAKER, THE BAKER'S WIFE, AND THE BAKER'S LITTLE BOY"—to come to Paris.
  C. REFORMING THE CHURCH AND CLERGY: The National Assembly brought the Church under state control, appropriating its property—which was used to back a new paper money—and requiring that priests accept the Civil Constitution of the French Clergy.
  D. THE REFORMS OF 1791 included a new constitution. Voting rights

were granted to affluent men, but women, slaves in the colonies, and many workers were excluded from the ranks of the "active" citizens.

E.   RESISTANCE AND REVOLUTION: Opposition to the Revolution began to surface, especially in the south and west, but this only served to further radicalize many supporters of the Revolution, especially the Parisian *sans-culottes*.

F.   The royal family's attempted FLIGHT TO VARENNES failed, and increased popular hostility toward the monarchy.

IV.   WAR AND THE SECOND REVOLUTION: The revolutionary left, fearful of invasion by foreign and émigré armies, went to war and replaced the monarchy with a republic.

A.   REACTIONS TO THE FRENCH REVOLUTION IN EUROPE were mixed. Liberals like Thomas Paine and Mary Wollstonecraft greeted it with enthusiasm; conservatives like Edmund Burke criticized it. When the kings of Austria and Prussia expressed their willingness to support Louis XVI, the Assembly declared war on Austria.

B.   The pressures and anxieties of war led to A SECOND REVOLUTION. The king was deposed in 1792, and, after a French victory at Valmy, a republic was declared. Louis XVI soon went to the guillotine, and divisions deepened in France, even among revolutionaries, and especially as military reversals heightened the population's insecurity.

C.   In 1793, a full-scale COUNTER-REVOLUTION broke out in western France.

D.   Faced with foreign invasion and civil war, the radical Jacobin-controlled government implemented THE TERROR. Under the leadership of the Committee of Public Safety, the revolutionary government centralized its operations and used forceful measures to put down the Vendéan and Federalist revolts, to win the war, and to bring radical revolutionaries under control. At the same time, leaders like Robespierre and Saint-Just sought to replace Old Regime culture with a new republican culture.

V.   During THE FINAL STAGES of the Revolution, the government of the Terror was replaced by the Directory.

A.   In THERMIDOR (July 1794), moderates in the government, fearful of being the next victims of the Terror, overturned the Committee of Public Safety. Robespierre went to the guillotine, and the radical revolution was ended.

B.   THE DIRECTORY: POLITICS AND SOCIETY: The new government represented a reaction against the asceticism of the Terror, and benefited the rich both politically and financially. With the end of price controls, a harsh winter in 1795, and continuing war, the poor suffered great hardships.

C.   INSTABILITY continued as the war dragged on and the Directory was assailed by royalists on the right and radicals on the left. General Napoleon Bonaparte was victorious in Italy, but other ventures proved less successful.

D.   In 1799, on THE EIGHTEENTH BRUMAIRE (November 9), Sieyès and Bonaparte staged a coup d'état against the Directory. Sieyès hoped that a new government with a stronger executive and support from the military might help to stabilize the French economy.

VI.   PERSPECTIVES ON THE FRENCH REVOLUTION

A.   EUROPEAN RESPONSES TO THE REVOLUTION: While the French revolutionary armies were often welcomed by Europeans in the territories these armies sought to "liberate," French rule often stimulated discontent and an increased sense of national identity among subject populations.

B. HISTORIANS' VIEWS OF THE REVOLUTION differ, ranging from older Marxist approaches to more recent "political culture" interpretations, but all agree that the French Revolution has had a major impact on modern history.

2. HISTORICAL GEOGRAPHY

Map Exercises

Familiarize yourself with the maps provided in your text, and then attempt to locate the following places on Blank Maps 12.1 and 12.2.

REVOLUTIONARY FRANCE

Provinces:	*Cities:*	*Departments:*
Alsace	Bordeaux	Gironde
Brittany	Caen	Vendée
Dauphiné	Lyon	
Franche-	Marseille	*Rivers, etc.:*
Comté	Paris	Loire River
Languedoc	Toulon	Quiberon
Normandy	Varennes	Bay
Provence	Versailles	Seine River

THE EXPANSION OF REVOLUTIONARY FRANCE

Adriatic Sea
Avignon

Batavian Republic
Cisalpine Republic

Corsica
Fleurus
Helvetic Republic
Ionian Islands
Jémappes
Ligurian Republic
Republic
   of Lucca
Nice
Parma

Parthenopean
   Republic
Piedmont
Roman Republic
Kingdom of
   Sardinia
Savoy
Grand Duchy of
   Tuscany
Valmy

Map Questions

What was the French revolutionaries' intent in replacing provinces with departments?

What new territories did France acquire between 1789 and 1799?

Locate the centers of counter-revolutionary and federalist activity in revolutionary France.

3. PEOPLE AND TERMS TO IDENTIFY

Louis XVI
Marie-Antoinette
The Estates-General
The National Assembly
The Bastille
Jean-Paul Marat
Émigrés
Assignats
The Civil Constitution of
   the Clergy

Georges-Jacques Danton
Olympe de Gouges
Jacobins
Sans-culottes
Girondins
Edmund Burke
Declaration of Pilnitz
Valmy
Vendée
Levée en masse

The Terror
Committee of Public
   Safety
Enragés
Maximilien Robespierre
De-christianization
Thermidor
The Directory
Eighteenth Brumaire

4. STUDY QUESTIONS

1. What caused the French monarchy's financial crisis of the 1780s? *Historical Continuities:* How had the French state financed its operations since 1500? What weaknesses were inherent in this system?

2. What was the National Assembly and why was it formed?

3. Why did ordinary French people support the efforts of the National Assembly? How did they express their support?

4. What was the "Great Fear"? What caused it and why was it significant?

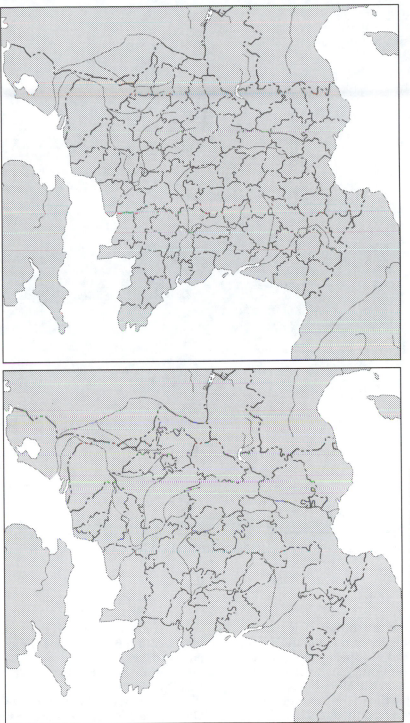

MAP 12.1   REVOLUTIONARY FRANCE

MAP 12.2   THE EXPANSION OF REVOLUTIONARY FRANCE

5. How did revolutionary legislation affect the practice of religion in France?

6. How did Europeans react to the French Revolution? Why were the governments of the other European nations so hostile to the Revolution?

7. What caused the French Revolution to enter a second, more radical phase?

8. From what disadvantages did the French revolutionary armies suffer going into war with Austria? Why were they so surprisingly successful?

9. What characterized the regions in which counter-revolutionary movements emerged?

10. What was the Terror? What caused it? Why did it end?

11. What were the weaknesses of the Directory? In what areas was it successful?

12. How did Napoleon seize power? Why was he able to do this?

13. *Historical Continuities:* What long-term impact do you expect French rule might have on conquered populations?

5. ANALYZING ART AND ARTIFACTS

What kind of emotional response is Jacques-Louis David's *Death of Marat* (p. 532 in the textbook) intended to elicit in the viewer? In what sense is this a "heroic" portrayal of the slain political leader? What is the political significance of this portrait?

How were ordinary supporters of the Revolution depicted in popular images of the period?

6. TECHNOLOGY AND HISTORY

Why do you think French revolutionaries introduced the guillotine (p. 528 in the textbook) as a means of execution? In what way was the guillotine a "humane" form of capital punishment? In what sense might its use be said to reflect Enlightenment values?

7. HISTORICAL ANALYSIS: INTERPRETIVE ESSAYS

1. What long-term conditions contributed to discontent with the French monarchy? What specific short-term factors precipitated the French Revolution?

2. Analyze the French Revolution as a fundamental change in European political culture. You may wish to contrast Old Regime political models with the new models of state and government formulated in "The Declaration of the Rights of Man and Citizen."

3. To what extent was the French Revolution a victory for liberty, equality, and fraternity?

4. *Historical Continuities:* What general, long-term trends in European history can explain the outbreak of revolutions (both successful and unsuccessful) in the latter part of the eighteenth century?

5. *Historical Continuities:* What different political lessons might nineteenth-century Europeans draw from the French Revolution in all its stages?

8. HISTORICAL VOICES: MEN, WOMEN, AND THE FRENCH REVOLUTION

A. The Rights of Man, The Rights of Woman

Like the representatives of the thirteen American colonies, the French members of the revolutionary National Assembly felt called upon to justify their actions to the world and to present a public declaration of their principles and goals. On August 26, 1789, they decreed the "Declaration of the Rights of Man and Citizen" as the preamble to a yet-to-be-written French Constitution. Following the line of political thought pioneered by Locke and elaborated by Montesquieu, Rousseau, and Jefferson, the French declaration represented a distillation of the fundamental premises of classical liberalism and became a rallying cry for liberal thinkers and activists throughout Europe.

Two years later, in 1791, the political activist Olympe de Gouges (1755–1793) published her own declaration of the "Rights of Woman." Modeled on the "Declaration of the Rights of Man and Citizen," de Gouges' revision was intended as a protest against the exclusion of French women from the ranks of those citizens whose rights had been guaranteed in 1789. Identifying a contradiction in the liberalism of the French revolutionaries, de Gouges argued that the tyrannical power of men over women was as objectionable as the despotism of the French monarchy. Her support for Marie Antoinette earned de Gouges the enmity of the revolutionary government, and she went to the guillotine in 1793, charged with the crime of being a royalist.

FROM *The Declaration of the Rights of Man and Citizen*

The representatives of the French people, constituted as the National Assembly, considering that ignorance, neglect or contempt for the rights of man are solely responsible for public misfortunes and the corruption of governments, have resolved to set forth the natural, inalienable and sacred rights of man in a solemn declaration, to the end that it may serve all the members of the body politic as a constant reminder of their reciprocal rights and duties; that the acts of the executive and legislative powers may be all the more respected because they can be constantly compared with the end of all political institutions; and that the demands of the citizens, grounded henceforth on simple and incontestable principles, should always tend to the maintenance of the Constitution and the common good.

Consequently the National Assembly, in the presence and under the auspices of the Supreme Being, recognizes and declares the following rights as belonging to man and the citizen:

1 Men are born free and remain free and equal in their rights. Social distinctions can only be founded on public utility.

2 The aim of every political association is the maintenance of the natural and imprescriptible rights of man. Those rights are those of liberty, property, security and resistance to oppression.

3 The fundamental source of all sovereignty resides in the nation. No body nor any individual may exercise any authority which does not derive explicitly from the sovereign nation.

FROM *Declaration of the Rights of Woman and Citizen* by Olympe de Gouges

The mothers, daughters, sisters, representatives of the nation, ask to constitute a National Assembly. Considering that ignorance, forgetfulness or contempt of the rights of women are the sole causes of public miseries, and of corruption of governments, they have resolved to set forth in a solemn declaration, the natural, unalterable and sacred rights of woman, so that this declaration, being ever present to all members of the social body, may unceasingly remind them of their rights and their duties; in order that the acts of women's power, as well as those of men, may be judged constantly against the aim of all political institutions, and thereby be more respected for it, in order that the complaints of women citizens, based henceforth on simple and indisputable principles, may always take the direction of maintaining the Constitution, good morals and the welfare of all.

In consequence, the sex superior in beauty and in courage in maternal suffering recognizes and declares, in the presence of and under the auspices of the Supreme Being, the following rights of woman and of the woman citizen:

Article I. Woman is born free and remains equal to man in rights. Social distinctions can be based only on common utility.

Article II. The aim of every political association is the preservation of the natural and imprescriptible rights of man and woman. These rights are liberty, prosperity, security and above all, resistance to oppression.

Article III. The source of all sovereignty resides essentially in the Nation, which is nothing but the joining together of Man and Woman; no body, no individual, can exercise authority that does not emanate expressly from it.

4 Liberty consists in being able to do anything which does not harm another: thus each man's exercise of his natural rights has no limits but those which guarantee the other members of society the enjoyment of these same rights. These limits can only be determined by the law. . . .

6 The law is the expression of the general will. Every citizen has the right, in person or by representation, to participate in the legislative process. The law must be the same for all, whether it punish or protect. Every citizen, being equal in its eyes, is equally admissible to every dignity, office and public employment in accordance with his ability and with no other distinction than that of his virtue and talent. . . .

10 No one must be troubled on account of his opinions, even his religious beliefs, provided that their expression does not disturb public order under the law.

11 Free expression of thought and opinions is one of the most precious rights of man. Accordingly every citizen may speak, write and publish freely, subject to the penalties for the abuse of this freedom provided for by the law. . . .

Article IV. Liberty and justice consist in giving back to others all that belongs to them; thus the only limits on the exercise of woman's natural rights are the perpetual tyranny by which man opposes her; these limits must be reformed by the laws of nature and of reason. . . .

Article VI. Law must be the expression of the general will: all citizens, men and women alike, must personally or through their representatives concur in its formation; it must be the same for all; all citizens, men and women alike, being equal before it, must be equally eligible for all high offices, positions and public employments, according to their abilities, and without distinctions other than their virtues and talents. . . .

Article X. No one ought to be disturbed for one's opinions, however fundamental they are; since a woman has the right to mount the scaffold, she must also have the right to address the House, provided her interventions do not disturb the public order as it has been established by law.

Article XI. The free communication of ideas and opinions is one of the most precious rights of woman, since this freedom ensures the legitimacy of fathers toward their children. Every woman citizen can therefore say freely: I am the mother of a child that belongs to you, without being forced to conceal the truth because of a barbaric prejudice; except to be answerable for abusers of this liberty as determined by law. . . .

Source: "The Declaration of the Rights of Man and Citizen." In *The French Revolution: The Fall of the Ancien Regime to the Thermidorian Reaction, 1785–1795,* pp. 114–117. Ed. and tr. John Hardman. New York: St. Martin's Press, 1982.

Source: Olympe de Gouges. "Declaration of the Rights of Woman and Citizen." In *European Women: A Documentary History, 1789–1945,* pp. 63–66. Eds. Eleanor S. Riemer and John C. Fout. New York: Schocken Books, 1980.

Questions

To what extent do these two documents draw on pre-existing political theory? How do they compare with the American "Declaration of Independence"?

How does Olympe de Gouges' reworking of the "Declaration of the Rights of Man and Citizen" transform its meaning?

How do you think male revolutionaries would have responded to de Gouges' declaration?

B. British Responses to the French Revolution: The Debate Between Edmund Burke and Mary Wollstonecraft

Born in Ireland, Edmund Burke (1729–1797) came to London as a young man to begin a successful career as a political writer and journalist. He was elected to Parliament in 1765 and served as a Member of Parliament for the next thirty years. Although he supported the American colonists in their conflict with Britain, he was fiercely critical of the French Revolution and of its British supporters. *Reflections on the Revolution in France*, written in 1790 in response to a French friend's letter, is an extended critique of specific aspects of the French Revolution, but it is also a general treatise that analyzes the foundations and functioning of state and society. In his championing of slow and cautious amelioration of existing political structures—as opposed to sudden, revolutionary change—and in his insistence on the importance of maintaining social hierarchies based on birth and wealth, Burke is often identified as the founding father of modern conservative political thought.

Burke's work elicited a passionate response from the British partisans of the Revolution, and no fewer than thirty "Answers to Burke" were published in the years following the appearance of *Reflections on the Revolution in France*. While Thomas Paine's *The Rights of Man* is the best known of these responses, Mary Wollstonecraft's *Vindication of the Rights of Men* was one of the earliest, and earned Wollstonecraft a prominent place in British liberal intellectual circles. Wollstonecraft (1759–1797), now famous for her *Vindication of the Rights of Woman*, a key text in the origins of modern feminism, derived her feminist theory from her classical liberalism. Like de Gouges, Wollstonecraft supported the French Revolution because she believed it would further the cause of human rights in general.

FROM *Reflections on the Revolution in France* by Edmund Burke

The people of England will not ape the fashions they have never tried, nor go back to those which they have found mischievous on trial. They look upon the legal hereditary succession of their crown as among their rights, not as among their wrongs; as a benefit, not as a grievance; as a security for their liberty, not as a badge of servitude. They look on the frame of their commonwealth, *such as it stands,* to be of inestimable value; and they conceive the undisturbed succession of the crown to be a pledge of the stability and perpetuity of all the other members of our constitution. . . .

You will observe, that from Magna Charta to the Declaration of Right, it has been the uniform policy of our constitution to claim and assert our liberties, as an *entailed inheritance* derived to us from our forefathers, and to be transmitted to our posterity; as an estate specially belonging to the people of this kingdom, without any reference whatever to any other more general or prior right. By this means our constitution preserves an unity in so great a diversity of its parts. We have an inheritable crown; an inheritable peerage; and a House of Commons and a people inheriting privileges, franchises, and liberties, from a long line of ancestors.

The policy appears to me to be the result of profound reflection; or rather the happy effect of following nature, which is wisdom without re-flection, and above it. A spirit of innovation is generally the result of a selfish temper, and confined views. People will not look forward to posterity, who never look backward to their ancestors. Besides, the people of England well know, that the idea of inheritance furnishes a sure principle of conservation, and a sure principle of transmission; without at all excluding a principle of improvement. It leaves acquisition free; but it secures what it acquires. Whatever advantages are obtained by a state proceeding on these maxims, are locked fast as in a sort of family settlement; grasped as in a kind of mortmain for ever. By a constitutional policy working after the pattern of nature, we receive, we hold, we transmit our government and our privileges, in the same manner in which we enjoy and transmit our property and our lives. The institutions of policy, the goods of fortune, the gifts of Providence, are handed down to us, and from us, in the same course and order. Our political system is placed in a just correspondence and symmetry with the order of the world, and with the mode of existence decreed to a permanent body composed of transitory parts; wherein, by the disposition of a stupendous wisdom, moulding together the great mysterious incorporation of the human race, the whole, at one time, is never old, or middle-aged, or young, but, in a condition of unchangeable constancy, moves on through the varied tenor of perpetual decay, fall, renovation, and progression. Thus, by preserving the method of nature in the conduct of the state, in what we improve, we are never wholly new; in what we retain, we are never wholly obsolete. By adhering in this manner and on those principles to our forefathers, we are guided not by the superstition of antiquarians, but by the spirit of philosophic analogy. In this choice of inheritance we have given to our frame of polity the image of a relation in blood; binding up the constitution of our country with our dearest domestic ties; adopting our fundamental laws into the bosom of our family affections; keeping inseparable and cherishing with the warmth of all their combined and mutually reflected charities, our state, our hearths, our sepulchres, and our altars. . . .

FROM *A Vindication of the Rights of Men* by Mary Wollstonecraft

The birthright of man, to give you, Sir, a short definition of this disputed right, is such a degree of liberty, civil and religious, as is compatible with the liberty of every other individual with whom he is united in a social compact, and the continued existence of that compact.

Liberty, in this simple, unsophisticated sense, I acknowledge, is a fair idea that has never yet received a form in the various governments that have been established on our beauteous globe; the demon of property has ever been at hand to encroach on the sacred rights of men, and to fence round with awful pomp laws that war with justice. But that it results from the eternal foundation of right—from immutable truth—who will presume to deny, that pretends to rationality—if reason has led them to build their morality and religion on an everlasting foundation—the attributes of God? . . .

I perceive, from the whole tenor of your Reflections, that you have a mortal antipathy to reason; but, if there is any thing like argument, or first principles, in your wild declamation, behold the result:—that we are to reverence the rust of antiquity, and term the unnatural customs, which ignorance and mistaken self-interest have consolidated, the sage fruit of experience: nay, that, if we do discover some errors, our *feelings* should lead us to excuse, with blind love, or unprincipled filial affection, the venerable vestiges of ancient days. These are gothic notions of beauty—the ivy is beautiful, but, when it insidiously destroys the trunk from which it receives support, who would not grub it up?

Further, that we ought cautiously to remain for ever in frozen inactivity, because a thaw, whilst it nourishes the soil, spreads a temporary inundation; and the fear of risking any personal present convenience should prevent a struggle for the most estimable advantages. This is sound reasoning, I grant, in the mouth of the rich and short-sighted.

Sources: Edmund Burke. *Reflections on the Revolution in France,* 1790. In *The Works of the Right Honourable Edmund Burke,* vol. 4, pp. 27, 35–37. London: Oxford University Press, 1907.
Mary Wollstonecraft. *A Vindication of the Rights of Men,* pp. 7–10. Delmar, NY: Scholars' Facsimiles and Reprints, 1975.

Questions
Why does Burke reject the "right to revolution"? What is Wollstonecraft's response to this argument?

What makes Burke a "conservative"? Wollstonecraft a "liberal"?

What does Burke mean when he calls British liberties an "entailed inheritance"? Why does Wollstonecraft reject this idea?

9. IMPORTANT HISTORICAL FACTS: STUDY DRILLS

A. Multiple Choice

1. In the late eighteenth century, the French monarchy was weakened by all of the following *except*
   A. a clergy hostile to the monarchical principle.
   B. an inept king and an unpopular queen.
   C. inadequate and inequitable taxation.
   D. a nobility eager to hold on to its privileges.
2. The third estate included all of the following *except*
   A. peasants.
   B. urban workers.
   C. priests.
   D. lawyers.
3. During the "Great Fear"
   A. French nobles attempted to flee the country.
   B. peasants were stirred to action by rumors of an aristocratic "famine plot."
   C. representatives of the third estate took an oath on a tennis court.
   D. the Bastille, a prison-fortress, was attacked by Parisians.
4. An ardent advocate of women's rights, she wrote *The Declaration of the Rights of Woman and Citizen,* and went to the guillotine during the Terror:
   A. Marie Antoinette
   B. Joan of Arc
   C. Charlotte Corday
   D. Olympe de Gouges
5. A *sans-culotte* could be identified by
   A. his fancy knee britches.
   B. his inherited wealth.
   C. his opposition to the Revolution.
   D. his tendency to call everyone "citizen."
6. Confronted with outbreaks of civil war in the provinces, the revolutionary government decreed mass conscription in 1793, calling on all loyal revolutionaries to take arms in support of the nation. This was known as
   A. the *levée en masse.*
   B. the Festival of Reason.
   C. the Seigneurial Reaction.
   D. the Assembly of Notables.
7. On September 20, 1792, the revolutionary army won its first significant victory, inspiring Goethe to declare, "a new epoch is beginning." The battle that turned the tide for the French, and prepared the way for the proclamation of the First French Republic, was known as
   A. the Vendée.
   B. Valmy.
   C. Varennes.
   D. the September Massacres.

8. Created by the Convention in March of 1793, this twelve-member body governed France during the Terror and included Robespierre as one of its leading figures:
   A. The Directory
   B. The National Assembly
   C. The Committee of Public Safety
   D. The Patriot Party
9. The radical revolutionary campaign to shut down religious institutions and destroy religious symbols that began in late 1793 was known as
   A. the Law of Suspects.
   B. the Civil Constitution of the Clergy.
   C. the Counter-Revolution.
   D. de-christianization.
10. The French established "Sister Republics" in all but
    A. Naples and Milan.
    B. Switzerland.
    C. Russia.
    D. The Netherlands.

B. Chronological Relationships

Arrange the following events in chronological order and explain the causal relationship between each matched set:

The French REPUBLIC is declared.
The counter-revolutionary VENDÉE rebellion begins.
The National Assembly abolishes the "FEUDAL regime."
France declares WAR on Austria.
The meeting of the ESTATES-General.
The government of the DIRECTORY is established.
The fall of the BASTILLE.
In THERMIDOR, Robespierre goes to the guillotine.
The Convention institutes "TERROR" against the enemies of the Revolution.
The meeting of the Assembly of NOTABLES.

1. _____
2. _____
Relationship:

3. _____
4. _____
Relationship:

5. _____
6. _____
Relationship:

7. _____
8. _____
Relationship:

9. _____
10. _____
Relationship:

C. Fill in the Blanks

1. Scheduled to meet on May 1st, 1789, the _____ would be made up of representatives selected from the nobility, the clergy, and "everybody else."
2. In search of guns and ammunition, the people of Paris attacked and captured _____ on July 14, 1789.
3. On the basis of land confiscated from the Catholic Church, the French revolutionary government issued a paper currency known as _____.
4. A populist orator who had denounced the distinction between "active" and "passive" citizens, _____ went to the guillotine for his "indulgent" belief that the Terror was no longer necessary.
5. The _____ were republicans, many of whom hailed from the Bordeaux region, and who agitated for a revolutionary war against the tyranny of European monarchs and nobles.
6. In the _____ King Leopold II of Austria and King Frederick William II of Prussia expressed their mutual desire to see order restored in France, generating anxiety about foreign invasion in France, and providing ammunition for those French revolutionaries who wished to go to war against the European monarchies.
7. In March 1793, a full-scale insurrection against the Revolution broke out in western France. This counter-revolutionary uprising was known as the _____.

8. The most radical of the revolutionary factions, the _____ called for strict enforcement of maximum limits on bread prices and intensification of the "de-christianization" campaign, but their leaders were struck down by the Committee of Public Safety.
9. Known as "The Incorruptible," _____ came to be feared as the mastermind of the Terror, and he was ousted from power in the month of "Thermidor."
10. On the _____ [November 9, 1799] the young Corsican general, Napoleon Bonaparte, staged a coup d'état (with his co-conspirator, Sieyès), overthrowing the Directory and taking effective control of the French government.

IMPORTANT HISTORICAL FACTS: STUDY-DRILL ANSWERS

A. Multiple Choice
1. A. a clergy hostile to the monarchical principle.
2. C. priests.
3. B. peasants were stirred to action by rumors of an aristocratic "famine plot."
4. D. Olympe de Gouges
5. D. his tendency to call everyone "citizen."
6. A. the *levée en masse.*
7. B. Valmy.
8. C. The Committee of Public Safety
9. D. de-christianization.
10. C. Russia.

B. Chronological Relationships
1. NOTABLES / 2. ESTATES
3. BASTILLE / 4. FEUDAL
5. WAR / 6. REPUBLIC
7. VENDÉE / 8. TERROR
9. THERMIDOR / 10. DIRECTORY

C. Fill in the Blanks
1. Estates-General
2. Bastille
3. assignats
4. Georges-Jacques Danton
5. Girondins
6. Declaration of Pilnitz
7. Vendée Rebellion
8. enragés
9. Maximilien Robespierre
10. Eighteenth Brumaire

13 *Napoleon and Europe*

1. CHAPTER OUTLINE

I. NAPOLEON'S RISE TO POWER was made possible by the French Revolution.
    A. THE YOUNG BONAPARTE was born in Corsica only shortly after it became French territory, and attended military school in France.
    B. NAPOLEON AND THE REVOLUTION: Siding with the Jacobins, Napoleon served as an officer in the revolutionary army and soon became commander of the Army of Italy.
II. CONSOLIDATION OF POWER: After campaigns in Italy and Egypt, Napoleon returned to France, where he helped to stage the Eighteenth Brumaire coup d'état against the ruling Directory.
    A. The ESTABLISHMENT OF THE CONSULAT involved the creation of a strong executive authority, headed by First Consul Napoleon.
    B. In the interests of ending religious discord, Napoleon negotiated and signed THE CONCORDAT with the pope in 1802.
    C. NAPOLEON'S LEADERSHIP: An "ever-restless spirit," Napoleon was a hardworking executive, but refused to delegate authority and became increasingly tyrannical and bellicose during the course of his reign.
    D. WARS OF CONQUEST AND EMPIRE: Having declared himself emperor, Napoleon once again went to war with Europe. After a series of brilliant campaigns, France ruled over the largest European empire since that of Rome.
    E. THE CORSICAN WARRIOR: Napoleon's military successes were based less on originality than on innovative implementation of strategy and tactics developed in the eighteenth century. Relying on "citizen-soldiers," Napoleon created a large, flexible, and highly mobile military machine.
III. THE FOUNDATIONS OF THE FRENCH EMPIRE
    A. INSTITUTIONAL FOUNDATIONS: IMPERIAL CENTRALIZATION was imposed in all matters of state, including finance and education.
    B. LEGAL FOUNDATIONS: THE NAPOLEONIC CODE provided a uniform law code for all of France (and much of the rest of Europe). Despite its social conservatism, especially regarding women and children, it formalized many of the legal gains of the revolutionary era.
    C. SOCIAL FOUNDATIONS OF THE EMPIRE: THE IMPERIAL HIERARCHY created by Napoleon was based not on inheritance but on service to the state. While reestablishing a titled elite, Napoleon preserved a certain degree of social mobility.
IV. THE TIDE TURNS AGAINST NAPOLEON: An overextended empire and ill-considered military

campaigns would eventually bring Napoleon down.

A. THE CONTINENTAL SYSTEM was designed to strangle British trade, but this policy was never successful, and Britain remained committed to defeating France.

B. Seeking to defeat Great Britain's ally Portugal, Napoleon found himself embroiled in THE PENINSULAR WAR, which tied down French troops in Spain and Portugal from 1808 to 1813.

C. STIRRINGS OF NATIONALISM IN NAPOLEONIC EUROPE: Especially in the Italian and German states, French invasion stimulated a new sense of national identity—and a desire for freedom from French rule.

D. MILITARY REFORMS IN PRUSSIA AND AUSTRIA were undertaken in response to devastating defeats by the French armies.

E. THE EMPIRE'S DECLINE AND THE RUSSIAN INVASION: In the face of growing resistance to his rule in France, Napoleon invaded Russia with his Grand Army. The Russians retreated, leaving Moscow in flames, and forcing Napoleon to march his troops back to France in the bitter Russian winter.

F. THE DEFEAT OF NAPOLEON came in 1814, when Austria, Britain, Prussia, and Russia successfully united against France.

V. MONARCHICAL RESTORATION AND NAPOLEON'S RETURN

A. Napoleon was sent into exile by the victorious allies and THE BOURBON RESTORATION was greeted with relief by most French people. However, many came to resent Louis XVIII's support of "Ultra-royalist" policies.

B. THE 100 DAYS: In a bold move, Napoleon escaped from Elba and returned to France, where he regained the support of his faithful army and the general public. He ruled for 100 days, but was decisively defeated by an allied army at Waterloo.

VI. NAPOLEON'S LEGACY: Napoleon left behind him a Europe much transformed by war, political and legal changes, and developing nationalism. He claimed to have sought the good of France and of Europe, but his personal ambition brought much death and disorder to the continent—and bequeathed a heroic myth to subsequent generations.

2. HISTORICAL GEOGRAPHY

Map Exercises

Familiarize yourself with the maps provided in your text, and then attempt to locate the following places on Blank Map 13.1.

NAPOLEONIC BATTLES

Austerlitz	Moscow
Borodino	Paris
Dresden	Smolensk
Friedland	Trafalgar
Jena	Ulm
Leipzig	Wagram
Lisbon	Waterloo
Madrid	

ITALY DURING THE NAPOLEONIC ERA

Campo Formio	Kingdom of
Corsica	Naples
Elba	Piedmont
Florence	Rome
Illyrian Provinces	Sardinia
Kingdom of Italy	Savoy
Milan	Sicily
Naples	Venice

Map Questions

How was the map of the German states redrawn during the Napoleonic era?

What territories did the Napoleonic Empire include at its greatest expanse?

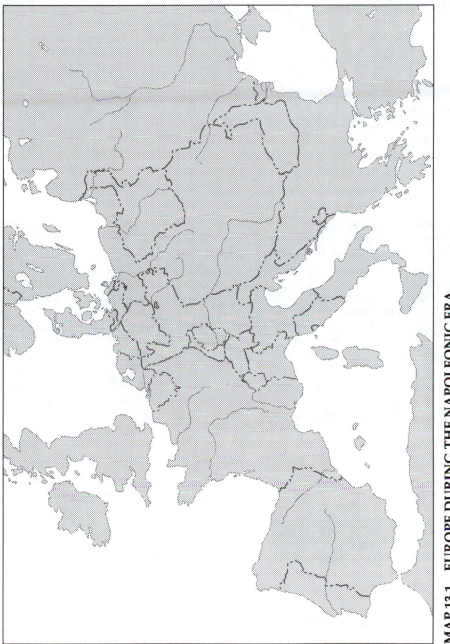

MAP 13.1   EUROPE DURING THE NAPOLEONIC ERA

3. PEOPLE AND TERMS TO IDENTIFY

Napoleon Bonaparte
Consulat
"Authority from above,
   confidence from below"
Concordat
Duke of Enghien
Toussaint L'Ouverture
Battle of Trafalgar

Confederation of the Rhine
Citizen-soldiers
Napoleonic Code
"A career open to all
   talents"
Notables
Continental System
Peninsular War

Talleyrand
Grand Army
Louis XVIII
Charter
100 Days
Waterloo

4. STUDY QUESTIONS

1. What factors in Napoleon's background help to explain his rise to power? *Historical Continuities*: To what extent was his dramatic ascent a product of the French Revolution?

2. Why did Napoleon negotiate a Concordat with the Catholic Church? *Historical Continuities:* To what extent was this agreement typical of previous arrangements made between French monarchs and the Church?

3. Why did France go back to war again in 1805?

4. How did Napoleon win so many battles?

5. To what extent was "centralization" a characteristic of all of Napoleon's initiatives?

6. Describe the type of social organization promoted by Napoleon through the Civil Code and through his creation of a service elite.

7. Why was Napoleon unable to defeat either Great Britain or Spain?

8. What were the distinctive characteristics of German nationalism?

9. How was Napoleon defeated? Was this defeat inevitable?

5. ANALYZING ART AND ARTIFACTS

How did fine art and popular representations of Napoleon serve to support (or deflate) the Napoleonic legend?

Historical Continuities: In what sense is David's *Bonaparte Leaping the St. Bernard* (p. 585) "romantic"? How does it depart

from the classicism of David's earlier painting, *The Death of Marat* (p. 532)?

6. TECHNOLOGY AND HISTORY

To what extent were Napoleon's military successes the result of technological innovations?

7. HISTORICAL ANALYSIS: INTERPRETIVE ESSAYS

1. Write an essay defending one of the following statements:
   Napoleon was an imperialist tyrant.
   Napoleon was one of the greatest
      rulers who ever lived.

2. What effect did Napoleon's reign have on Europe as a whole?

3. *Historical Continuities:* Did Napoleon end or continue the French Revolution?

4. *Historical Continuities:* In what sense might Napoleon's government be considered the first "modern" (as opposed to early modern) regime?

8. HISTORICAL VOICES: THE NAPOLEONIC LEGACY

A. Napoleon Regulates Marriage and the Family

The French Civil (or "Napoleonic") Code and the French Penal Code, promulgated in 1804 and 1810 respectively, contributed to the completion of the codification of law begun at the time of the Revolution of 1789. The Napoleonic Code served as the foundation for the civil law not only of France but also of Louisiana and much of continental Europe and Latin America.

If the Napoleonic Code ratified many of the civil liberties gained during the revolutionary period, it also reestablished the legal authority of fathers and husbands, which had been substantially diminished during the revolutionary era. Rejecting the liberal feminism of thinkers like the Marquis de Condorcet and Olympe de Gouges, Napoleon and his legal consultants gave the political and economic inequality of women (and children) a firm basis in law. Similarly, Napoleonic lawmakers gave legal sanction to the sexual double standard, establishing harsh penalties for a married woman's adulterous relations but turning a blind eye to her husband's sexual adventures, except in the most extreme cases. Similarly, an unwed mother was prohibited from seeking child support from the father of her child unless she could prove that she had been the victim of an abduction.

FROM Napoleon's Civil Code of 1804

Article 19. A French woman who marries a foreign national takes her husband's nationality. If she becomes a widow, she recovers her French nationality if she is living in France, or if she returns to France with the King's authorization and having declared that she wishes to establish permanent residency in the country.

Article 37. Witnesses to civil proceedings must be male, [and] at least twenty-one years of age. . . .

Article 108. A married woman can have no other domicile than that of her husband. . . .

Article 144. A man younger than eighteen years of age, and a woman younger than fifteen years of age, cannot enter into a marriage contract. . . .

Article 148. A son under the age of twenty-five, and a daughter under the age of twenty-one, cannot enter into a marriage contract without the consent of his or her father and mother; in case of disagreement, the consent of the father suffices. . . .

Article 212. Husband and wife owe each other faithfulness, support, and assistance.

Article 213. A husband owes protection to his wife, a wife obedience to her husband.

Article 214. A wife is obligated to live with her husband, and to follow him wherever he judges it appropriate to reside: A husband is obligated to receive his wife [in his domicile] and to furnish her with all that is necessary for her survival, in accordance with her faculties and station.

Article 215. A wife cannot file a civil suit without the authorization of her husband, even if she is a public merchant, or is not in a joint-property marriage, or is legally separated from her husband. . . .

Article 229. A husband can file for divorce on the grounds of the adultery of his wife.

Article 230. A wife can file for divorce on the grounds of the adultery of her husband, if her husband has kept his mistress in the conjugal domicile. . . .

Article 340. Paternity suits are forbidden. In the case of abduction, if the period at which time the abduction took place corresponds with that of conception, the abductor can, at the request of the interested parties, be declared the father of the child.

FROM Napoleon's Penal Code

Article 337. A wife convicted of adultery will be subject to a prison sentence of at least three months and of no more than two years.

Her husband retains the right to end this imprisonment by consenting to take his wife back.

Article 338. The accomplice of an adulterous wife will be punished with a comparable term of imprisonment, and, in addition, a fine of between 24,000 and 480,000 francs.

The only proofs which can be admitted as evidence against the accused accomplice are, besides being caught in the act, those resulting from letters or other documents written by the accused.

Article 339. A husband who has kept his mistress in the conjugal domicile, and who has been convicted as a result of his wife's legal complaint, will be punished with a fine of between 24,000 and 480,000 francs.

Sources: Petits Codes Dalloz. *Code Civil annoté d'après la doctrine et la jurisprudence,* 56th ed., pp. 15, 45, 87, 94, 96, 118, 119, 125, 175. Trans. Kathleen M. Nilan. Paris: Jurisprudence Générale Dalloz, 1957.

Petits Codes Dalloz. *Code Pénal annoté d'après la doctrine et la jurisprudence,* pp. 226, 227. Trans. Kathleen M. Nilan. Paris: Jurisprudence Générale Dalloz, 1954.

Questions

By what logic did the Civil Code establish that a French woman who married a non-French husband would lose her French citizenship?

Given the disabilities imposed on women by the Civil Code, why do you think that women were allowed to marry at an earlier age than men?

To what extent do the Civil and Penal Codes represent an attempt to regulate female sexuality?

B. The Napoleonic Legend

Admired and reviled during his lifetime, Napoleon continued to elicit adoration and outrage after his death. Seen by some French moderates as the savior of the Revolution, he was hated by liberals for his autocracy and by conservatives for his opportunism. Whether loved or hated, his meteoric career cast a long shadow on European culture and politics throughout the nineteenth century.

The first generation of romantics was torn between its admiration for Napoleon's heroism and his almost superhuman individual capacities and its contempt for his failure to either uphold the liberal gains of the Republic or restore the Monarchy and his often brutal and exploitative treatment of subject populations. Both liberals and royalists found much to praise and criticize, but few could resist the temptation to mythologize the life and actions of this great man.

The following selection of French assessments of Napoleon demonstrates the diversity of responses to the legacy of the emperor. The first citation, written by Germaine de Staël (1766–1817), an ardent liberal and an early proponent of romanticism in France, reveals de Staël's dislike for Napoleon, mingled though it is with a certain grudging admiration for the political finesse of the man who banished her from Paris for her opposition to his political regime. In the second, René de Chateaubriand (1768–1848), another early French romantic, but one who felt a deep sentimental attachment to both legitimism and Catholic Christianity, describes his own mixed feelings about Napoleon. Chateaubriand rallied to Napoleon's government as a result of the Concordat with the pope, and he served Napoleon as ambassador to Rome, but he resigned in 1804, after the execution of the duke d'Enghien on trumped-up charges. The final passage, the poem "The Grandmother's Tale," by the very successful songwriter Pierre-Jean de Béranger (1780–1857), presents a more populist portrait of the emperor. Here Napoleon appears as a man of the people, the "little corporal," who led France to victory, but whose successes did not distance him from the concerns of common folk. While de Staël's and Chateaubriand's comments on Napoleon reflect the often critical opinions of the educated elite, Béranger's poem clearly exhibits the lingering sympathy for the emperor among many members of the general public.

FROM *Ten Years of Exile* by Germaine de Staël

Bonaparte's government is characterized by a profound contempt for all of the intellectual riches of human nature: virtue, the dignity of the soul, religion, enthusiasm, these are, in his eyes, the *eternal enemies of the continent*, to avail myself of his favorite expression. He would like to reduce man to nothing but force and cunning, and would name everything else stupidity or madness. Above all others, the English irritate him because they have discovered a means of achieving success with honesty, a thing which Napoleon would like to make people think is impossible. This beacon of light in the world hurt his eyes from the first days of his reign; and unable to destroy it with his weapons, he has never ceased to direct against it all of the artillery of his false reasoning.

I do not believe that Bonaparte, having taken over as head of state, had at that time formed the plan of establishing a universal monarchy. But I do believe that his intent was captured in what he said to a man I count among my friends, a few days after the 18th of Brumaire: "One must," he said, "do something new every three months if one wants to capture the imagination of the French nation. With her, he who does not move forward is lost." He promised himself to encroach each day a bit further on the liberty of France, and on the independence of Europe, but, without losing sight of his final goal, he knew how to adapt himself to circumstances. He circumvented an obstacle, when that obstacle was too strong; he stopped completely when the opposing wind was too violent. That man, at bottom so impatient, has the talent of waiting things out when necessary. He takes this from the Italians, who know how to restrain themselves in order to attain their passions' goal, as if they had cold-bloodedly chosen this goal. It is through the art of alternating between cunning and force that he subjugated Europe. . . .

FROM *The Memoirs of Chateaubriand* by René de Chateaubriand

A monstrous pride and an incessant affectation spoil Napoleon's character. At the time of his dominion, what need had he to exaggerate his stature, when the God of Armies had furnished him with the war chariot "whose wheels are living"?

He took after the Italian blood; his nature was complex: great men, a very small family upon earth, unhappily find only themselves to imitate them. At once a model and a copy, a real personage and an actor representing that personage, Napoleon was his own mime; he would not have believed himself a hero, if he had not dressed himself up in a hero's costume. . . .

That Bonaparte, following up the successes of the Revolution, every-where disseminated principles of independence; that his victories helped to relax the bonds between the peoples and the kings, and snatched those peoples from the power of the old customs and the an-cient ideas; that, in this sense, he contributed to the social enfranchise-ment: these are facts which I do not pretend to contest; but that, of his own will, he laboured scientifically for the political and civil deliverance of the nations; that he established the narrowest despotism with the idea of giving to Europe and to France in particular the widest Constitution; that he was only a tribune disguised as a tyrant: all this is a supposition which I cannot possibly adopt.

Bonaparte, like the race of princes, desired nothing and sought noth-ing save power, attaining it, however, through liberty, because he made his first appearance on the world's stage in 1793. The Revolution, which was Napoleon's wet-nurse, did not long delay in appearing to him as an enemy; he never ceased beating her. . . .

The Emperor meddled with everything; his intelligence never rested; he had a sort of perpetual agitation of ideas. In the impetuousness of his nature, instead of a free and continuous train, he advanced by leaps and bounds, he flung himself upon the universe and shook it; he would have none of it, of that universe, if he was obliged to wait for it: an incompre-hensible being, who found the secret of debasing his most towering ac-tions by despising them, and who raised his least elevated actions to his own level. Impatient of will, patient of character, incomplete and as though unfinished, Napoleon had gaps in his genius: his understanding resembled the sky of that other hemisphere under which he was to go to die, the sky whose stars are separated by empty spaces.

FROM *The Grandmother's Tale.* by Pierre-Jean de Béranger

His fame shall never pass away!
  Beside the cottage-hearth the hind
  No other theme shall list to find
For many and many a distant day.
When winter nights their gloom begin,
  And winter embers ruddy glow,
Round some old gossip closing in,
  They'll beg a tale of long ago—
"For all," they'll say, "he wrought us ill,
  His glorious name shall ne'er grow dim,
The people love, yes, love him still,
  So, Grandmother, a tale of him,
        A tale of him!"

"One day past here I saw him ride,
  A caravan of kings behind;
  The time I well can call to mind,
I hadn't then been long a bride.
I gazed out from the open door,
  Slowly his charger came this way;
A little hat, I think, he wore,
  Yes, and his riding coat was grey.
I shook all over as quite near,
  Close to this very door he drew—

'Good-day,' he cried, 'good-day, my
        dear!' "—
  "What, Grandmother, he spoke to you,
        He spoke to you?"

"The following year I chanced to be
  In Paris; every street was gay,
  He'd gone to Notre Dame to pray,
And passed again quite close to me!
The sun shone out in all its pride,
  With triumph every bosom swelled,
'Ah, what a glorious scene!' they cried,
  'Never has France the like beheld!'
A smile his features seemed to wear,
  As on the crowds his glance he threw,
For he'd an heir, at last, an heir!"—
  "Ah, Grandmother, what times for you,
        What times for you!"

"Then came for France that dreadful day
  When foes swept over all the land;
  Undaunted he alone made stand,
As tho' to keep the world at bay!—
One winter's night, as this might be,
  I heard a knocking at the door;
I opened it; great heavens! 'twas he!
  A couple in his wake, no more;
Then sinking down upon a seat,
  Ay, 'twas upon this very chair,
He gasped 'Defeat! ah God, defeat!' "—
  "What, Grandmother, he sat down *there*,
        He sat down *there*?"

"He called for food; I quickly brought
  The best I happened to have by;
  Then when his dripping clothes were dry,
He seemed to doze awhile, methought;
Seeing me weeping when he woke,
  'Courage,' he cried, 'there's still a chance;
I go to Paris, one bold stroke,
  And Paris shall deliver France!'
He went; the glass I'd seen him hold,
  The glass to which his lips he'd set,
I've treasured since like gold, like gold!"—
  "How, Grandmother, you have it yet,
        You have it yet?"

"'Tis there. But all, alas, was o'er;
  He, whom the Pope himself had crown'd,
  The mighty hero world-renown'd,
Died prisoner on a far-off shore.
For long we none believed the tale,
  They said that he would reappear,
Across the seas again would sail,

To fill the universe with fear!
But when we found that he was dead,
When all the shameful truth we knew,
The bitter, bitter tears I shed!"—
"Ah, Grandmother, God comfort you,
God comfort you!"

Sources: Madame la baronne de Staël. *Dix Années d'exil.* In *Oeuvres complètes de Mme la baronne de Staël, publiées par son fils,* vol. 15, pp. 14–15. Trans. Kathleen M. Nilan. Paris: Treuttel and Würtz, 1821.

François René, vicomte de Chateaubriand. *The Memoirs of Chateaubriand,* vol. 3, pp. 199–201. London: Freemantle and Co., 1902.

Pierre-Jean de Béranger. "The Grandmother's Tale." In *Songs of Béranger,* pp. 56–59. Trans. William Toynbee. London: Walter Scott, 1892.

Questions

What did de Staël and Chateaubriand admire about Napoleon? Why did they ultimately reject him?

Why do you think the grandmother in Béranger's poem feels such sympathy for Napoleon?

With which of these three assessments do you most agree? Why?

9. IMPORTANT HISTORICAL FACTS: STUDY DRILLS

A. Multiple Choice

1. Napoleon Bonaparte was, by birth
   A. Genoese.
   B. French.
   C. Corsican.
   D. English.
2. In his role as executive, Napoleon exercised "authority from above," but he allowed the French people to demonstrate their "confidence from below" through
   A. public demonstrations.
   B. democratic elections of government officials.
   C. plebiscites.
   D. an uncensored press.
3. The duke of Enghien died because
   A. Napoleon needed an excuse to declare himself emperor.
   B. he had conspired to return the Bourbons to the throne of France.
   C. he had fought in the Battle of Waterloo.
   D. he had violated the Napoleonic Code.
4. The French sugar island of Haiti first gained its independence under the leadership of
   A. Pascale di Paoli.
   B. Toussaint L'Ouverture.
   C. the Notables.
   D. Spanish guerrillas.
5. The Napoleonic Code did all of the following *except*
   A. establish a uniform code of law for all of France.
   B. guarantee freedom of religion.
   C. guarantee women voting rights.
   D. protect property rights.
6. Napoleon's motto, "a career open to all talents," demonstrated his support for
   A. absolute social equality.
   B. the abolition of all titles and similar social distinctions.
   C. university-level education for all French people.
   D. social mobility based on ability and service to the state.
7. At the beginning of the 1812 campaign against Russia, the "Grand Army" consisted of
   A. 40,000 troops.
   B. 100,000 troops.
   C. 300,000 troops.
   D. 600,000 troops.
8. After Napoleon's defeat in 1814, he was replaced on the French throne by
   A. Talleyrand.
   B. Louis XVIII.

C. Sieyès.
D. the Duchess of Parma.
9. Napoleon's return to power in 1815 was known as
A. the Bourbon Restoration.
B. the Directory.
C. the Concordat.
D. the 100 Days.
10. Napoleon's last battle was fought at
A. Waterloo.
B. Austerlitz.
C. Trafalgar.
D. St. Helena.

B. Chronological Relationships
1. List the following military events in chronological order. In a brief sentence explain their historical significance.
The Peace of Amiens
The Battle of Austerlitz
The Battle of Friedland
The Battle of Jena
The Battle of the Nile
The Peninsular War
The Invasion of Russia
The Siege of Toulon
The Battle of Trafalgar
The Battle of Wagram
The Battle of Waterloo
2. *Historical Continuities:* Draw a timeline detailing the changing political regimes in France during the period between 1789 and 1815.

C. Fill in the Blanks
1. The government known as the _____ was established in France in 1799, after Napoleon and his co-conspirators staged a coup d'état.
2. In an effort to make peace with the Catholic Church, Napoleon negotiated and signed an agreement with the pope known as a _____.
3. Although Admiral Nelson would die as a result of wounds suffered during the _____, this naval engagement brought a decisive end to French hopes of invading England.
4. In an effort to consolidate his German holdings, Napoleon abolished the Holy Roman Empire and replaced it with the _____.
5. During the French Revolution and the reign of Napoleon, mercenaries were replaced by _____, troops who fought not for money but out of commitment to the French nation.
6. As opposed to the titled nobles of the Old Regime, who inherited their status, the _____ of the Napoleonic era earned their place in the elite through service to the state.
7. Napoleon's _____ was intended to "strangle" British commerce by depriving it of European markets, thereby forcing the British government to negotiate an end to its war with France.
8. When Napoleon attempted to capture both Spain and Portugal for the French Empire, his army met with considerable resistance from guerrilla fighters and became embroiled in the long _____.
9. A former bishop, _____ served as Napoleon's minister of foreign affairs until 1807. A proponent of the "party of peace," he helped to negotiate the restoration of Bourbon rule in 1814.
10. Although "Ultra-royalists" like the count of Artois wished to reestablish an absolute monarchy in 1814, Louis XVIII agreed to rule as a constitutional monarch, guaranteeing the maintenance of representative government and "public liberties" in the _____.

IMPORTANT HISTORICAL FACTS: STUDY-DRILL ANSWERS

A. Multiple Choice
1. B. French.
2. C. plebiscites.
3. A. Napoleon needed an excuse to declare himself emperor.
4. B. Toussaint L'Ouverture.
5. C. guarantee women voting rights.
6. D. social mobility based on ability and service to the state.
7. D. 600,000 troops.
8. B. Louis XVIII.
9. D. the 100 Days.
10. A. Waterloo.

B. Chronological Relationships

1. The Siege of Toulon (1793)
   The Battle of the Nile (1798)
   The Peace of Amiens (1802)
   The Battle of Trafalgar (October 21, 1805)
   The Battle of Austerlitz (December 2, 1805)
   The Battle of Jena (1806)
   The Battle of Friedland (1807)
   The Peninsular War (1808–1813)
   The Battle of Wagram (1809)
   The Invasion of Russia (1812)
   The Battle of Waterloo (1815)

2. 1789–1792 The Constitutional Monarchy
   1792–1795 The First French Republic
   1795–1799 The Directory
   1799–1804 The Consulate
   1804–1814 The First Empire
   1814   First Bourbon Restoration
   1814–1815 100 Days
   1815–1830 Second Bourbon Restoration

C. Fill in the Blanks

1. Consulat
2. Concordat
3. Battle of Trafalgar
4. Confederation of the Rhine
5. Citizen-soldiers
6. Notables
7. Continental System
8. Peninsular War
9. Talleyrand
10. Charter

14 Challenges to Restoration Europe

1. CHAPTER OUTLINE

I. THE POST-NAPOLEONIC SETTLEMENT: After the fall of Napoleon, the monarchs of Europe attempted to reestablish the balance of power between their states, and to rebuild a more conservative social and political order.
  A. By THE TREATY OF PARIS the Bourbons were returned to power, but, thanks to the efforts of Talleyrand, France did not lose any of its pre-revolutionary territory.
  B. DIPLOMATIC MANEUVERING AT THE CONGRESS OF VIENNA took place behind the scenes. Metternich and Castlereagh dominated the territorial negotiations, while Tsar Alexander I worked for the founding of a "Holy Alliance" of Christian monarchs.
  C. THE CONGRESS SYSTEM instituted at Vienna was intended to protect dynastic legitimacy and territorial integrity. The territorial settlements included the creation of a German Confederation.
  D. THE CONCERT OF EUROPE: In the hopes of preserving the Congress system, the Great Powers agreed to meet annually.
II. RESTORATION EUROPE: After 1815, monarchs and nobles sought to "restore" the state system, opposing liberal and nationalist movements in the name of conservative principles.
  A. CONSERVATIVE IDEOLOGY developed as a reaction against the excesses of the French Revolution. Its proponents argued that an alliance of church and monarchical state was essential to the maintenance of social order.
  B. RESTORATION OF MONARCHS, NOBLES, AND CLERGY: Throughout Europe, the power and authority of the traditional elite was revived.
III. Restoration conservatism was confronted with STIRRINGS OF REVOLT throughout Europe.
  A. LIBERAL MOVEMENTS drew on the ideals of the Enlightenment and the French Revolution, and their leaders called for civil liberties and constitutional government. In Germany and Italy, liberalism and nationalism were closely linked.
  B. LIBERAL REVOLTS IN SPAIN, PORTUGAL, AND ITALY occurred in the early 1820s. The Congress powers (minus Britain) intervened in Spain, returning absolute power to Ferdinand VII.
  C. LIBERAL STIRRINGS IN GERMANY: German students demonstrated for liberal and nationalist reforms; the kings of Austria and Prussia responded with the repressive Carlsbad Decrees.

D. THE GREEK REVOLT: Conservatives chose to support Christian Greeks in a nationalist revolt against the Muslim Ottoman Empire, undermining the very principles of dynastic legitimacy the Congress system had been designed to uphold.

E. THE DECEMBRIST REVOLT IN RUSSIA failed to liberalize the tsarist state, but it was indicative of a growing liberalism among the Russian educated elite.

IV. THE BOURBON RESTORATION IN FRANCE AND THE REVOLUTION OF 1830: Louis XVIII's Charter established a conservative constitutional monarchy in France.

A. Conservative ULTRA-ROYALISTS rejected any compromise with liberalism, insisting on a complete reestablishment of French absolutism.

B. THE REVOLUTION OF 1830 broke out after the government of the very conservative Charles X, Louis XVIII's successor, attempted to override the constitutional guarantees of the Charter. French liberals offered the throne to Louis-Philippe, who agreed to rule as a constitutional monarch.

V. LIBERAL ASSAULTS ON THE OLD ORDER: Other liberal movements followed on the heels of the French Revolution of 1830.

A. THE REVOLT IN BELGIUM was successful and ended in the creation of an independent Belgian state.

B. LIBERALIZATION IN SWITZERLAND was also markedly successful, resulting in a period of social and political "regeneration."

VI. NATIONALIST STRUGGLES: Like liberalism, nationalism threatened the Congress system, especially in Central Europe.

A. THE REVOLT IN POLAND resulted in temporary independence for the Poles, but it was soon put down by Russian troops, and Poland was absorbed into the Russian Empire.

B. UPRISINGS IN ITALY AND SPAIN also failed. The Italian states remained dominated by foreign powers, and Spain fell under the rule of a conservative general.

C. GERMAN NATIONALISM IN CENTRAL EUROPE had a powerful influence on intellectuals, but German liberals were more moderate and cautious than their British and French counterparts. Many hoped that the individual German states would gradually move to institute liberal reforms.

VII. CRISIS AND COMPROMISE IN GREAT BRITAIN: Despite considerable tensions within British society, revolution was avoided by means of compromise between the landed elite and the merchant middle class.

A. RELIGIOUS AND ELECTORAL REFORM: Catholics were gradually granted full political rights in the 1820s, while pressure for electoral reform grew among the middle class and workers.

B. THE REFORM BILL OF 1832 doubled the electorate, strengthening the political power of the middle class and enabling the passage of liberal measures like the banning of slavery and the regulation of child labor.

C. THE REPEAL OF THE CORN LAWS AND CHARTISM: In 1832, the protectionist Corn Laws were repealed in the face of rising protest, but workers' demands for an increased political role, expressed in the Chartist movement, went largely unheeded.

VIII. CONCLUSION

2. HISTORICAL GEOGRAPHY

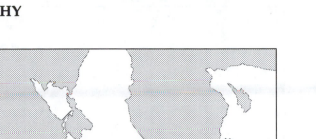

MAP 14.1 EUROPE IN 1815

MAP 14.2   THE BIRTH OF BELGIUM

Map Exercises

Familiarize yourself with the maps provided in your text, and then attempt to locate the following places on Blank Maps 14.1 and 14.2.

EUROPE IN 1815

Austria
Bavaria
Denmark
Dutch Republic
France
German
    Confederation
Great Britain
Habsburg Empire
Illyria
Lombardy-Venetia
Ottoman Empire
Papal States

Kingdom of Poland
Portugal
Kingdom of Prussia
Kingdom of
    Piedmont-
    Sardinia
Southern
    Netherlands
Spain
Swiss
    Confederation
Kingdom of the
    Two Sicilies

THE BIRTH OF BELGIUM

Amsterdam
Antwerp
Belgium
Bruges
Brussels
Ghent
The Hague
Liège
Luxembourg

Maastricht
Meuse River
Mosel River
Netherlands
Rhine River
Rotterdam
Scheldt River
Tournai
Ypres

Map Questions

Compare Map 13.1 (The Empire of Napoleon, p. 560) with Map 14.1 (Europe after the Congress of Vienna, 1815, p. 593). Describe the major territorial settlements reached at the Congress of Vienna.

In what parts of Europe did most of the liberal revolts take place? The nationalist revolts?

3. PEOPLE AND TERMS TO IDENTIFY

Congress of Vienna
Metternich
Holy Alliance
German Confederation
Concert of Europe
Conservatism
Volk
Junkers
Liberalism
Carbonari

Monroe Doctrine
Carlsbad Decrees
Philhellenic Movement
Decembrist Revolt
Ultras
French Revolution
   of 1830
Louis-Philippe
Belgium
Chopin

Mazzini
Rossini's *William Tell*
Hegel
Zollverein (German
   Customs Union)
Catholic Emancipation
   Act
Reform Bill of 1832
Repeal of the Corn Laws
Chartism

4. STUDY QUESTIONS

1. What were the goals of the key participants in the Congress of Vienna? *Historical Continuities:* To what extent did the Vienna settlement represent an attempt to turn the clock back to 1789?

2. How did the territorial settlements reached at Vienna serve to create a new balance of power in Europe?

3. *Historical Continuities:* What was being "restored" in Restoration Europe?

4. Describe the basic tenets of early-nineteenth-century conservatism. Who were the conservatives?

5. Describe the basic tenets of early-nineteenth-century liberalism. Who were the liberals?

6. Why did the Greek Revolt pose a problem for European conservatives?

7. Who supported liberal reform in Russia? Who opposed it?

8. What did the French "Ultras" want?

9. What caused the French Revolution of 1830?

10. Why were the Belgians successful and the Poles unsuccessful in their respective revolts?

11. Why were the efforts of Italian nationalists like Mazzini unsuccessful during this period?

12. How did German liberalism differ from French and British liberalism?

13. *Historical Continuities:* Why was there no revolution in Britain during the eighteenth and nineteenth centuries?

5. ANALYZING ART AND ARTIFACTS

Compare the portraits of Charles X (p. 612) and Simon Bolívar (p. 603). In what ways are these two leaders represented as the embodiments of conservatism and liberalism, respectively.

What is the political meaning of Delacroix's *Massacre at Chios* (p. 607)? How is this meaning conveyed in the painting?

How are the political and economic leaders of France represented in Honoré Daumier's caricatures (pp. 610 and 615)?

6. TECHNOLOGY AND HISTORY

Historical Continuities: The picture on p. 636 is the first contemporary photographic image to appear in your text. How do you expect that the new technology of photography affected nineteenth-century Europeans' perceptions of their world? To what political purposes might this invention be put?

7. HISTORICAL ANALYSIS: INTERPRETIVE ESSAYS

1. How successful was the Congress of Vienna in "restoring" the Old Regime?

2. Why was the conservative state structure reestablished by the Congress of Vienna increasingly threatened by opposition movements in the years between 1815 and 1848?

3. What is the relationship between liberalism and nationalism? To what extent are these two ideologies compatible or incompatible?

4. *Historical Continuities:* What were the eighteenth-century origins of nineteenth-century liberalism?

5. *Historical Continuities:* To what extent are liberalism and democracy compatible? Under what conditions do you expect a nineteenth-century liberal would accept an extension of the suffrage to women and/or the working classes?

8. HISTORICAL VOICES: THE CONSERVATIVE REVIVAL AND THE LIBERAL RESPONSE

A. The Restoration of Throne and Altar

Born in the Savoy, a holding of the Italian Kingdom of Piedmont-Sardinia, Joseph de Maistre was by language and culture French. A devout Catholic and a fiercely monarchist noble, he chose to emigrate from his native city of Chambéry when it was captured by French armies under Napoleon. Maistre lived at first in Switzerland, but left for Russia in 1803, where he served as an envoy of the king of Sardinia until 1817. After his recall from Russia, Maistre settled in Turin and continued in the service of the Sardinian state. While he published a variety of political writings, his best known works are *On the Papacy* (1819) and *Saint-Petersburg Evenings* (1821).

Along with Edmund Burke and the Vicomte de Bonald, Maistre became one of the most important late-eighteenth-century adversaries of the Enlightenment and the French Revolution, establishing himself as the champion of a political theory steeped in Christian religiosity. According to Maistre, human beings are fundamentally depraved beings desperately in need of the guidance provided by kings and priests. Maistre's nationalism reflects this fundamentally theological orientation: each nation is a creation of God and has a unique, preordained role to play in God's plan for humanity. Thus, the French Revolution can be said to have had a "satanic character" insofar as it represents a rejection of this divine "mission."

Already in 1796, in his *Considerations on France*, Maistre had launched a scathing attack on secularism and republicanism. His arguments, elaborated in subsequent works, provided a theoretical basis for the legitimist revival of the years following Napoleon's defeat at Waterloo, and served as a blueprint for reactionary initiatives like the "Holy Alliance." In the following passages from this work, Maistre discusses the role of Providence in human life and national politics, and he condemns the secular philosophies of the eighteenth century that inspired the French Revolution.

FROM *Considérations sur la France* by Joseph de Maistre

We are all attached to the throne of the Supreme Being by a supple chain, which restrains us without reducing us to servitude.

What is most admirable in the universal order of things is the action of free beings held under the hand of the divine. Freely slaves, they act at one and the same time both voluntarily and necessarily: they really do what they wish, but without being able to upset the general plans. Each of these beings occupies the center of a sphere of activity whose diameter varies at the pleasure of the *eternal Geometer,* who is able to extend, restrain, stop or direct their will without altering its nature.

Each nation, like each individual, has been given a mission which it must accomplish. France exercises a veritable magistracy over Europe, which it would be useless to deny, and which she has abused in the most sinful manner. Most importantly, she was the leader of the [European]religious system, and it is not without reason that her King was known as *"Very Christian"* . . . Now, since [France] has used her influence to repudiate her vocation and to demoralize Europe, one should not be astonished if she is recalled to her duty by terrible means.

. . . any assault on sovereignty, *in the name of the Nation,* is always a more or less national crime; because it is always more or less the fault of the Nation that a certain number of sedition-mongers have been placed in such a position to commit this crime in the name [of the Nation]. Thus, it is undoubtedly true that the death of Louis XVI was not *wanted* by all French people; but the great majority of of the people *wanted,* for more than two years, all of the follies, all of the injustices, all of the assaults which led to the disaster of the 21st of January [1793].*

Now, all national crimes against sovereignty are punished immediately and terribly; that is a law that has never suffered an exception. . . . Every drop of Louis XVI's blood cost France torrents of blood; four million French people, perhaps, paid with their heads for the great national crime of an antireligious and antisocial insurrection, crowned by an act of regicide.

Pay careful attention then, all of you who have not yet learned enough from history. You said that the king's scepter supported the pope's tiara. Well! There is no longer a scepter in the great arena: it is broken, and the pieces have been thrown in the mud. You did not know to what point the influence of a rich and powerful priesthood could uphold the dogmas that it preached. . . . There are no more priests: they have been expelled, slaughtered, degraded; they have been despoiled; and those who escaped the guillotine, the stake, the dagger, the firing squad, drowning, and deportation, are today the recipients of the charity they once gave away. You feared the power of custom, the ascendancy of authority, the illusions of the imagination. None of that exists anymore: there is no more custom; there is no master; each man's spirit is his alone. Philosophy gnawed away the cement that held men together, and there are no longer any moral communities. Civil authority, favoring with all its might the overthrow of the old system, gives to the enemies of Christianity all of the support it once gave to Christianity itself. The human spirit takes every shape imaginable in the hopes of combating the old national religion. These efforts are applauded and rewarded, and contrary efforts are treated as crimes. You no longer have anything to fear from the enchantment of the eyes, which are always the first to be deceived. Stately show, vain ceremonies, no longer overawe men who have seen a mockery made of everything for the last seven years. The temples are closed, and are opened only for noisy debates and the bacchanalias of an unrestrained people. The altars have been overturned; filthy animals have been paraded through the streets wearing bishops' vestments; communion cups have been used in abominable orgies; and upon those altars, which the ancient faith surrounded with adoring cherubs, naked prostitutes have been paraded. So-called

---

*The date on which Louis XVI was executed.

"philosophy" has no more grievances, then; all human fortunes are in its favor; everything is done for it and against its rival. If it is victorious, it will not say, like Caesar: "I came, I saw, and I conquered"; but it will, after all, have conquered: it can clap its hands and sit proudly on an overturned cross. But if Christianity emerges from this terrible ordeal purer and more vigorous; if the Christian Hercules, by his own force alone, lifts up *the son of the earth,* and crushes him in his arms, *patuit Deus* [God will endure].—People of France! Make way for the Very Christian King, carry him yourselves to his ancient throne; lift his banner, and see that his golden coins, traveling again from one pole to the other, carry to all regions the triumphal motto: CHRIST RULES, HE REIGNS, HE IS VICTOR!

Source: Joseph de Maistre. *Considérations sur la France,* pp. 11, 16–17, 77–79. Trans. Kathleen M. Nilan. Paris: Nouvelle Librairie Nationale, 1907.

Questions
    What does Maistre mean when he says that human beings act "both voluntarily and necessarily"?
    According to Maistre, what were the results of Enlightenment thought and the French Revolution?
    Given Maistre's arguments, what significance do you expect he would ascribe to the Bourbon Restoration of 1815?

B. Youthful Nationalism Challenges "Grey-Headed" Tradition

Born in the Republic of Genoa, which was absorbed by the Kingdom of Piedmont-Sardinia in 1814, Giuseppe Mazzini (1805–1872) was at least three generations younger than Maistre, and worlds removed from the Catholic legitimist's political and religious orientation. An ardent and romantic nationalist, Mazzini dedicated his life to the cause of Italian unification. Despite his sincere religiosity, Mazzini was not a Christian. A staunch republican, he rejected both monarchist and papal solutions to the problem of Italian disunity, and spent much of his life in exile from his beloved Italy.

In 1832 Mazzini, then twenty-seven years old and living in Marseille, France, founded "Young Italy," a secret organization dedicated to the cause of Italian unification. Mazzini had been deeply disappointed by the collapse of the Italian revolutionary movement in 1830, which he blamed on "grey-headed men, educated under the old system of ideas, distrustful of the young, and still under the influence of the terror inspired by the excesses of the French Revolution." He thus called on the young to work toward a unified—and democratic—Italian nation.

The following excerpts from "General Instructions for the Members of Young Italy" (issued around the time of the launching of Young Italy in 1832) clearly demonstrate the distinctive synthesis of romanticism, nationalism, and liberalism that typified much of the nationalist rhetoric of the early nineteenth century.

Interestingly, the American edition of Mazzini's writings within which these excerpts were published includes an introduction written by William Lloyd Garrison, one of the most radical of the American anti-slavery activists. Garrison was drawn to Mazzini because of the Italian nationalist's broad-minded dedication to the eradication of oppression, not only in Italy but around the world. In his introduction, Garrison quotes from a letter written by Mazzini to an American abolitionist, in which Mazzini expressed his awareness of the connections between his Italian nationalist movement and the American anti-slavery movement:

    . . . We are fighting the same sacred battle for freedom and the emancipation of the oppressed: you sir, against *Negro*, we against *white* slavery. . . . May the day soon arrive in which the word

BONDAGE will disappear from our living languages, and only point out a historical record!

FROM *Life, Writings, and Political Principles* **by Joseph Mazzini**

Young Italy is a brotherhood of Italians who believe in a law of Progress and Duty, and are convinced that Italy is destined to become one nation,—convinced also that she possesses sufficient strength within herself to become one, and that the ill success of her former efforts is to be attributed not to the weakness, but to the misdirection of the revolutionary elements within her,—that the secret of force lies in constancy and unity of effort. They join this association in the firm intent of consecrating both thought and action to the great aim of reconstituting Italy as one independent sovereign nation of free men and equals. . . .

By Italy we understand,—1. Continental and peninsular Italy, bounded on the north by the upper circle of the Alps, on the south by the sea, on the west by the mouths of the Varo, and on the east by Trieste; 2. The islands proved Italian by the language of the inhabitants, and destined, under a special administrative organization, to form a part of the Italian political unity. By the Nation we understand the universality of Italians bound together by a common pact, and governed by the same laws. . . .

Young Italy is Republican and Unitarian. Republican,—Because theoretically every nation is destined, by the law of God and humanity, to form a free and equal community of brothers; and the republican is the only form of government that insures this future. Because all true sovereignty resides essentially in the nation, the sole progressive and continuous interpreter of the supreme moral law. Because, whatever be the form of privilege that constitutes the apex of the social edifice, its tendency is to spread among the other classes, and by undermining the equality of the citizens, to endanger the liberty of the country. Because, when the sovereignty is recognized as existing not in the whole body, but in several distinct powers, the path to usurpation is laid open, and the struggle for supremacy between these powers is inevitable; distrust and organized hostility take the place of harmony, which is society's law of life. Because the monarchical element being incapable of sustaining itself alone by the side of the popular element, it necessarily involves the existence of the intermediate element of an aristocracy—the source of inequality and corruption to the whole nation. Because both history and the nature of things teach us that elective monarchy tends to generate anarchy; and hereditary monarchy tends to generate despotism. Because, when monarchy is not, as in the Middle Ages, based upon the belief now extinct in right divine, it becomes too weak to be a bond of unity and authority in the state. Because the inevitable tendency of the series of progressive transformations taking place in Europe, is towards the enthronement of the republican principle, and because the inauguration of the monarchical principle in Italy would carry along with it the necessity of a new revolution shortly after. . . .

Young Italy is Unitarian,—Because, without unity, there is no true nation. Because, without unity, there is no real strength; and Italy, surrounded as she is by powerful, united, and jealous nations, has need of strength before all things. Because federalism, by reducing her to the political impotence of Switzerland, would necessarily place her under the

influence of one of the neighboring nations. Because federalism, by re-
viving the local rivalries now extinct, would throw Italy back upon the
Middle Ages. . . .

National unity, as understood by Young Italy, does not imply the
despotism of any, but the association and concord of all. The life inherent
in each locality is sacred. Young Italy would have the *administrative* organization designed upon a broad basis of religious respect for the liberty
of each commune, but the *political* organization, destined to represent
the nation in Europe, should be one and central. Without unity of religious belief, and unity of social pact; without unity of civil, political, and
penal legislation, there is no true nation.

Source: Joseph Mazzini. *Life, Writings, and Political Principles,* pp. 62, 64–65, 67–68. Intro.
William Lloyd Garrison. New York: Hurd & Houghton, 1872.

Questions

What does Mazzini mean by "Italy"?

What does Mazzini mean when he says that Young Italy is "Republican and Unitarian"?

How do you think Maistre would have responded to Mazzini's arguments?

9. IMPORTANT HISTORICAL FACTS: STUDY DRILLS

A. Multiple Choice

1. The Holy Alliance affirmed the
religious basis of the Congress system.
It was drafted by
   A. Emperor Francis I of Austria.
   B. King Louis XVIII of France.
   C. Tsar Alexander I of Russia.
   D. Pope Pius VII.

2. These Prussian nobles owned 40
percent of the land, maintained a
stranglehold over the military officer
corps, and looked with contempt on
the untitled bourgeoisie:
   A. *volk*
   B. Junkers
   C. Young Germans
   D. Burschenschaften

3. All of the following are tenets of
nineteenth-century conservatism
except:
   A. The church and the state are the
twin pillars of social order.
   B. The power of the king comes from
God and is inviolable.
   C. Revolutionary change is bad.
   D. All human beings are endowed
with certain "natural rights."

4. All of the following are tenets of
nineteenth-century liberalism *except:*
   A. Separation of church and state.

B. Freedom of the press.
C. The maintenance of a hereditary
nobility.
D. Constitutional government.

5. In 1823, the United States declared
that North and South America were
not open to future colonization by any
European powers. This declaration
was known as
   A. Manifest Destiny.
   B. the American Declaration of
Independence.
   C. the Monroe Doctrine.
   D. the Charter.

6. In 1819, a liberal German student
murdered a conservative historian
believed to be a tsarist spy. This
resulted in
   A. the Six Acts.
   B. the Carlsbad Decrees.
   C. the Decembrist Revolt.
   D. the Massacre of Chios.

7. Louis-Philippe was asked to take the
throne of France in 1830 because
   A. he knew how to hold his Bourbon.
   B. he was ardently conservative.
   C. he was a liberal relative of the
ruling Bourbons.
   D. he had helped to execute Louis
XVI.

8. The residents of the Belgian state created in 1830 spoke
   A. Dutch and German.
   B. Belgian.
   C. English.
   D. Flemish and French.

9. The Zollverein was created in 1834 in order to
   A. regulate the price of wheat.
   B. remove customs barriers between German states.
   C. demonstrate the liberal sentiments of German students.
   D. provide a platform for protests against Enlightenment thought.

10. The Catholic Emancipation Act
    A. allowed British Catholics to become Members of Parliament.
    B. freed all Catholics imprisoned in the Ottoman Empire.
    C. freed all slaves in the British colonies.
    D. exempted all French Catholics from papal control.

B. Chronological Relationships

Place each of the following events on a timeline, and identify the date on which each occurred. Which of the above events would you consider liberal victories? Conservative victories? Why?

Charles X inherits the French throne.
General Narváez takes power in Spain.
Greece becomes an independent kingdom under King Otto I.
Louis-Philippe becomes "King of the French."
Simón Bolívar liberates Venezuela from Spanish rule.
The British Parliament passes the Catholic Emancipation Act.
The Carlsbad Decrees.
The Congress of Vienna.
The Decembrist Revolt is suppressed in Russia.
The German Customs Union is established.

C. Matching Exercise: Historical Actors

_____ Carbonari
_____ Chartist
_____ Chopin
_____ Decembrist
_____ Hegel
_____ Mazzini
_____ Metternich
_____ Philhellene
_____ Ultra
_____ William Tell

A. A British working-class activist who agitated for universal suffrage in the 1830s and 1840s (and probably belonged to the London Workingmen's Association).
B. A fanatical French royalist.
C. A fourteenth-century Swiss patriot who became the subject of an anti-Austrian opera by Italian composer Rossini.
D. A German philosopher whose nationalism was expressed in a reverence for a strong state.
E. A leading figure at the Congress of Vienna and a strong proponent of conservative political principles.
F. A member of a Russian secret society, which rose up in revolt against Tsar Nicholas I in 1825.
G. A member of an Italian revolutionary society sworn to secrecy by a charcoal mark on his forehead.
H. An Italian lawyer and revolutionary who campaigned all over Europe for the creation of a unified Italian republic.
I. A Polish composer who moved to France, but continued to inspire Polish nationalists with his polonaises.
J. Like Byron and Shelley, a lover of all things Greek.

IMPORTANT HISTORICAL FACTS: STUDY-DRILL ANSWERS

A. Multiple Choice
1. C. Tsar Alexander I of Russia.
2. B. Junkers
3. D. All human beings are endowed with certain "natural rights."
4. C. The maintenance of a hereditary nobility.
5. C. the Monroe Doctrine.
6. B. the Carlsbad Decrees.
7. C. he was a liberal relative of the ruling Bourbons.
8. D. Flemish and French.
9. B. remove customs barriers between German states.
10. A. allowed British Catholics to become Members of Parliament.

B. Chronological Relationships

1814–1815	The Congress of Vienna.	CONSERVATIVE
1819	The Carlsbad Decrees.	CONSERVATIVE
1821	Simón Bolívar liberates Venezuela.	LIBERAL
1824	Charles X inherits the French throne.	CONSERVATIVE
1825	The Decembrist Revolt is suppressed in Russia.	CONSERVATIVE
1829	Parliament passes the Catholic Emancipation Act.	LIBERAL
1830	Louis-Philippe becomes "King of the French."	LIBERAL
1832	Greece becomes an independent kingdom.	LIBERAL
1834	The German Customs Union is established.	LIBERAL
1843	General Narváez takes power in Spain.	CONSERVATIVE

C. Matching Exercise: Historical Actors

G. Carbonari
A. Chartist
I. Chopin
F. Decembrist
D. Hegel
H. Mazzini
E. Metternich
J. Philhellene
B. Ultra
C. William Tell

15 The Middle Classes in the Era of Liberalism

1. CHAPTER OUTLINE

I. DIVERSITY OF THE MIDDLE CLASSES: The members of the nineteenth-century bourgeoisie ranged from the most affluent bankers to the most modest shopkeepers.

   A. VARIATIONS IN BOURGEOIS EUROPE: In Western Europe, the bourgeoisie played a significant role in society and commanded considerable respect; in Eastern Europe, the middle classes were minuscule and exercised little political power.

   B. THE ENTREPRENEURIAL IDEAL AND SOCIAL MOBILITY: The middle classes revered the respectable "self-made man" who moved up in society as a result of hard work, self-discipline, and thrift.

   C. The RISING PROFESSIONS: Lawyers, doctors, and other professionals struggled to improve their status, sometimes establishing professional organizations like the British Medical Society.

II. Despite considerable national differences, a distinctive MIDDLE-CLASS CULTURE developed throughout Europe.

   A. MARRIAGE AND FAMILY: The family served as crucial focus for middle-class life. Bourgeois men and women increasingly insisted on marrying for love, and they began to limit the number of their children.

   B. SEPARATE SPHERES: Middle-class men were expected to participate in the public sphere of work and politics, while middle-class women were held to be the guardians of the private sphere of domesticity. Some feminists protested women's exclusion from public life, but women remained subject to their fathers' or husbands' authority.

   C. A CULTURE OF COMFORT grew up around the well-furnished middle-class home. Increasing leisure time created a growing demand for diversions like novels and sight-seeing.

   D. EDUCATION: Middle-class men attended secondary schools and universities in growing numbers, but the middle-class remained ambivalent about the utility of education, especially for women and the working poor.

   E. Despite disenchantment with the organized church and secularizing tendencies, the middle classes remained deeply attached to RELIGION. It reinforced their sense of confidence and respectability and was believed to have a "moralizing" effect on workers.

   F. ASSOCIATIONAL LIFE AND PUBLIC SERVICE: Clubs and other voluntary organizations satisfied middle-class needs for socializing and for charitable activities.

III. LIBERALISM AND ITS AMBIGUITIES
   A. LIBERALS AND THE FRANCHISE: Most liberals favored expanding the electorate, but most also rejected universal manhood suffrage.
   B. LIBERALS AND LAISSEZ-FAIRE: Liberals rejected state interference in the workings of the economy, and insisted that governments pass only those laws that would provide "the greatest good for the greatest number."
   C. Yet an increasing number of liberals came to support an expansion of STATE INTERVENTION in public life, either out of fear of working-class radicalism or out of a growing belief in the necessity of social justice.

IV. A reaction against the aristocratic classicism of the eighteenth-century, ROMANTICISM was a complex cultural phenomenon, emphasizing the individual fulfillment dear to the European middle classes.
   A. ROMANTIC LITERATURE AND PAINTING rejected the objectivity and rationality of the Enlightenment in favor of the subjectivity and emotionality of works like *The Raft of the Medusa* and *Faust*.
   B. ROMANTIC MUSIC was also emotional and passionate and enjoyed considerable popularity among the general public.

V. CONCLUSION

2. HISTORICAL GEOGRAPHY

Map Exercise
   Review the maps provided in the previous chapter (pp. 593, 620, 623 in the textbook), and then attempt to locate the following cities on Blank Map 15.1.

REVIEW OF EUROPEAN CITIES

Amsterdam	Belgrade	Bordeaux	Manchester
Athens	Berlin	Brussels	Marseille
		Constantinople	Munich
		Copenhagen	Naples
		Frankfurt	Paris
		Hamburg	Rome
		Lisbon	St. Petersburg
		London	Vienna
		Madrid	Warsaw

3. PEOPLE AND TERMS TO IDENTIFY

Bourgeoisie	Comfort	Utilitarianism
Respectability	Baedeker Guides	Iron Law of Wages
Self-Made Man	Thomas Arnold	John Stuart Mill
British Medical Society	Sunday Schools	Romanticism
Separate Spheres	Laissez-faire	Beethoven

4. STUDY QUESTIONS

1. *Historical Continuities:* Where do the terms *bourgeois* and *burgher* come from? What does this etymology tell you about the origins of the European middle classes?

2. What differentiated the nineteenth-century middle classes from the upper and lower classes? What were the minimum requirements for entry into the bourgeoisie?

3. What is "respectability"? Why was it so important to the nineteenth-century middle classes?

4. What role did the family play in middle-class life?

5. Describe the "separate spheres" in which middle-class men and women lived.

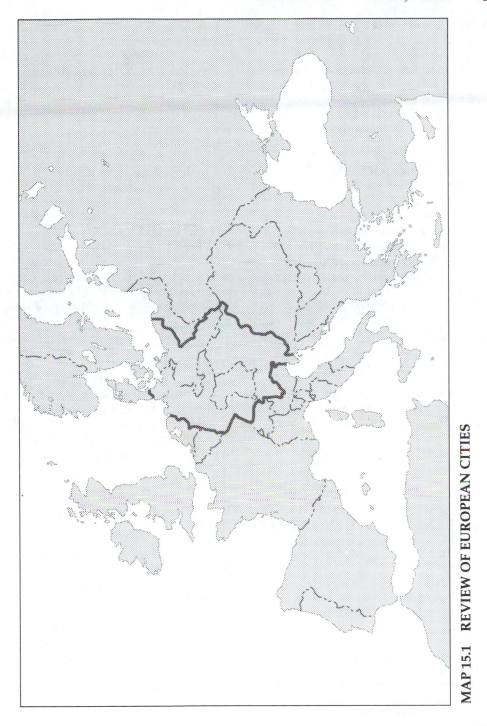

MAP 15.1 REVIEW OF EUROPEAN CITIES

6. What functions did education, religion, and voluntary associations serve in middle-class culture?

7. What means did the middle-classes use to "moralize" the working classes? Why?

8. Why did liberals reject state intervention in the economy? When were they willing to tolerate state intervention in other areas of public life?

9. In what sense was romanticism an expression of middle-class cultural values and ideals?

5. ANALYZING ART AND ARTIFACTS

What do the illustrations presented in the text tell you about the material conditions of middle-class life? How did the European bourgeoisie decorate the interiors of its homes? How did worker housing differ from middle-class housing?

What makes the portraits of the Imperial Guard and of the poet Goethe (pp. 664 and 665 in the textbook) "romantic" in their style and subject matter?

6. TECHNOLOGY AND HISTORY

In what sense is the flush toilet a quintessentially middle-class technology? What is the larger historical significance of this innovation?

7. HISTORICAL ANALYSIS: INTERPRETIVE ESSAYS

1. *Historical Continuities:* To what extent were the European middle classes a product of the rise of cities and towns?

2. Write the biography of a "typical" middle-class woman.

3. How might a man of very humble origins make his way into the middle class?

4. Defend this statement: "The single most important characteristic of the nineteenth-century European middle classes was individualism."

8. HISTORICAL VOICES: PRIVATE AND PUBLIC LIVES OF THE NINETEENTH-CENTURY MIDDLE CLASSES

A. Coventry Patmore and the "Angel in the House"

Coventry Patmore's four part novel in verse, *The Angel in the House,* was one of the most popular English-language poems of the mid-nineteenth century. A lyric celebration of courtship and marriage, it helped to promote a new, intensely idealized model of companionate marriage based on love and mutual respect. Although today's readers may find the poem excessively sentimental, Patmore's account of the road to married bliss delighted its Victorian audience.

Coventry Patmore (1823–1896) himself enjoyed a very happy first marriage to a minister's daughter, and the poem is at least in part autobiographical. The son of an unsuccessful investor, Patmore found financial security as an employee of the British Museum, and personal satisfaction in his role as husband and father to six children. A deeply religious man, he converted to Catholicism after the death of his beloved first wife, and later remarried—again for love. In the late 1870s, he began a long poem about the soul's "marriage" to God, but destroyed the manuscript on the advice of a spiritual advisor.

As its title suggests, *The Angel in the House* (published in four parts between 1854 and 1863) portrays the family sphere as a refuge of love and spiritual values, presided over by an "angelic" and fundamentally chaste wife and mother. The first passage cited below celebrates the joys of domesticity in a description of the tenth anniversary of the marriage of the narrator and his wife Honoria. In the second passage the enduring happiness of this marriage is explained as a result of the sexual purity of Honoria and the sexual restraint of her husband.

FROM *The Angel in the House* by **Coventry Patmore**

Her sons pursue the butterflies,
   Her baby daughter mocks the doves
With throbbing coo; in his fond eyes
   She's Venus with her little Loves;
Her footfall dignifies the earth,
   Her form's the native-land of grace,
And, lo, his coming lights with mirth
   Its court and capital her face!
Full proud her favour makes her lord,
   And that her flatter'd bosom knows.
She takes his arm without a word,
   In lanes of laurel and of rose.
Ten years to-day has she been his.
   He but begins to understand,
He says, the dignity and bliss
   She gave him when she gave her hand.
She, answering, says, he disenchants
   The past, though that was perfect; he
Rejoins, the present nothing wants
   But briefness to be ecstasy.
He lauds her charms; her beauty's glow
   Wins from the spoiler Time new rays;
Bright looks reply, approving so
   Beauty's elixir vitæ, praise.
Upon a beech he bids her mark
   Where, ten years since, he carved her name;
It grows there with the growing bark,
   And in his heart it grows the same.
For that her soft arm presses his
   Close to her fond, maternal breast;
He tells her, each new kindness is
   The effectual sum of all the rest!
And, whilst the cushat, mocking, coo'd,
   They blest the days they had been wed,
At cost of those in which he woo'd,
   Till everything was three times said. . . .

THE MARRIED LOVER
Why, having won her, do I woo?
   Because her spirit's vestal grace
Provokes me always to pursue,
   But, spirit-like, eludes embrace;
Because her womanhood is such
   That, as on court-days subjects kiss
The Queen's hand, yet so near a touch
   Affirms no mean familiarness,
Nay, rather marks more fair the height
   Which can with safety so neglect

To dread, as lower ladies might
    That grace could meet with disrespect,
Thus she with happy favour feeds
    Allegiance from a love so high
That thence no false conceit proceeds
    Of difference bridged, or state put by;
Because, although in act and word
    As lowly as a wife can be,
Her manners, when they call me lord
    Remind me 'tis by courtesy;
Not with her least consent of will,
    Which would my proud affection hurt,
But by the noble style that still
    Imputes an unattain'd desert;
Because her gay and lofty brows,
    When all is won which hope can ask,
Reflect a light of hopeless snows
    That bright in virgin ether bask;
Because, though free of the outer court
    I am, this Temple keeps its shrine
Sacred to Heaven; because, in short
    She's not and never can be mine.

Source: Coventry Patmore. *The Angel in the House,* pp. 112–114, 183–184. London: George Routledge and Sons, 1905.

Questions
To what extent is this representation of marriage "middle class"?
Is this a "romantic" poem?
Why do you think nineteenth-century feminists would have objected to this portrayal of womanhood? Does it seem objectionable today? Why or why not?

B. John Stuart Mill and the Liberty of the Individual

There is, on first glance, little in common between Patmore, a minor poet of a distinctly religious bent, and John Stuart Mill (1806–1873), one of the most important liberal (and agnostic) thinkers of the nineteenth century. However, both men were deeply marked by the romantic movement and by new attitudes about the happiness to be derived from marital and family relations.

Mill was the son of the philosopher and historian, James Mill, an unaffectionate and austere utilitarian, who raised John Stuart to be a sort of intellectual child prodigy. Having been started on Greek by his father at the age of three, Mill mastered several additional languages (including Latin), advanced mathematics, and political economy by his early teens, and

published his first article—an essay on economics—when he was seventeen. In 1826, Mill, who had become what he himself described in his *Autobiography* as "a mere reasoning machine," suffered a "crisis in [his]mental history," characterized by a sense of "dry heavy dejection." As a result, he rejected the Enlightenment's single-minded emphasis on reason in favor of romanticism's cultivation of the emotions. While Mill could never be accused of having allowed his sensibility to overwhelm his common sense, he acquired a "sentimental education" from poetry, a literary genre his father rejected as lacking in utility. A few years after this turning point in his life, Mill met Harriet Taylor, a married woman who was to be the great love—and intellectual companion—of his life. Having already shared ten years of companionship, the couple finally married in 1851, after the death of Taylor's husband.

Throughout his life, Mill remained committed to the basic tenets of political liberalism, but he rejected the atomistic individualism of thinkers like his father. As an adult, Mill came to believe that governmental guarantees of fundamental civil liberties profited the community as much as the isolated individual. Unlike the most strident advocates of laissez-faire policies, Mill argued that democratically elected governments had a duty to intervene in support of economic and social justice, even if this meant placing limits on individual freedom. However, as is apparent in the following passage from *On Liberty*, published in 1859, shortly after his wife's death, Mill never abandoned his deep commitment to the rights of the individual.

FROM *Essay on Liberty* by John Stuart Mill

The object of this Essay is to assert one very simple principle, as entitled to govern absolutely the dealings of society with the individual in the way of compulsion and control, whether the means used be physical force in the form of legal penalties, or the moral coercion of public opinion. That principle is, that the sole end for which mankind are warranted, individually or collectively in interfering with the liberty of action of any of their number, is self-protection. That the only purpose for which power can be rightfully exercised over any member of a civilized community, against his will, is to prevent harm to others. His own good, either physical or moral, is not a sufficient warrant. He cannot rightfully be compelled to do or forbear because it will be better for him to do so, because it will make him happier, because, in the opinions of others, to do so would be wise, or even right. These are good reasons for remonstrating with him, or reasoning with him, or persuading him, or entreating him, but not for compelling him, or visiting him with any evil, in case he do otherwise. To justify that, the conduct from which it is desired to deter him must be calculated to produce evil to some one else. The only part of the conduct of any one, for which he is amenable to society, is that which concerns others. In the part which merely concerns himself, his independence is, of right, absolute. Over himself, over his own body and mind, the individual is sovereign.

It is, perhaps, hardly necessary to say that this doctrine is meant to apply only to human beings in the maturity of their faculties. We are not speaking of children, or of young persons below the age which the law may fix as that of manhood or womanhood. Those who are still in a state to require being taken care of by others, must be protected against their own actions as well as against external injury. For the same reason, we may leave out of consideration those backward states of society in which the race itself may be considered as in its nonage. The early difficulties in the way of spontaneous progress are so great, that there is seldom any choice of means for overcoming them; and a ruler full of the spirit of improvement is warranted in the use of any expedients that will attain an end, perhaps otherwise unattainable. Despotism is a legitimate mode of government in dealing with barbarians, provided the end be their improvement, and the means justified by actually effecting that end. Liberty, as a principle, has no application to any state of things anterior to the time when mankind have become capable of being improved by free and equal discussion. Until then, there is nothing for them but implicit obedience to an Akbar or a Charlemagne, if they are so fortunate as to find one. But as soon as mankind have attained the capacity of being guided to their own improvement by conviction or persuasion (a period long since reached in all nations with whom we need here concern ourselves), compulsion, either in the direct form or in that of pains and penalties for non-compliance, is no longer admissible as a means to their own good, and justifiable only for the security of others. . . .

Each is the proper guardian of his own health, whether bodily, or mental or spiritual. Mankind are greater gainers by suffering each other to live as seems good to themselves, than by compelling each to live as seems good to the rest.

Though this doctrine is anything but new, and, to some persons, may have the air of a truism, there is no doctrine which stands more directly opposed to the general tendency of existing opinion and practice. . . .

It will be convenient for the argument, if, instead of at once entering upon the general thesis, we confine ourselves in the first instance to a single branch of it, on which the principle here stated is, if not fully, yet to a certain point, recognized by the current opinions. This one branch is the Liberty of Thought. . . .

If all mankind minus one, were of one opinion, and only one person were of the contrary opinion, mankind would be no more justified in silencing that one person, than he, if he had the power, would be justified in silencing mankind. Were an opinion a personal possession of no value except to the owner; if to be obstructed in the enjoyment of it were simply a private injury, it would make some difference whether the injury was inflicted only on a few persons or on many. But the peculiar evil of silencing the expression of an opinion is, that it is robbing the human race; posterity as well as the existing generation; those who dissent from the opinion, still more than those who hold it. If the opinion is right, they are deprived of the opportunity of exchanging error for truth: if wrong, they lose, what is almost as great a benefit, the clearer perception and livelier impression of truth, produced by its collision with error. . . .

Strange it is, that men should admit the validity of the arguments for free discussion, but object to their being "pushed to an extreme," not seeing that unless the reasons are good for an extreme case, they are not good for any case. Strange that they should imagine that they are not assuming infallibility when they acknowledge that there should be free discussion on all subjects which can possibly be *doubtful*, but think that some particular principle or doctrine should be forbidden to be questioned because it is *so certain*, that is, because *they are certain* that it is certain. To call any proposition certain, while there is any one who would deny its certainty if permitted, but who is not permitted, is to assume that we ourselves, and those who agree with us, are the judges of certainty, and judges without hearing the other side.

Source: John Stuart Mill. *On Liberty.* In Harvard Classics, vol. 25. New York: P. F. Collier, 1909.

Questions

When does a government have a right to curtail individual liberties, according to Mill?

Why does Mill deprive children and "barbarians" of the liberties of civilized adults? What does this tell you about his conception of civil society?

In what ways do guarantees of individual freedom of expression benefit society as a whole?

9. IMPORTANT HISTORICAL FACTS: STUDY DRILLS

A. Multiple Choice

1. Among the European bourgeoisie, respectability might be said to have replaced
   A. hard work.
   B. inherited title.
   C. debauchery.
   D. comfort.
2. The "self-made man" was an example of
   A. ennoblement.
   B. upward social mobility.
   C. professionalization.
   D. a country gentleman.
3. Founded in 1832, it was intended to encourage standardized training and scientific research, as well as enhancing professional identity:
   A. The Jockey Club
   B. *The Magazine of Domestic Economy*
   C. The National Gallery
   D. The British Medical Society
4. Within their "separate sphere," middle-class women were expected to do all of the following *except:*
   A. educate children.
   B. supervise the household and its servants.
   C. assume personal control of financial assets.
   D. provide moral and religious guidance within the family.
5. The middle-class "culture of comfort" included all of the following amenities *except:*
   A. Wedgwood china.
   B. flush toilets.
   C. public gardens.
   D. colorful and ornate men's clothing.
6. When Europeans went sight-seeing, they were likely to take along
   A. a Baedeker guide-book.
   B. *The Pickwick Papers.*
   C. *The Wealth of Nations.*
   D. a camera.
7. Sunday schools were attended by
   A. the children of workers.
   B. university students.
   C. middle-class children.
   D. members of the clergy.
8. When liberal economists said, "Laissez-faire" ("Leave it alone"), they meant
   A. government should not interfere with commerce.
   B. government should not interfere with religion.
   C. government should not abolish tariffs and toll barriers.
   D. merchants should not interfere with government.
9. For utilitarians like Bentham, the sole measure of a law was whether it
   A. served religion.
   B. provided the greatest good for the greatest number.
   C. supported the power of the governing authorities.
   D. protected minority rights.
10. All of the following settings might have inspired a romantic artist *except:*
    A. a formal eighteenth-century garden.
    B. a storm at sea.
    C. ancient ruins.
    D. a Hungarian folk melody.

B. Chronological Relationships

Make a timeline illustrating the chronological relationship between the individuals listed in Study Drill C.

C. Matching Exercise: Historical Actors

_____ Thomas Arnold
_____ Jane Austen
_____ Ludwig von Beethoven
_____ Jeremy Bentham
_____ Henry Lord Brougham
_____ Sarah Stickney Ellis
_____ Théodore Géricault
_____ Johann Wolfgang von Goethe
_____ Thomas Malthus
_____ Harriet Taylor Mill
_____ John Stuart Mill
_____ Hannah More
_____ Niccolò Paganini
_____ Robert Peel
_____ David Ricardo
_____ Friedrich von Schiller
_____ Franz Schubert
_____ Percy Bysshe Shelley
_____ Adam Smith
_____ William Wordsworth

A. This British feminist argued in favor of women's rights in *The Enfranchisement of Women* (1807–1858).

B. A British utilitarian, his motto was: "The greatest good for the greatest number" (1748–1832).

C. A popular British author, she promoted female domesticity as a means of preserving national stability (1812–1872).

D. Born in Vienna, this composer incorporated folk songs into his musical works (1797–1828).

E. After he became deaf and heard only "the harmonies of his soul," this German composer produced increasingly romantic works (1770–1827).

F. Author of *The Wealth of Nations*, he popularized laissez-faire economic theory (1723–1790).

G. Co-author of the *Lyrical Ballads*, he found his inspiration in England's Lake District (1779–1850).

H. Despite his liberalism, this British thinker supported a certain degree of state intervention in the interests of social justice (1806–1873).

I. Having predicted that population growth would always outstrip food production, this British clergyman argued that education would make the poor more resigned to their suffering (1766–1834).

J. He founded the Society for the Diffusion of Useful Knowledge in the interests of educating the working poor (1778–1868).

K. In "The Aesthetic Education of Mankind," this German romantic argued that freedom could be found through Beauty (1759–1805).

L. In *Faust*, this German romantic author described a misunderstood heroic individual (1749–1832).

M. In "Hymn to Apollo," this short-lived British romantic glorified the lofty role of the poet (1792–1822).

N. His *Principles of Political Economy and Taxation* assumed that the "iron law of wages" would always keep workers' pay low (1772–1823).

O. A "self-made man," he became prime minister of Britain (1788–1850).

P. This British writer favored teaching poor children to read, but not to write (1745–1833).

Q. A celebrated Italian violinist, he thrilled audiences with his "bewitching" performances (1782–1840).

R. This French romantic painter was drawn to dramatic scenes of shipwrecks and battle (1791–1824).

S. Her witty novels demonstrated the virtues of middle-class respectability (1775–1817).

T. This headmaster of Rugby School introduced significant reforms into British secondary schools (1795–1842).

IMPORTANT HISTORICAL FACTS: STUDY-DRILL ANSWERS

A. Multiple Choice
1. B. inherited title.
2. B. upward social mobility.
3. D. The British Medical Society
4. C. assume personal control of financial assets.
5. D. colorful and ornate men's clothing.
6. A. a Baedeker guide-book.
7. A. the children of workers.
8. A. government should not interfere with commerce.
9. B. provided the greatest good for the greatest number.
10. A. a formal eighteenth-century garden.

B. Chronological Relationships

1723–1790 Smith
    1745–1833 More
    1748–1832 Bentham
    1749–1832 Goethe
        1759–1805 Schiller
            1766–1834 Malthus
                1770–1827 Beethoven
                1772–1823 Ricardo
                1775–1817 Austen
                1778–1868 Brougham
                1779–1850 Wordsworth
                    1782–1840 Paganini
                    1788–1850 Peel
                        1791–1824 Géricault
                        1792–1822 Shelley
                        1795–1842 Arnold
                        1797–1828 Schubert
                            1806–1873 John Stuart Mill
                            1807–1858 Harriet Taylor Mill
                          1812–1872 Ellis

C. Matching Exercise: Historical Actors

T. Thomas Arnold
S. Jane Austen
E. Ludwig von Beethoven
B. Jeremy Bentham
J. Henry Lord Brougham
C. Sarah Stickney Ellis
R. Théodore Géricault
L. Johann Wolfgang von Goethe
I. Thomas Malthus
A. Harriet Taylor Mill

H. John Stuart Mill
P. Hannah More
Q. Niccolò Paganini
O. Robert Peel
N. David Ricardo
K. Friedrich von Schiller
D. Franz Schubert
M. Percy Bysshe Shelley
F. Adam Smith
G. William Wordsworth

16 The Industrial Revolution, 1800–1850

1. CHAPTER OUTLINE

I. While historians once emphasized suddenness of change and technological innovation in their analyses of the Industrial Revolution, recent historians focus more on continuities in economic and industrial developments. They recognize the following as PRECONDITIONS FOR TRANSFORMATION:

   A. Between 1800 and 1850, Europe experienced a DEMOGRAPHIC EXPLOSION. Despite continued high rates of mortality, especially among the poor and infants, life expectancies increased for all Europeans.

   B. THE EXPANDING AGRICULTURAL BASE supported this population growth, especially in Western Europe, where the consolidation of land under cultivation and the commercialization of agriculture greatly increased crop yields.

   C. TRAINS AND STEAMBOATS, and better roads, improved transportation and contributed significantly to industrial development, as well as increasing opportunities for travel.

II. A VARIETY OF NATIONAL INDUSTRIAL EXPERIENCES: While northwestern nations like Great Britain and Belgium industrialized rapidly, other regions lagged behind, especially in Southern and Eastern Europe.

   A. IN THE VANGUARD: BRITAIN'S ERA OF MECHANIZATION began in the eighteenth century, giving the "workshop of the world" a head start on other industrializing nations.

   B. INDUSTRIALIZATION IN FRANCE was slower than in England, due in part to less efficient agriculture, weak financial institutions, and less liberal commercial policies.

   C. INDUSTRIALIZATION IN THE GERMAN STATES was less rapid than that to the west, but the Zollverein, a customs union established in 1834, and the efforts of industrialists like Alfred Krupp created a base for future industrial development.

   D. SPARSE INDUSTRIALIZATION IN SOUTHERN AND EASTERN EUROPE: The economies of nations such as Spain and Russia were still dominated by the traditional agricultural sector. In Southern and Eastern Europe, industrialization was slowed by underdeveloped natural resources, lack of government support, and inadequate transportation.

III. IMPACT OF THE INDUSTRIAL REVOLUTION: Despite dramatic changes in the European economy, most ordinary people's lives were only gradually affected by industrialization.

A. CONTINUITIES ON THE LAND: Landless agricultural laborers faced declining wages, due to a surplus of farm workers, and unemployment as a result of mechanization. Peasants' lives remained hard, especially in Southern and Eastern Europe, and some lashed out in desperate protest.

B. Urban Growth and URBANIZATION: The European population urbanized rapidly between 1800 and 1850. As cities grew, especially in Western Europe, the rich and the poor moved into separate neighborhoods, and serious strains were placed on existing urban resources, such as housing and water supplies.

C. MIGRATION AND MOBILITY: Faced with hardship in rural areas, and new opportunities in the cities, many Europeans chose to move, either to the nearest big town or to the distant New World. Urban growth relied almost entirely on this influx of migrants.

IV. INDUSTRIAL WORK AND WORKERS: Industrialization brought new hardships and was rejected by machine-breaking Luddites and criticized by novelists such as Charles Dickens.

A. GENDER AND FAMILY IN THE INDUSTRIAL AGE: Women's work in the factories and in cottage industry played a crucial role in industrialization. Due to the growing separation between home and workplace, working women were torn between the conflicting demands of childrearing and wage labor. Women found employment in a variety of occupations, including textile production, domestic service, and prostitution.

B. CHILD LABOR also contributed to the development of industry, despite the dangers posed to young children by factory and mine work. Beginning in the 1830s, some governments passed laws intended to mitigate the worst evils of child labor.

C. STANDARDS OF LIVING OF THE LABORING POOR: Historians continue to debate the question of whether or not workers' lives were improved or worsened by the Industrial Revolution. Clear benefits were realized after 1850, but in the first half of the century industrialization brought much misery.

D. POOR RELIEF was sometimes provided by the state, but private charity continued to be the most important source of assistance for the poor.

E. THE QUESTION OF CLASS CONSCIOUSNESS: As traditional patterns and institutions of labor disappeared, workers—and especially urban artisans—began to develop a sense of their solidarity as members of the working class.

F. WORKERS' ASSOCIATIONS AND SOCIAL PROTEST: Workers organized to protest their conditions and to protect their interests as workers. Organizations such as friendly societies and trade unions were formed, and workers agitated for political and economic rights.

V. THE ORIGINS OF EUROPEAN SOCIALISM lay in a growing concern over the economic and social inequalities created by industrialization.

A. UTOPIAN SOCIALISTS hoped to answer the "social question" by building a perfect and harmonious society. Their plans were sometimes fanciful, but their critique of liberalism and capitalism was highly influential among workers.

B. PRACTICAL SOCIALISTS looked for more realistic solutions, calling on the state or workers themselves to improve social conditions. Some socialists, such as Flora Tristan, linked the emancipation of women to the emancipation of workers.

C. KARL MARX AND THE ORIGINS OF "SCIENTIFIC SOCIALISM": Marx rejected the "unscientific" approach of other socialists, arguing that economic relations are governed by scientific laws. He posited a class struggle between the capitalist bourgeoisie and the industrial proletariat and insisted that revolution, and the subsequent establishment of a communist society, was inevitable.

VI. CONCLUSION: Industrialization brought dramatic benefits, especially in the lives of the European elite, but it also brought misery to many workers. Upper-class observers increasingly feared the social and political disorder occasioned by worker poverty and political radicalism.

2. HISTORICAL GEOGRAPHY

MAP 16.1 INDUSTRIAL BRITAIN

Map Exercises

Familiarize yourself with the maps provided in your text, and then attempt to locate the following places on Blank Maps 16.1 and 16.2.

INDUSTRIAL BRITAIN

Birmingham	Leeds
Bristol	Liverpool
Edinburgh	London
Glasgow	Manchester
Lancaster	Sheffield

INDUSTRIAL EUROPE

Berlin	Brussels
Bordeaux	Catalonia

Dresden	Paris
Florence	Rhineland
Frankfurt	Ruhr
Genoa	Saxony
Hamburg	Silesia
Lyon	Turin
Marseille	Venice
Munich	Vienna

Map Questions

Which regions in Europe had the highest concentration of railroad lines by 1851?

Which regions of Central Europe were included in the Zollverein of 1834?

3. PEOPLE AND TERMS TO IDENTIFY

Industrial Revolution	Suburbs	Class consciousness
Irish potato famine	Little Ireland	Friendly Societies
Commercialization of agriculture	Luddites	Saint-Simon
Railroads	Registered prostitute	Phalanstery
Workshop of the World	The British Factory Act of 1833	Flora Tristan
Articles of Paris	Manchester	"Property is theft"
Zollverein	Handloom weavers	Karl Marx
Alfred Krupp	The Poor Law Amendment Act of 1834	Proletariat
Captain Swing		

4. STUDY QUESTIONS

1. How have historians' interpretations of the Industrial Revolution changed in recent years?

2. Why did the European population increase dramatically between 1800 and 1850? *Historical Continuities:* To what extent does this "demographic explosion" represent a departure from earlier patterns of European population growth?

3. In what sense were improvements and innovations in transportation a precondition for industrialization?

4. Why *did* the Industrial Revolution begin in England? Why did Southern and Eastern Europe lag behind?

5. How did rural life change between 1800 and 1850?

6. How did urban life change between 1800 and 1850?

7. What role did women play in the Industrial Revolution?

8. Did the standard of living of the laboring poor increase or decrease during the first half of the nineteenth century?

9. How did workers respond to the changes wrought by industrialization?

10. Outline the differences between utopian socialism, practical socialism, and scientific socialism.

11. *Historical Continuities:* How do conservatism, liberalism, and socialism differ?

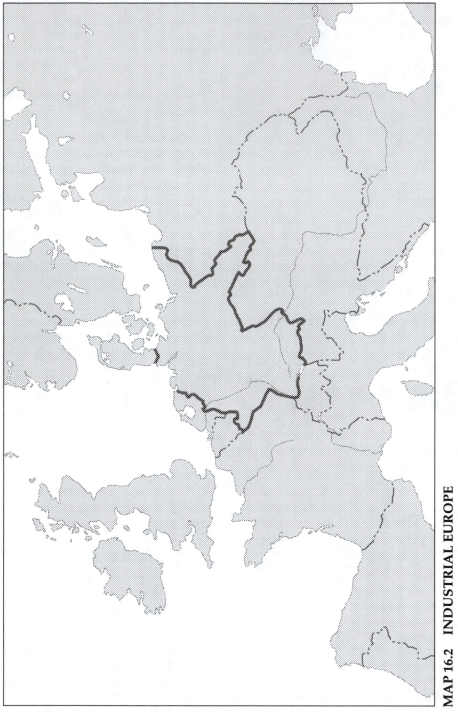

MAP 16.2   INDUSTRIAL EUROPE

5. ANALYZING ART AND ARTIFACTS

How did artists illustrate the changes brought by industrialization? What does Honoré Daumier's *Third Class Carriage* (p. 679), for example, suggest about artists' attitudes toward new technologies and toward the working poor?

Do you find the illustration of a young girl working in a coal mine (p. 698) shocking? Why or why not? Why do you think it would have shocked many Europeans living during the first half of the nineteenth century?

In what sense is the plan for the phalanstery that is reproduced in your text on p. 710 a representative expression of utopian-socialist thought? Does the phalanstery embrace or reject industrial architecture?

6. TECHNOLOGY AND HISTORY

Make a list of all of the different ways the railroad helped to promote industrialization.

How were early factories laid out? (See the illustration on p. 683 for an example.) How did the architecture of the factory contribute to worker productivity?

7. HISTORICAL ANALYSIS: INTERPRETIVE ESSAYS

1. *Historical Continuities:* To what extent was the Industrial Revolution of 1800 to 1850 a product of eighteenth-century developments?

2. What specific conditions were conducive to the industrialization of any given region or nation?

3. Write the life history of a factory worker born in 1800.

4. If you had been living in the first half of the nineteenth century, how would you have answered the "social question"?

5. Was Karl Marx right?

8. HISTORICAL VOICES: CLASS RELATIONS IN THE INDUSTRIAL ERA

A. Workers and Employers in Elizabeth Gaskell's *Mary Barton*

Orphaned of her mother at an early age, Elizabeth Stevenson (1810–1865) grew up in her aunt's home in the rural town of Knutsford, England. At the age of twenty-two she married William Gaskell, a young Unitarian minister, and the couple settled in the rapidly growing industrial city of Manchester. During the early years of her marriage, Elizabeth Gaskell lived an unexceptional and apparently contented life, busying herself with the rearing of six children and the charitable work expected of a minister's wife. However, in 1845 her dearly beloved son died and Gaskell began to write to alleviate her grief, apparently at the suggestion of her husband. Her first novel, *Mary Barton*, published in October 1848, was an immediate—and controversial—success, and remains one of the most compelling of the many "social problem" novels of the period.

Set in Manchester in the hard years of the 1830s, *Mary Barton* is the story of John Barton, a factory worker embittered by poverty and the death of his wife, and his daughter, Mary, a young working woman struggling to maintain her virtue against the blandishments of a mill-owner's son. Intended as an even-handed account of the conditions that drove some workers to strike and some—like John Barton—to more desperate measures, the book was criticized at the time of its appearance as being overly sympathetic to workers. Gaskell's next novel, *North and South*, attempted to redress the balance by focusing on the difficulties experienced by factory owners.

In the following scene from *Mary Barton*, factory owners and striking workers meet to negotiate their differences over wages and work conditions. The Manchester textile industry is experiencing a slump, but neither workers nor masters are willing to discuss their problems openly and as equals. This lack of communication causes a fatal rift between the two groups, and results in a series of tragic events.

FROM *Mary Barton* by Elizabeth Gaskell

So class distrusted class, and their want of mutual confidence wrought sorrow to both. The masters would not be bullied, and compelled to reveal why they felt it wisest and best to offer only such low wages; they would not be made to tell that they were even sacrificing capital to obtain a decisive victory over the continental manufacturers. And the workmen sat silent and stern with folded hands, refusing to work for such pay. There was a strike in Manchester. . . .

The day arrived on which the masters were to have an interview with a deputation of the work-people. The meeting was to take place in a public room, at an hotel; and there, about eleven o'clock, the mill-owners, who had received the foreign orders, began to collect. . . .

. . . Some were for a slight concession, just a sugar-plum to quieten the naughty child, a sacrifice to peace and quietness. Some were steadily and vehemently opposed to the dangerous precedent of yielding one jot or one tittle to the outward force of a turn-out. It was teaching the work-people how to become masters, said they. Did they want the wildest thing hereafter, they would know that the way to obtain their wishes would be to strike work. Besides, one or two of those present had only just returned from the New Bailey, where one of the turn-outs had been tried for a cruel assault on a poor north-country weaver, who had attempted to work at the low price. They were indignant, and justly so, at the merciless manner in which the poor fellow had been treated; and their indignation at wrong, took (as it often does) the extreme form of revenge. . . . They forgot that the strike was in this instance the consequence of want and need, suffered unjustly, as the endurers believed; for, however insane, and without ground of reason, such was their belief, and such was the cause of their violence. . . .

No one thought of treating the workmen as brethren and friends, and openly, clearly, as appealing to reasonable men, stating exactly and fully the circumstances which led the masters to think it was the wise policy of the time to make sacrifices themselves, and to hope for them from the operatives. . . .

The door was now opened, and the waiter announced that the men were below . . .

Tramp, tramp, came the heavy clogged feet up the stairs; and in a minute five wild, earnest-looking men stood in the room. . . . Had they been larger-boned men, you would have called them gaunt; as it was, they were little of stature, and their fustian clothes hung loosely upon their shrunk limbs. In choosing their delegates, too, the operatives had had more regard to their brains, and power of speech, than to their wardrobes . . . It was long since many of them had known the luxury of a new article of dress; and air-gaps were to be seen in their garments. Some of the masters were rather affronted at such a ragged detachment coming between the wind and their nobility; but what cared they?

At the request of a gentleman hastily chosen to officiate as chairman, the leader of the delegates read, in a high-pitched, psalm-singing voice, a paper, containing the operatives' statement of the case at issue, their complaints, and their demands, which last were not remarkable for moderation. . . .

The masters could not consent to the advance demanded by the workmen. They would agree to give one shilling per week more than they had previously offered. Were the delegates empowered to accept such offer?

They were empowered to accept or decline any offer made that day by the masters. . . .

They came back, and positively declined any compromise of their demands. . . .

Towards seven o'clock that evening, many operatives began to assemble in a room in the Weavers' Arms public-house, a room appropriated for "festive occasions," as the landlord, in his circular, on opening the premises, had described it. But, alas! it was on no festive occasion that they met there this night. . . .

John Barton began to speak; they turned to him with great attention. "It makes me more than sad, it makes my heart burn within me, to see that folk can make a jest of striving men; of chaps who comed to ask for a bit o' fire for th' old granny, as shivers i' th' cold; for a bit o' bedding, and some warm clothing to the poor wife who lies in labour on th' damp flags; and for victuals for the childer, whose little voices are getting too faint and weak to cry aloud wi' hunger. For, brothers, is not them the things we ask for when we ask for more wage? We donnot want dainties, we want bellyfuls; we donnot want gimcrack coats and waist-coats, we want warm clothes; and so that we get 'em, we'd not quarrel wi' what they're made on. We donnot want their grand houses, we want a roof to cover us from the rain, and the snow, and the storm; ay, and not alone to cover us, but the helpless ones that cling to us in the keen wind, and ask us with their eyes why we brought 'em into th' world to suffer?" He lowered his deep voice almost to a whisper—

"I've seen a father who had killed his child rather than let it clem* before his eyes; and he were a tender-hearted man."

*clem = starve

Source: Mrs. [Elizabeth] Gaskell. "Meeting Between Masters and Workmen." In *Mary Barton*, pp. 208–212, 216–217. New York: G. P. Putnam's Sons, 1906.

Questions

Is Gaskell even-handed in her treatment of workers and masters? Why do you think many of her contemporaries criticized her treatment of this subject matter?

How might this strike be ended and the best interests of both masters and workers served, according to Gaskell?

B. Proletariat and Bourgeoisie in Karl Marx's *Communist Manifesto*

In February 1848, on the eve of the outbreak of revolution throughout Europe, Karl Marx (1818–1883) and Friedrich Engels (1820–1895) published *The Communist Manifesto*. Rejecting the conciliatory tone adopted that same year by the devout Gaskell, Marx and Engels urged industrial workers—the "proletariat"—to rise up in revolt against the oppressive class system created by industrial capitalism.

In Marx and Engels' "scientific" analysis of nineteenth-century class relations, the bourgeoisie—the owners of the means of production—are described as ruling over an economically dispossessed and politically disenfranchised proletariat. The two classes, both of which had arisen out of the new modes of production generated by the Industrial Revolution, would inevitably come into open conflict with one another, as the contradictions inherent in the capitalist economy necessarily resulted in ever more serious crises of overproduction and widespread unemployment. Eventually, revolution would erupt, and the victorious proletariat would abolish the class system and private property itself.

Marx, the son of a German lawyer, and Engels, the son of a successful German factory owner, were both by their birth members of the bourgeoisie, but they saw themselves as "bourgeois ideologists" (see below) who had identified the class struggle as the motive force of historical change and had subsequently gone over to the side of the proletariat. As Marx and Engels saw it, educated and enlightened bourgeois could provide leadership to the workers in their coming battle with the capitalist bourgeoisie.

In the following passages from their inflammatory and highly influential pamphlet, Marx and Engels describe the origins of the bourgeoisie and the proletariat, and analyze the economic relations existing between the two classes.

FROM *Manifesto of the Communist Party* by Karl Marx and Friedrich Engels

The history of all hitherto existing societies is the history of class struggles.

Freeman and slave, patrician and plebeian, lord and serf, guild-master and journeyman, in a word, oppressor and oppressed, stood in constant opposition to one another, carried on an uninterrupted, now hidden, now open fight, a fight that each time ended, either in a revolutionary re-constitution of society at large, or in the common ruin of the contending classes.

. . . Our epoch, the epoch of the bourgeoisie, possesses, however, this distinctive feature: it has simplified the class antagonisms: Society as a whole is more and more splitting up into two great hostile camps, into two great classes, directly facing each other: Bourgeoisie and Proletariat.

The bourgeoisie, wherever it has got the upper hand, has put an end to all feudal, patriarchal, idyllic relations. It has pitilessly torn asunder the motley feudal ties that bound man to his "natural superiors," and has left remaining no other nexus between man and man than naked self-interest, than callous "cash payment." It has drowned the most heavenly ecstasies of religious fervor, of chivalrous enthusiasm, of philistine sentimentalism, in the icy water of egotistical calculation. It has resolved personal worth into exchange value. And in place of the numberless and feasible chartered freedoms, has set up that single, un-conscionable freedom—Free Trade. In one word, for exploitation, veiled by religious and political illusions, naked, shameless, direct, brutal exploitation.

. . . The bourgeoisie has torn away from the family its sentimental veil, and has reduced the family relation to a mere money relation.

. . . The bourgeoisie cannot exist without constantly revolutionizing the instruments of production, and thereby the relations of production, and with them the whole relations of society. Conservation of the old modes of production in unaltered form, was, on the contrary, the first condition of existence for all earlier industrial classes. Constant revolutionizing of production, uninterrupted disturbance of all social conditions, everlasting uncertainty and agitation distinguish the bourgeois epoch from all earlier ones.

. . . Modern bourgeois society with its relations of production, of exchange and of property, a society that has conjured up such gigantic means of production and of exchange, is like the sorcerer, who is no longer able to control the powers of the nether world whom he has called up by his spells. For many a decade past the history of industry and commerce is but the history of the revolt of modern productive forces against modern conditions of production, against the property relations that are the conditions for the existence of the bourgeoisie and of its rule. It is enough to mention the commercial crises that by their periodical return put on its trial, each time more threateningly, the existence of the entire bourgeois society. In these crises a great part not only of the existing products, but also of the previously created productive forces, are periodically destroyed. In these crises there breaks out an epidemic that, in all earlier epochs, would have seemed an absurdity—the epidemic of over-production. . . .

The weapons with which the bourgeoisie felled feudalism to the ground are now turned against the bourgeoisie itself.

But not only has the bourgeoisie forged the weapons that bring death to itself; it has also called into existence the men who are to wield those weapons—the modern working class—the proletarians.

In proportion as the bourgeoisie, i.e., capital, is developed, in the same proportion is the proletariat, the modern working class, developed—a class of laborers, who live only so long as they find work, and who find work only so long as their labor increases capital. These laborers, who must sell themselves piece-meal, are a commodity, like every article of commerce, and are consequently exposed to all the vicissitudes of competition, to all the fluctuations of the market.

Owing to the extensive use of machinery and to division of labor, the work of the proletarians has lost all individual character, and consequently, all charm for the workman. He becomes an appendage of the machine, and it is only the most simple, most monotonous, and most easily acquired knack, that is required of him. Hence, the cost of production of a workman is restricted, almost entirely, to the means of subsistence that he requires for his maintenance, and for the propagation of his race. . . .

Modern industry has converted the little workshop of the patriarchal master into the great factory of the industrial capitalist. Masses of laborers, crowded into the factory, are organized like soldiers. As privates of the industrial army they are placed under the command of a perfect hierarchy of officers and sergeants. Not only are they slaves of the bourgeois class, and of the bourgeois State; they are daily and hourly enslaved by the machine, by the over-looker, and, above all, by the individual bourgeois manufacturer himself. The more openly this despotism proclaims gain to be its end and aim, the more petty, the more hateful and the more embittering it is.

The less the skill and exertion of strength implied in manual labor, in other words, the more modern industry becomes developed, the more is the labor of men superseded by that of women. Differences of age and sex have no longer any distinctive social validity for the working class. All are instruments of labor, more or less expensive to use, according to their age and sex.

. . . This organization of the proletarians into a class, and consequently into a political party, is continually being upset again by the competition between the workers themselves. But it ever rises up again, stronger, firmer, mightier. It compels legislative recognition of particular interests of the workers, by taking advantage of the divisions among the bourgeoisie itself. . . .

. . . in times when the class struggle nears the decisive hour, the process of dissolution going on within the ruling class, in fact within the whole range of society, assumes such a violent, glaring character, that a small section of the ruling class cuts itself adrift, and joins the revolutionary class, the class that holds the future in its hands. Just as, therefore, at an earlier period, a section of the nobility went over to the bourgeoisie, so now a portion of the bourgeoisie goes over to the proletariat, and in particular, a portion of the bourgeois ideologists, who have raised themselves to the level of comprehending theoretically the historical movement as a whole.

Of all the classes that stand face to face with the bourgeoisie today, the proletariat alone is a really revolutionary class. The other classes decay and finally disappear in the face of Modern Industry; the proletariat is its special and essential product. The lower middle class, the small manufacturer, the shopkeeper, the artisan, the peasant, all these fight against the bourgeoisie, to save from extinction their existence as fractions of the middle class. They are therefore not revolutionary, but conservative. Nay more, they are reactionary, for they try to roll back the wheel of history. . . .

In the conditions of the proletariat, those of old society at large are already virtually swamped. The proletarian is without property; his relation to his wife and children has no longer anything in common with the bourgeois family-relations; modern industrial labor, modern subjection to capital, the same in England as in France, in America as in Germany, has stripped him of every trace of national character. Law, morality, religion, are to him so many bourgeois prejudices, behind which lurk in ambush just as many bourgeois interests.

. . . All previous historical movements were movements of minorities, or in the interests of minorities. The proletarian movement is the self-conscious, independent movement of the immense majority, in the interests of the immense majority. . . .

The essential condition for the existence, and for the sway of the bourgeois class, is the formation and augmentation of capital; the condition for capital is wage-labor. Wage-labor rests exclusively on competition between the laborers. The advance of industry, whose involuntary promoter is the bourgeoisie, replaces the isolation of the laborers, due to competition, by their revolutionary combination, due to association. The development of Modern Industry, therefore, cuts from under its feet the very foundation on which the bourgeoisie produces and appropriates products. What the bourgeoisie, therefore, produces, above all, is its own grave-diggers. Its fall and the victory of the proletariat are equally inevitable.

. . . Let the ruling classes tremble at a Communistic revolution. The proletarians have nothing to lose but their chains. They have a world to win.

WORKING MEN OF ALL COUNTRIES, UNITE!

Source: Karl Marx and Friedrich Engels. *Manifesto of the Communist Party.* From the English edition of 1888, ed. Friedrich Engels.

Questions

According to Marx and Engels, who are the bourgeoisie and the proletariat?

Why is a clash between these two classes inevitable?

To what extent does Gaskell's description of negotiations between factory workers and factory owners support Marx and Engel's arguments?

9. IMPORTANT HISTORICAL FACTS: STUDY DRILLS

A. Multiple Choice

1. The commercialization of agriculture was typified by:
   A. the consolidation of agricultural land through enclosure.
   B. subsistence farming.
   C. the subdivision of agricultural land into small family plots.
   D. a decrease in productivity.

2. The building of railroads did all of the following *except:*
   A. facilitate the transport of coal.
   B. provide investment opportunities for the middle class.
   C. allow increased opportunities for tourism.
   D. encourage people to stay in rural areas.

3. The Zollverein was
   A. a cannon factory based in the Ruhr.
   B. a Prussian workers' association.
   C. a German customs union.
   D. a Silesian handloom.

4. As cities grew, workers tended to move to
   A. America.
   B. the elite quarters.
   C. rural areas.
   D. industrial suburbs.

5. The British Factory Act of 1833
   A. abolished the Speenhamland System.
   B. placed restrictions on the labor of children.
   C. created new factories.
   D. allowed the creation of workers' unions.

6. Through the works of Gaskell and Engels, the city of Manchester became known for
   A. its rustic beauty and small farms.
   B. its utopian-socialist community.
   C. its bustling port.
   D. its downtrodden factory workers.

7. The Poor Law Amendment Act of 1834
   A. established residential workhouses for the poor.
   B. supplemented the wages of poor workers.
   C. abolished private poor relief.
   D. made impoverishment a hanging offense.

8. Workers' perception that they were members of a working class with interests different from those of employers has been labeled
   A. trade unionism.
   B. de-skilling.
   C. class consciousness.
   D. socialism.

9. Friendly Societies were:
   A. cabarets
   B. workers' associations
   C. employers' associations
   D. church organizations

10. Followers of utopian-socialist Charles Fourier hoped to build ideal communities known as
    A. villages of cooperation.
    B. phalansteries.
    C. Coketowns.
    D. Icaria.

B. Chronological Relationships

1. Population Growth: Using the figures provided in Table 16.1 (p. 672 of the text), draw a line or bar graph comparing the different nations' population growth rates between 1800 and 1850. How had the size of these populations changed during this period? Which nations experienced the most dramatic growth?
   Historical Continuities: Compare these figures with those provided in Chapter 9 [Table 9.1, p. 371].

2. Identify the date at which each of the following events occurred and arrange them in chronological order.
   Alfred Krupp displays a cannon at the Crystal Palace.
   A steamship sails from Liverpool to Boston in sixteen days.
   The German States form a Zollverein, or customs union.
   Galician peasants rise up in revolt and slaughter nobles.
   Friedrich Engels publishes *Conditions of the Working Class in England.*
   Glove makers in Nottingham smash a thousand stocking-frames.
   The French government passes its first child labor law.
   The first passenger train begins service between Liverpool and Manchester.

British Parliament repeals the
Combination Acts.

French Saint-Simonian women found a
newspaper that publishes articles
written exclusively by women.

C. Matching Exercise: Historical Actors

_____ Alfred Krupp
_____ Captain Swing
_____ Count Henri de Saint-Simon
_____ Flora Tristan
_____ Handloom weavers
_____ Luddites
_____ Pierre-Joseph Proudhon
_____ Proletariat
_____ Registered prostitutes
_____ The Irish

A. These Silesian artisans saw their wages
    drop by three-quarters between 1805
    and 1833 as mechanization undermined
    the cash value of their skills.
B. An anarchist socialist who called for
    the abolition of the state and who
    argued, in a famous formulation, that
    private property is theft.
C. Said to be the leader of the
    unemployed rural workers who
    smashed threshing machines in
    England in the early 1830s.
D. A utopian socialist who suggested
    that, while society could do without
    dukes, princes, and bishops, it could
    not do without bankers, artisans, and
    farmers.
E. Fleeing the potato famine of the late
    1840s, they migrated to England,
    where they faced considerable
    discrimination.
F. These glove makers smashed
    stocking-frames in an attempt to
    maintain traditional methods of
    production.
G. Workers whose only capital was their
    labor, they would be the "grave
    diggers" of the bourgeoisie, according
    to Marx.
H. Their activities policed by the state,
    they were forced to have regular
    medical exams in order to limit the
    spread of venereal disease.
I. A "practical" socialist who linked
    feminism with socialism and who
    called for the creation of "workers'
    palaces."
J. Having inherited a small steel
    manufacturing firm in the Ruhr, he
    eventually built it into a very
    successful company specializing in
    arms production.

IMPORTANT HISTORICAL FACTS: STUDY-DRILL ANSWERS

A. Multiple Choice

1. A. the consolidation of agricultural
   land through enclosure.
2. D. encourage people to stay in rural
   areas.
3. C. a German customs union.
4. D. industrial suburbs.
5. B. placed restrictions on the labor of
   children.
6. D. its down-trodden factory workers.
7. A. established residential workhouses
   for the poor.
8. C. class consciousness.
9. B. workers' associations
10. B. phalansteries.

B. Chronological Relationships
1. Population Growth Bar Graph

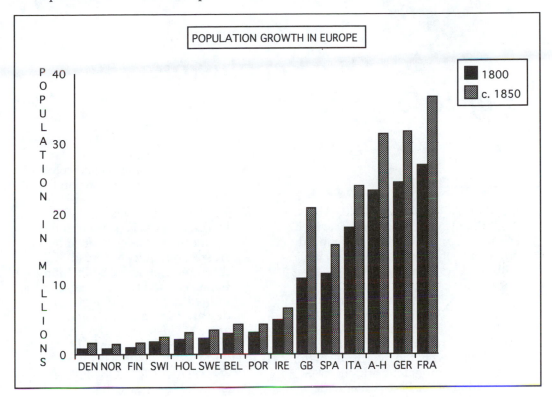

POPULATION GROWTH IN EUROPE

Legend: ■ 1800   ▨ c. 1850

Y-axis: POPULATION IN MILLIONS (0, 10, 20, 30, 40)

X-axis: DEN NOR FIN SWI HOL SWE BEL POR IRE GB SPA ITA A-H GER FRA

2.

1811–1812	Glove makers in Nottingham smash a thousand stocking-frames.
1816	A steamship sails from Liverpool to Boston in sixteen days.
1824	British Parliament repeals the Combination Acts.
1830	The first passenger train begins service between Liverpool and Manchester.
1832	French Saint-Simonian women found a newspaper that publishes articles written exclusively by women.
1834	The German States form a Zollverein, or customs union.
1841	The French government passes its first child labor law.
1844	Friedrich Engels publishes *Conditions of the Working Class in England.*
1846	Galician peasants rise up in revolt and slaughter nobles.
1851	Alfred Krupp displays a cannon at the Crystal Palace.

C. Matching Exercise: Historical Actors

J. Alfred Krupp
C. Captain Swing
D. Count Henri de Saint-Simon
I. Flora Tristan
A. Handloom weavers
F. Luddites
B. Pierre-Joseph Proudhon
G. Proletariat
H. Registered prostitutes
E. The Irish

17 The Revolutions of 1848

1. CHAPTER OUTLINE

I. REVOLUTIONARY MOBILIZATION: A continent-wide food crisis provided an opportunity for liberal and radical opponents of existing regimes to unite with workers against conservative governments and to agitate for a variety of political and social reforms.

  A. THE FEBRUARY REVOLUTION IN FRANCE: In early 1848, an electoral reform movement culminated in the overthrow of the Orléanist monarchy and the creation of the Second Republic. Moderate liberals and radicals soon divided over reform policies, and the first election to the newly created National Assembly returned a conservative majority.

  B. REVOLUTION IN THE GERMAN STATES: In March 1848, radicals and liberals in the German states followed the lead of their French counterparts and rebelled against existing regimes. They were joined by artisans and peasants, who had been suffering the hardships of the "hungry forties."

  C. REVOLUTION IN CENTRAL EUROPE: In the Austrian Empire, radicals and liberals called for economic and political reforms, while Magyars and Czechs demanded greater political autonomy. The emperor was forced not only to liberalize his government but also to grant considerable freedom to Hungary.

  D. The REVOLUTION IN THE ITALIAN STATES started in the northern regions controlled by Austria but quickly spread throughout the peninsula. Many Italians hoped for the creation of a unified Italy, but the Austrian defeat of an Italian nationalist army at Custoza precluded the immediate realization of this goal.

II. THE ELUSIVE SEARCH FOR REVOLUTIONARY CONSENSUS: After initial successes, the revolutionary union of liberals, radicals, and nationalists collapsed, leaving the way open for the resurgence of conservative regimes.

  A. CRISIS IN FRANCE: In June 1848 the republican provisional government moved to close the National Workshops, prompting a short but bloody battle between workers (and their sympathizers) and government forces. At the end of the year, Louis Napoleon Bonaparte was elected president by an overwhelming majority.

  B. In the German states, THE FRANKFURT PARLIAMENT attempted to create a unified Germany under a constitutional monarchy, but it failed to win support from either the ruling elites or the common people, and ended in total failure.

III. COUNTER-REVOLUTION: Throughout Europe, conservatives

took advantage of divisions between radical and liberal revolutionaries, and moved to reestablish the power of autocratic regimes.

A. COUNTER-REVOLUTION IN CENTRAL EUROPE: Under the leadership of Prince Schwarzenberg, the Austrian monarchy used military force to suppress a workers' revolt in Vienna and a nationalist revolt in Hungary. Rulers of the German states also reasserted their power, abrogating recently granted constitutions and depriving the few remaining representative assemblies of any effective power.

B. PRUSSIAN-AUSTRIAN RIVALRY increased as the autocratic rulers of the two states attempted to lay claim to a dominant position in Central Europe. Tensions between Austria and Prussia nearly resulted in war, but Prussia backed down (in the face of a Russian military threat) in 1850.

C. THE COUNTER-REVOLUTION IN THE ITALIAN STATES: With the help of French troops, the pope returned to power in Rome. One by one, the other liberal regimes established in 1848 collapsed, putting an end to hopes for an immediate unification of the Italian states.

D. THE AGONY OF THE FRENCH SECOND REPUBLIC: After the June Days, democratic-socialists sought to build support for radical republicanism throughout France, but their efforts were forcibly repressed by the government. Having seized power the year before, Louis Napoleon declared himself Napoleon III in 1852, ending the Second Republic and establishing the Second Empire in its place.

IV. THE LEGACY OF 1848: Monarchs responded to the Revolutions of 1848 by building professional armies, which would support the cause of counter-revolution. Despite the resurgence of autocracy after 1848, the legacy of the revolutions included an apprenticeship in republicanism in France and nationalism in Italy, Germany, and among ethnic minorities in the Austrian Empire, and the arrival of mass politics on the European scene.

2. HISTORICAL GEOGRAPHY

Map Exercises

Familiarize yourself with the map provided in your text, and then attempt to locate the following places on Blank Map 17.1.

REVOLUTION IN CENTRAL EUROPE

Baden	Nassau
Berlin	Posen
Budapest	Prague
Cracow	Rhineland
Dresden	Schleswig
Frankfurt	Stuttgart
Galicia	Transylvania
Moldavia	Vienna
Moravia	Wallachia
Munich	Westphalia

REVOLUTION IN ITALY

Dalmatia	Palermo
Florence	Parma
Milan	Piedmont-Sardinia
Modena	Rome
Naples	Venice

Map Questions

Which regions of Europe saw the most revolutionary activity in 1848? Which saw the least?

Which European cities served as centers of revolution?

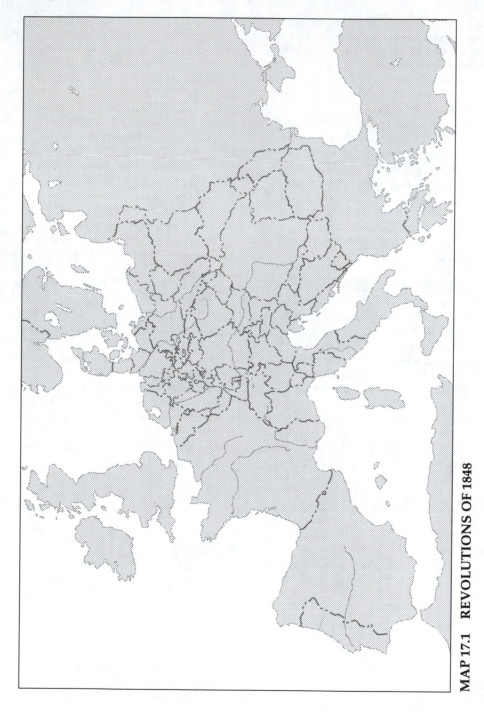

MAP 17.1 REVOLUTIONS OF 1848

3. PEOPLE AND TERMS TO IDENTIFY

Second French Republic
Louis Napoleon Bonaparte
   (Napoleon III)
National Workshops
Frederick William IV
Lajos Kossuth
Robot
The Battle of Custoza

June Days
Frankfurt
   Parliament
Kleindeutsch vs.
   Grossdeutsch
The Basic Rights of the
   German People
Pan-Slav Congress

Prince Felix zu
   Schwarzenberg
The Humiliation of
   Olmütz
Roman Republic
Giuseppe Garibaldi
Montagnards
Falloux Law

4. STUDY QUESTIONS

1. *Historical Continuities:* What caused the Revolutions of 1848?

2. Why were French revolutionaries unable to unite against conservatives?

3. What role did nationalist aspirations play in the German, Italian, and Austrian Revolutions of 1848?

4. Why did a violent civil war break out in France in June of 1848?

5. Why did the Frankfurt Parliament's attempt to unify the German states end in abject failure?

6. Why were counter-revolutionary initiatives successful in the aftermath of the Revolutions of 1848?

7. What caused the conflict between Austria and Prussia after 1848?

8. Why did the attempt to unify Italy fail?

9. *Historical Continuities:* To what extent were the Revolutions of 1848 a short-term failure and a long-term success?

5. ANALYZING ART AND ARTIFACTS

How were the various Revolutions of 1848 represented in the visual imagery of the period?

What did the "liberty tree" (shown on pp. 719 and 745 in the textbook) symbolize to revolutionaries and counter-revolutionaries?

6. TECHNOLOGY AND HISTORY

Why did revolutionaries find it so easy to overthrow monarchical leaders in 1848? What military reforms did monarchs institute after 1848 to keep this from happening again?

7. HISTORICAL ANALYSIS: INTERPRETIVE ESSAYS

1. *Historical Continuities:* What long-term political trends made the Revolutions of 1848 possible?

2. Imagine you are a police spy working for one of the monarchs deposed by the Revolutions of 1848. Write a report outlining the differences between radical and liberal revolutionaries, and explaining the ways in which conservative supporters of the monarch might take advantage of these differences to return him to power.

3. What caused the failure of the nationalist movements of 1848? What would it take for them to succeed in the future?

4. You are a British diplomat stationed in Vienna. Write an assessment of the foreign policy implications of the Revolutions of 1848.

8. HISTORICAL VOICES: REVOLUTION AND REACTION IN 1848

As revolution swept across Europe in February and March of 1848, people from all walks of life joined together both in celebration and in battle. In the major cities of continental Europe—Paris, Rome, Berlin, Vienna—a mood of mingled anxiety and exaltation brought urban residents out into the streets, at first to gather in peaceable protest, but soon to confront government troops from behind hastily constructed barricades. In the heady excitement of these days, eyewitnesses wrote often breathless descriptions of their experiences, some to reassure distant friends and family about their safety, others to inform the world about the momentous events taking place around them. The four accounts reproduced below were all written by individuals with first-hand experience of the revolution.

Although of Irish descent, the Baroness Bonde (1817–1900) lived in Paris for much of her life. As a young child she witnessed the tumult of the Revolution of 1830 in Paris, and was in the French capital for the events of 1848 as well. Bonde's family were strong supporters of the Orleanist monarchy, and had socialized extensively with the French aristocracy. Writing to a close friend in London, the future baroness described the outbreak of revolution in Paris in letters marked by an often piquant—if not very republican— wit. Commenting on the panicked flight of many members of the upper classes from Paris, she explained that two noblewomen "were so frightened that they dressed as peasants, got a barrowful of eggs and left Paris, shouting the *Marseillaise* out of tune; if I had done anything of the sort, I never could see an egg again without blushing." While she criticized the French king Louis-Philippe for his cowardice, Baroness Bonde was no partisan of radicalism, as is demonstrated by her anxious remarks about a "communist" takeover.

FROM *Paris in '48* by Baroness Bonde

Paris, Thursday, Feb. 24th, 1848.

My Dear Mrs. Ashburnham,

We are in the midst of a revolution more fearful than that of 1830, because the mob are beginning to pillage. I am just returned from a visit to Mons. de Tracy, where the Lafayettes live, and where I hoped to hear some news. On our road we found two barricades, and the troops returning with lowered muskets. Though there are a hundred thousand regular troops in Paris, and two hundred pieces of cannon, the King has given way, and we are wholly and solely defended by the National Guard some of whom are disaffected, at least to the dynasty. The twelve colonels of the twelve legions went to the Tuileries yesterday, and said that unless electoral reform were granted and a change of Ministry, they could not answer for their men. His Majesty gave way, and sent for Molé.*

This, however, was only one step in the fatal course of concession, and, after some fighting on the boulevard, in which about fifty persons were killed, Odilon Barrot was entrusted with the formation of the Ministry.† He is trying to form a cabinet with Dufaure, Thiers, Rémusat, and

---

*It is interesting to see how this action of the King appeared to a contemporary; in itself it was rather reactionary, for Molé, who had been minister under Napoleon, was a great upholder of the royal prerogative, belonged to the old order of things, and was entirely out of sympathy with the forward movements of the time. [Ed. note]

†Barrot had withstood Louis Philippe's personal policy, and was leader of the dynastic Opposition. [Ed. note]

Lamoricière, but perhaps it is already too late even for this extreme *parti.* The Chamber is dissolved, the town in a state of siege, and Bugeaud military governor. Perhaps even now Ledru Rollin, a Liberal to the verge of Communism, is invested with the dictatorship.*

. . . The King's abdication is called for at every barricade, and his extreme cowardice has greatly damped the ardour of his partisans. A fortnight ago this movement might have been prevented; now, no one knows what he is driving at. E. is in a dreadful state, as her husband was on duty all Tuesday, and is just returned to the barricade. He arrested three men himself, and as yet has escaped unhurt, but you may imagine how anxious we are. . . . The Rue Basse du Rempart was running with blood this morning, and some people say they still hear a fusillade. The *rappel* and the *générale* are beating everywhere, and one cannot but feel nervous when one thinks of the spirit of anarchy and rapine that is abroad. All the shops are shut, even in our own peaceful *quartier,* and as we were going down the Rue d'Astorg, we saw a band of marauders who were attempting to force Madame de Noailles' house, repulsed by the National Guard. Bakers, wine-merchants, and *charcutiers* have been pillaged. Most of the houses with railings have been attacked, and the iron or wooden palings turned into weapons of offence. An American living in the Rue de Ponthieu has been pillaged, and his pictures cut to pieces with swords. I saw a National Guard disarmed by some boys under twenty, and I assure you it is a service of no small danger to join the patrols. I spend most of the day with E., who is already worn out with anxiety, and quite ill. . . . I must, of course, send this per post, as the Embassy is inaccessible; besides, I am sure that in this case you will not mind. I shall write again to-morrow if there is anything settled. . . . I have no time for more details; I am just in time for post. . . . I have just heard there has been a fusillade on the Place de la Concorde—a few killed, many wounded. How will all this end?

P.S.—I open my letter to say that the King has abdicated, and is off. The Comte de Paris is proclaimed, and the Duchesse d'Orléans Regent. It is a frightful state of things. . . .

*Ledru Rollin represented Socialism in the Chamber, and supported the demand for universal suffrage. He was not made dictator, but became Minister of the Interior in the Provisional Government, and subsequently stood for the Presidency. [Ed. note]

Margaret Fuller (1810–1850), an American living in Rome in 1848, was, as opposed to the Baroness Bonde, an ardent supporter of the revolution who actively promoted the republican and nationalist movements in the Italian states. The first woman to have been assigned to the post of chief literary critic for the *New York Tribune,* Fuller was already a well-known journalist in 1848, and her letters describing events in Italy were written for publication in the *Tribune.* Recently married to the Marquis Ossoli, an Italian republican who served as a captain of Rome's revolutionary Civic Guard, Fuller was one of the few Americans to remain in Italy during the years of revolution. The description of the outbreak of revolution in Rome cited below appeared in a letter Fuller wrote on March 29, 1848.

Although pregnant in 1848, Fuller took a strong interest in events in Rome, and in 1849 ran a hospital for Italian republicans who had been wounded while fighting French troops sent to defend the pope by Louis Napoleon Bonaparte. Returning to America in 1850, Fuller, her husband, and their infant son were killed in a tragic shipwreck off the New England coast and her manuscript on the revolution was lost.

FROM *At Home and Abroad* **by Margaret Fuller**

The news of the dethronement of Louis Philippe reached us just after the close of the Carnival. It was just a year from my leaving Paris. I did not think, as I looked with such disgust on the empire of sham he had established in France, and saw the soul of the people imprisoned and held fast as in an iron vice, that it would burst its chains so soon. Whatever be the result, France has done gloriously; she has declared that she will not be satisfied with pretexts while there are facts in the world,—that to stop her march is a vain attempt, though the onward path be dangerous and difficult. It is vain to cry, Peace! peace! when there is no peace. The news from France, in these days, sounds ominous, though still vague. It would appear that the political is being merged in the social struggle: it is well. Whatever blood is to be shed, whatever altars cast down, those tremendous problems MUST be solved, whatever be the cost! That cost cannot fail to break many a bank, many a heart, in Europe, before the good can bud again out of a mighty corruption. To you, people of America, it may perhaps be given to look on and learn in time for a preventive wisdom. You may learn the real meaning of the words FRATERNITY, EQUALITY: you may, despite the apes of the past who strive to tutor you, learn the needs of a true democracy. You may in time learn to reverence, learn to guard, the true aristocracy of a nation, the only really nobles,— the LABORING CLASSES.

And Metternich, too, is crushed; . . . I have seen the Austrian arms dragged through the streets of Rome and burned in the Piazza del Popolo. . . .

When the double-headed eagle was pulled down from above the lofty portal of the Palazzo di Venezia, the people placed there in its stead one of white and gold, inscribed with the name ALTA ITALIA,* and quick upon the emblem followed the news that Milan was fighting against her tyrants,—that Venice had driven them out. . .—and that Modena, that Parma, were driving out the unfeeling and imbecile creatures who had mocked Heaven and man by the pretence of government there.

With indescribable rapture these tidings were received in Rome. Men were seen dancing, women weeping with joy along the street. The youth rushed to enroll themselves in regiments to go to the frontier. . . .

*"Great Italy"

Revolution came to the German states in mid-March as well. In the Prussian capital of Berlin, the revolution began peacefully, if exuberantly. However, when shots were fired as soldiers attempted to clear a crowd from the square in front of the royal palace, fighting broke out and barricades went up. The eyewitness account presented below narrates these events, emphasizing the solidarity of the people of Berlin in opposition to the king's troops.

FROM *Rhyme and Revolution in Germany* **by J. G. Legge**

At one moment everybody was rejoicing and shouting "Hurrah!" and a few minutes later all was changed to yells of rage and cries for revenge. In one hour the appearance of the city was entirely different, its physiognomy quite transformed. "To the church towers!" was the cry "To the alarm bells!" and the church doors were broken open by force, for no one would wait till the sexton arrived with the keys. . . . As if by magic barricades arose. At every street corner people gathered, young and old, of high and low degree, to build barricades. Stalls, carriages, omnibuses, cabs, heavy transport wagons, postal and brewery carts and scaffolding poles were collected by thousands of hands in all parts of the city. Even women and children took part; the unity which prevailed in building was marvellous. All were equal; *e.g.,* two men would be seen dragging a beam, one a workman with a torn shirt and the other a well-dressed gentleman. The chief materials of the barricades nearly everywhere were torn up pavements, stone flags, beams, and the many boards and planks lying across the gutters, or carriages, carts, etc., which were upset. Beds, sacks of flour, and furniture were brought out of the houses; every one gave willingly what he had, gates, doors, fences, palings, hooks, bars, etc. Everything was done in perfect order, and everywhere with the same remarkable speed and contempt of death. People co-operated throughout. . . . At that moment there were only two parties: citizen and soldier, the people and the troops. The women made coffee, cut sandwiches, and handed food out into the street for the workmen and the fighters. In the streets bullets were moulded and lance tips forged; many zinc bars brought from workshops, lead and so on were cut up into small pieces to load the muskets. . . .

Throughout Europe, university students played a crucial role in the revolution. In Vienna, the capital of Habsburg Austria, students joined in the initial outburst of protest and then, after their initial demands had been satisfied, organized themselves to patrol the city and maintain order. The young student Adolf Pichler shared the enthusiastic response of the people of Vienna to the outbreak of revolution in Austria, and he took pride in being a member of one of the student patrols that helped to prevent pillage and arson. Pichler was a dedicated German nationalist, and his impassioned description of the raising of the German colors in early April provides evidence of the strongly nationalist tone of much revolutionary activity in Central Europe.

FROM *Rhyme and Revolution in Germany* by J. G. Legge

Sunday, 2nd April. What a joyful surprise; the black, red, and gold flag is floating on St. Stephen's tower in the morning air. It seemed like a dream and a fairy-tale to me. During the night men came to the university and handed the flag to the detachment of students on guard with the request that they should put it up. Twelve of them sprang up, climbed the stairs of the tower, and then in the darkness of night clambered out on to the crockets and hoisted the symbol of German unity. That is how the story generally went.—Very early in the morning we hastened to the university. We saw two more German flags hung out in the street; with what enthusiasm were they greeted! Viennese women had sent us these banners. How great and noble the women of Vienna were in this excited time! The flame of liberty was at its purest in their hearts; they loved liberty with the supreme love of woman, with all their soul. We at once decided, after singing, "What is the German's Fatherland," to march to the Stephansplatz. The blue sky of spring shone down upon us, the flags steamed and waved in the procession, the air was full of the sound of bells. How impressive and how powerful were the tones of the German anthem! Then to the statue of the last German Kaiser—to Joseph! . . . From there we went to the Palace Square. . . . Lovely women looked down from the windows. A student could not resist the impulse to lay his hand on the German ribbon and to call to them, "Look, these are the colours with which you must adorn yourselves in future!"—"Yes, yes," they answered, "so we shall." And they waved joyfully to us. We came to attention in front of the palace. The Kaiser appeared at the window and was welcomed with rejoicing. (In reply to a short address by a student the Kaiser returned thanks "with joyful emotion.") . . . Then the flag waved, we hastened to the palace gate, and a few moments afterwards the flag was fluttering from the window where the Kaiser had been standing shortly before. He appeared once more, went up to the flag and laid his hand on the pole, with the Kaiserin at his left hand. Students in their uniform surrounded them. The German Flag on the Imperial Palace at Vienna! We extended our arms, emotion stifled every sound, there was only one thought and one feeling: Germany, Germany!

Sources: Baroness Bonde. *Paris in '48: Letters from a Resident Describing the Events of the Revolution,* pp. 6–9. Ed. C. E. Warr. New York: James Pott & Co., 1903.
    Margaret Fuller Ossoli. *At Home and Abroad: or, Things and Thoughts in America and Europe,* pp. 305–307. Boston: Roberts Brothers, 1874.
    J. G. Legge. *Rhyme and Revolution in Germany: A Study in German History, Life, Literature and Character,* 1813–1850, pp. 286, 272. New York: Brentanos, 1919.

Questions
What do these accounts tell you about ordinary people's experience of revolution?

How did individual responses to the revolution differ? How can these differences be explained?

How do you think you would have responded to the revolution? Would it make a difference if you lived in Paris, as opposed to Rome, or Berlin, or Vienna?

9. IMPORTANT HISTORICAL FACTS: STUDY DRILLS

A. Multiple Choice

1. Revolution broke out in 1848 in each of the following places *except:*
   A. France.
   B. Prussia.
   C. England.
   D. Austria.
2. The government established in France as the result of the February Revolution was known as
   A. the Second Republic.
   B. the Second Empire.
   C. the Democratic-Socialist Republic.
   D. the July Monarchy.
3. In 1848 the king of Prussia was
   A. Ferdinand I.
   B. Francis Joseph.
   C. Frederick William IV.
   D. Charles Albert.
4. The Hungarian nationalist movement was led by a noble lawyer by the name of
   A. Klemens von Metternich.
   B. Lajos Kossuth.
   C. Giuseppe Garibaldi.
   D. Joseph Jelačić.
5. During the June Days
   A. the banning of a reform banquet in France resulted in the outbreak of revolution.
   B. Bavarian demonstrators rose up against the rule of Ludwig I.
   C. French government troops killed between 1500 and 3000 insurgents.
   D. the first meeting of the Frankfurt Parliament took place.
6. The Frankfurt Parliament's "Basic Rights of the German People" proclaimed everything *except:*
   A. freedom of speech.
   B. legal equality for Jews.
   C. the abolition of private property.
   D. the end of seigneurial obligations.

7. After being appointed the head of the Austrian government in late 1848, this counter-revolutionary noble convinced Ferdinand I to abdicate in favor of his more able son:
   A. Prince Felix zu Schwarzenberg
   B. Prince Klemens von Metternich
   C. Prince Alfred Windischgrätz
   D. Alexander von Bach

8. The Roman Republic was established in 1849 after the pope was forced to flee the Papal States, but it was soon defeated by
   A. the Inquisition.
   B. Croatian troops led by Joseph Jelačić.
   C. Austrian troops led by Count Joseph Radetzky.
   D. French troops sent by Louis Napoleon.

9. The Montagnards were
   A. Italian supporters of Garibaldi.
   B. Swiss laborers.
   C. French democratic-socialists.
   D. Hungarian nationalists.

10. Passed in March 1850 by the French Assembly, the Falloux Law was a conservative measure which
    A. imposed censorship on the press.
    B. allowed the Catholic Church to open secondary schools.
    C. outlawed the singing of *The Marseillaise*.
    D. ended universal manhood suffrage.

B. Chronological Relationships

List the following events in chronological order:

Prussia is forced to sign the "humiliation of Olmütz."

In the early stages of the revolution in Austria, Emperor Ferdinand I leaves Vienna out of fear of becoming a prisoner of the revolution.

Faced with the outbreak of revolution in Prussia, Frederick William IV replaces his conservative cabinet with a more liberal one.

The French government closes the National Workshops and French workers rise up in revolt.

The Roman Republic is proclaimed.

Revolution breaks out in Paris after a reform banquet is banned.

Louis Napoleon Bonaparte declares himself emperor of the French.

The Frankfurt Parliament proclaims the Basic Rights of the German People.

An Italian nationalist army is defeated by an Austrian army at Custoza.

The Hungarian Diet proclaims Magyar independence.

C. Fill in the Blanks

1. Elected largely on the merit of his uncle's name, _____ became president of France in December 1848, and declared himself emperor in 1852.

2. The _____ were created as a form of assistance for unemployed French workers. Their abolition in mid-1848 led to the outbreak of a bloody civil war between workers and government troops.

3. _____ was the labor service Austrian peasants owed to their lords. This seigneurial obligation was deeply resented by the peasantry, and was abolished by Emperor Ferdinand in 1848 in an effort to forestall rural rebellion.

4. In August 1848, an Italian nationalist army was defeated by Austrian general Radetzky at the _____.

5. In May 1848, the German Constituent National Assembly, known as the _____, convened for the first time. It attempted to create a unified German state under a constitutional monarchy, but it failed to gain support and was forced to disband by mid-1849.

6. Supporters of the _____ policy wished to exclude Austria from a united Germany.

7. Supporters of the _____ policy wished to include Austria in a united Germany.

8. In June 1848, Czechs hosted a _____ in Prague. The assembled delegates, united only by their shared ethnicity but divided by their differing national experiences, failed to agree on anything other than their common dislike of the Habsburg regime.

9. Fearing the expansion of Prussian power in Central Europe, the Russian

tsar threatened to intervene on the side of Austria in late 1849. The Prussian government backed down, and signed the _____, an agreement to demobilize its army.

10. Italian republican nationalist _____ gathered a volunteer army in Lombardy, which he brought to the aid of the besieged Republic of Rome, but the republic fell to French bombardment in June 1849.

IMPORTANT HISTORICAL FACTS: STUDY-DRILL ANSWERS

A. Multiple Choice
1. C. England.
2. A. the Second Republic.
3. C. Frederick William IV.
4. B. Lajos Kossuth.
5. C. French government troops killed between 1500 and 3000 insurgents.
6. C. the abolition of private property.
7. A. Prince Felix zu Schwarzenberg
8. D. French troops sent by Louis Napoleon.
9. C. French democratic-socialists.
10. B. allowed the Catholic Church to open secondary schools.

B. Chronological Relationships

February 1848 — Revolution breaks out in Paris after a reform banquet is banned.

March 1848 — Faced with the outbreak of revolution in Prussia, Frederick William IV replaces his conservative cabinet with a more liberal one.

May 1848 — In the early stages of the revolution in Austria, Emperor Ferdinand I leaves Vienna out of fear of becoming a prisoner of the revolution.

June 1848 — The French government closes the National Workshops and French workers rise up in revolt.

August 1848 — An Italian nationalist army is defeated by an Austrian army at Custoza.

December 1848 — The Frankfurt Parliament proclaims the Basic Rights of the German People.

February 1849 — The Roman Republic is proclaimed.

April 1849 — The Hungarian Diet proclaims Magyar independence.

November 1850 — Prussia is forced to sign the "humiliation of Olmütz."

December 1852 — Louis Napoleon Bonaparte declares himself emperor of the French.

C. Fill in the Blanks
1. Louis Napoleon Bonaparte
2. National Workshops
3. Robot
4. the Battle of Custoza
5. Frankfurt Parliament
6. Kleindeutsch
7. Grossdeutsch
8. Pan-Slav Congress
9. the humiliation of Olmütz
10. Giuseppe Garibaldi

18 The Era of National Unification

1. CHAPTER OUTLINE

I. Many factors, including linguistic, economic, and ideological differences, militated against THE POLITICAL UNIFICATION OF ITALY. However, nationalist sentiment was on the upswing in Italy after 1848, promoting the possibility of an Italian "resurgence" (*Risorgimento*).

   A. LEADERSHIP FOR ITALIAN UNIFICATION came from Victor Emmanuel II, liberal king of Piedmont-Sardinia, and his prime minister Cavour, and from republican nationalist Mazzini.

   B. ALLIANCES AND WARFARE TO FURTHER ITALIAN UNIFICATION: Cavour formed an alliance with France against Austria in 1858, and war broke out between Piedmont-Sardinia, France, and the Habsburg empire in 1859. France signed a separate peace with Austria, but Piedmont-Sardinia was still able to annex a considerable amount of territory at the end of the war, uniting virtually all of northern and central Italy under the leadership of Piedmont-Sardinia.

   C. GARIBALDI AND THE LIBERATION OF SOUTHERN ITALY: Urged on by Cavour, the colorful republican nationalist Garibaldi and his "red shirt" army invaded Sicily. Garibaldi's continued successes in southern Italy aroused Cavour's concern, and the prime minister sent troops to meet Garibaldi in the Papal States, where the two armies cooperated in capturing a part of the pope's territories.

   D. COMPLETION OF THE UNIFICATION OF ITALY: In 1866, Italy gained the Austrian territory of Venetia as a result of its participation in the Austro-Prussian War. Finally, in 1871, Rome was also incorporated into the Italian state. Political unification had been achieved, but Italians were still divided by marked economic and social differences, especially between affluent northerners and poor southerners.

II. THE UNIFICATION OF GERMANY was desired by many Germans but it too faced considerable obstacles. Middle-class nationalists feared a new outbreak of worker radicalism; they were divided over "small German" and "big German" approaches to unification; and they worried that if either Prussia or Austria led the drive toward unification, the result would be an autocratic regime rather than a liberal national state.

   A. WILLIAM I, BISMARCK, AND THE RESOLUTION OF THE CONSTITUTIONAL CRISIS:

The course of German unification was determined by the accession of William I to the Prussian throne and his appointment of the formidable Bismarck as chief minister. Faced with the Prussian Parliament's refusal to approve new taxes to finance reforms in the military, Bismarck simply ignored the liberal opposition, building the power of the Prussian state through autocratic policies and hard-headed opportunism. He argued that Prussia would take a dominant position in a united Germany not as a result of its liberalism but of its power.

B. ALLIANCES AND WARFARE TO ESTABLISH PRUSSIAN LEADERSHIP: Bismarck then proceeded to go to war in the interest of increasing Prussian power within the German state system, first allying with Austria against Denmark over Schleswig and Holstein, and then turning on Austria over the same territory. In 1866, Prussian troops defeated the Austrian army at the Battle of Sadowa.

C. THE NORTH GERMAN CONFEDERATION was formed after Sadowa and united much of northern Germany under the leadership of Prussia. Bismarck's great success won him the support even of many liberals, who were willing to compromise their political principles in the interest of national power.

D. THE FRANCO-PRUSSIAN WAR AND GERMAN UNIFICATION: Following a final successful war—against an isolated France—Bismarck united Germany under the rule of William I, who became emperor of Germany in 1871. The new German state was an autocratic monarchy dominated by the Junker aristocracy and Prussian military officers.

III. NATIONAL AWAKENINGS IN THE HABSBURG LANDS: Weakened by Italian and German unification, the Austrian Empire nevertheless survived, despite conflicts generated by the growth of nationalist movements among its multi-ethnic population.

A. DIVERSITY AND COHESION IN THE HABSBURG EMPIRE: The Austrian Empire was a linguistic and ethnic patchwork, but factors like the tradition of Habsburg rule, the use of German as a common language, the solidarity of the ruling elites across ethnic lines, and the nearly universal adherence to Catholicism created a certain cultural unity.

B. REPRESSION OF NATIONALISM IN THE HABSBURG EMPIRE was unrelenting. After the revolutionary episode of 1848, Francis Joseph moved to restore the absolutist state within the empire, using the military, the police, and the Church to reimpose order.

C. POLITICAL CRISIS AND FOREIGN POLICY DISASTERS: Within the Empire, Francis Joseph's attempts to liberalize his neo-absolutist regime met with little success. In international affairs, the Austrians met with one disaster after another, including defeat by the Prussians in 1866.

D. CREATION OF THE DUAL MONARCHY: In response to Magyar demands for increased autonomy, Francis Joseph formulated the Compromise of 1867, which created the Dual Monarchy of Austria-Hungary. This satisfied the Magyars, but did not satisfy other ethnic minorities within the empire.

IV. CONCLUSION

2. HISTORICAL GEOGRAPHY

MAP 18.1   UNIFICATION OF ITALY

Map Exercises

Familiarize yourself with the maps provided in your text, and then attempt to locate the following places on Blank Maps 18.1 and 18.2.

UNIFICATION OF ITALY

Kingdom of the
   Two Sicilies

Lombardy
Magenta

Marche
Modena
Naples
Nice
Palermo
Papal States
Parma
Piedmont-
   Sardinia

Romagna
Rome
Sardinia
Savoy
Solferino
Turin
Tuscany
Umbria
Venetia

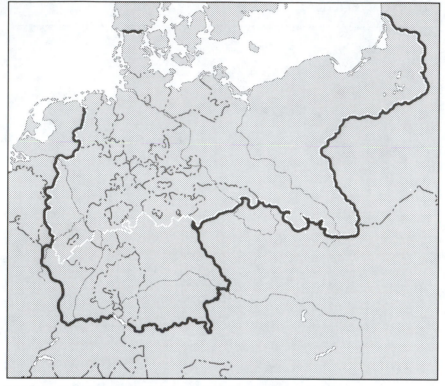

MAP 18.2   UNIFICATION OF GERMANY

UNIFICATION OF GERMANY

Alsace	Pomerania
Austria	Posen
Baden	Sadowa
Bavaria	Saxony
Berlin	Schleswig
Brandenburg	Sedan
East Prussia	Silesia
Hanover	Westphalia
Holstein	West Prussia
Lorraine	Württemberg

Map Questions

How did the unification of Italy and Germany affect the borders of the other sovereign European states?

Where were the different ethnic minorities under the rule of Austria concentrated in the empire?

3. PEOPLE AND TERMS TO IDENTIFY

Risorgimento
Victor Emmanuel II
Count Camillo di Cavour
Giuseppe Mazzini
Giuseppe Garibaldi
William I
National Union

Count Otto von Bismarck
Realpolitik
Schleswig and Holstein
Battle of Sadowa
North German
    Confederation
Franco-Prussian War

Emperor Francis Joseph
Ringstrasse
Alexander von Bach
Dual Monarchy
Compromise (*Ausgleich*) of
    1867
Nationality Law of 1868

4. STUDY QUESTIONS

1. *Historical Continuities:* Why did the Italian states remain disunited for so long?

2. How did Italy finally achieve its political unification?

3. What factors worked against German unification?

4. *Historical Continuities:* What is *Realpolitik*? How does it differ from earlier approaches to national politics and international relations?

5. Why did Bismarck succeed in unifying Germany under the leadership of the Prussian state? How might this be contrasted with Cavour's approach to Italian unification?

6. In an age of growing nationalism, what held together the Austrian Empire?

7. Why was the Dual Monarchy created? Was it a satisfactory solution to the Austro-Hungarian Empire's nationalities problem?

5. ANALYZING ART AND ARTIFACTS

How is nationalist ideology expressed in the photographs and other illustrations presented in the text?

How are Italian and German national leaders represented in images produced for mass consumption during the era of national unification?

6. TECHNOLOGY AND HISTORY

How did new technologies affect warfare in the mid-nineteenth century?

To what extent were the dramatic successes of the Prussian military dependent on new technologies?

7. HISTORICAL ANALYSIS: INTERPRETIVE ESSAYS

1. *Historical Continuities:* What long-term historical factors made possible the unification of both Germany and Italy in the mid-nineteenth century?

2. Compare and contrast the political strategies of Cavour and Bismarck. Why was each of these political leaders successful in his pursuit of unification?

3. What impact did international Great-Power rivalries have on the unification of Italy and Germany?

4. *Historical Continuities:* What role did nationalism play in the history of Europe between 1815 and 1871?

8. HISTORICAL VOICES: LEADERS IN THE CAMPAIGN FOR NATIONAL UNIFICATION

A. A French Liberal Compares Cavour with Bismarck

Italian and German unification shared certain common characteristics. In each case, the creation of a unified national state was a final product of the rise of nationalist movements in the first half of the nineteenth century, and it represented the accession of minor European states— Prussia and Piedmont-Sardinia—to Great-Power status through territorial aggrandizement. However, European observers also noted significant differences in the ways in which the two states had been built and in their respective governmental systems. The new nation of Germany was governed by a traditional autocrat who ruled in the interests of the Junker aristocracy. Italy, on the other hand, was led by a constitutional monarch who had agreed to share power with the liberal elite in the interest (at least in theory) of all Italians.

For moderate European liberals, the differences between the two new nations seemed to find their clearest expression in the contrasting characters of the two men who led the Italian and German unification movements. Camillo di Cavour (1810–1861), on the one hand, was often described as a model statesman who had skillfully directed the campaign to unite the Italian states under the leadership of the liberal Piedmontese monarchy. Otto von Bismarck (1815–1893), on the other hand, was seen as a crafty conservative who had forced the weaker German states to accept domination by Prussia and the German people to accept an illiberal and autocratic regime. While Bismarck was often condemned for his high-handed, anti-democratic governing style, Cavour was praised for his moderation—for being, as Cavour himself said, an "honest middle-course man"— and his respect for (and mastery of) parliamentary politics and the people's will.

In the introduction to his biography of Cavour, written in 1877, the liberal journalist Charles de Mazade could not refrain from comparing the Italian prime minister to Germany's "iron chancellor." At the very moment that French liberals were struggling to defend a still-weak Republic from a monarchist takeover (see Chapter 21), Mazade reflected on the differences between the Italian and German nation-builders. Mazade's remarks reveal both his own anti-German prejudices—shared by many of his compatriots, who were still stinging from the defeat of 1870—and his sympathy for Cavour, one of the "most illustrious of the favorites of fortune in our century."

FROM *The Life of Count Cavour* by Charles de Mazade

The signal superiority of Count Cavour consists in his having been a real Liberal, in the strongest and fullest acceptation of the word. The liberty in which he believed, both from instinct and reason, was to him no empty formula, nor was it an engine of destruction, or an implement of war against the Church or the State; it was a regular system of public guarantees, impartially applied and patiently worked out, as free from subterfuge as from violence. In the working of institutions, even in the boldest undertakings, he carried a mind free alike from revolutionary prejudice and timid scruples. Confidence was a part of his nature, and, granting whatsoever was due to liberty, he was still, and above all, the man made to govern. . . .

. . . It is now difficult to speak of Count Cavour without being reminded of the Prussian minister who has been enabled to perform in Germany what the Piedmontese minister achieved in Italy. Events are interlinked; men follow but do not always resemble one another. I have no desire to undervalue the German chancellor; coming from a Frenchman this would be childish and unworthy. In Prince Bismarck we have good reason to see an enemy, and we do not combat him with idle disparagements. All we can say is, that if Count Cavour and Prince Bismarck appear to have a similar fortune, at least till now, in analogous undertakings, they differ in genius, character, and mode of proceeding, as widely as Italy differs from Germany.

Several private letters written by Prince Bismarck in the course of his career have been published within the last few years; and they unveil a strangely complex nature; they reveal the whole man. A man assuredly of powerful originality, impetuous, crabbed, abrupt, and familiar; of feudal stamp, a Teuton by temperament and education; mixing confidential communications as to his capacities as a drinker, and the effects of moonlight on the banks of the Rhine, with visions of grandeur and power; a Mephistophelean politician and diplomatist, despising diplomatic and parliamentary formulas; impatient for action at all cost, *ferro et* *igne,** and defining himself with the air of a ruffled giant, from a heap of violent contradictions, in his disturbing and discomposed figure of conqueror.

That is not the portrait of Count Cavour, whom his contemporaries knew and saw at his work. Doubtless, Prince Bismarck is a great German. Count Cavour was rather, and in the broad humane sense, a great man. He, too, had strength of will and genius, but with perfect cordiality and a very taking charm. Prince Bismarck began by showing himself independent of his parliament, and even in some degree ridiculing it; he provoked the conflict and defied "rebellious" majorities; and if he ended in overruling the Chambers, it was by making his power and success a necessity to his country. Count Cavour worked always with the aid of public opinion and of parliament on his side. What he had been aided by liberty in accomplishing, he leaned on liberty to consolidate, with no despotic impatience, no persecution of beliefs.

*"Iron and fire."

Source: Charles de Mazade. *The Life of Count Cavour,* pp. vii–xi. London: 1877.

Questions

What does Mazade mean when he calls Cavour "a real Liberal"?

Why would a Frenchman like Mazade be predisposed to see Cavour as a hero and Bismarck as a villain?

B. Bismarck Wins Over a Hesitant King to the Cause of German Unification

In the nineteenth century, Prussian power was based not on extensive territorial holdings, but on forceful leadership and a powerful, well-disciplined military. Otto von Bismarck, who had been named chancellor of Prussia in 1862, realized that German unification under the leadership of the Hohenzollern dynasty would be possible only through skillful diplomacy coupled with a willingness to use force when necessary—and expedient.

When William I of Prussia came to power in 1861, he was torn between his inherited allegiance to absolutism and his personal inclination toward a more liberal, constitutional monarchy. Convinced by his advisors to bring the conservative Bismarck into his government, William nevertheless hesitated to commit himself to a break with the Reichstag, the Prussian parliament. After one of his first pronouncements as chancellor—the famous "iron and blood" speech—Bismarck hastened to meet with William in order to convince him to spearhead the unification initiative—even if this meant ruling without the Reichstag. Having gained William's confidence, Bismarck then proceeded to make Prussia the leading player in the movement toward the establishment of a unified Germany. In 1871 William was crowned emperor of Germany and made Bismarck chancellor of the newly created state.

In the following excerpt from Bismarck's memoirs (written after the chancellor had been removed from office in 1890 by the new emperor, William II), Bismarck recounts how he won William I's allegiance to the cause of conservative nationalism in 1861.

FROM *Bismarck: The Man and the Statesman* by Otto, Prince von Bismarck

In the beginning of October I went as far as Jüterbogk to meet the King, . . . and waited for him in the still unfinished railway station, filled with third-class travellers and workmen, seated in the dark on an overturned wheelbarrow. My object in taking this opportunity for an interview was to set his Majesty at rest about a speech made by me in the Budget Commission on September 30, . . .

. . . I had indicated plainly enough the direction in which I was going. Prussia—such was the point of my speech—as a glance at the map will show, could no longer wear unaided on its long narrow figure the panoply which Germany required for its security; it must be equally distributed over all German peoples. We should get no nearer the goal by speeches, associations, decisions of majorities; we should be unable to avoid a serious contest, a contest which could only be settled by blood and iron. In order to secure our success in this, the deputies must place the greatest possible weight of blood and iron in the hands of the King of Prussia, in order that according to his judgment he might throw it into one scale or the other. . . .

I had some difficulty in discovering from the curt answers of the officials the carriage in the ordinary train, in which the King was seated by himself in an ordinary first-class carriage. . . . When I begged for permission to narrate the events which had occurred during his absence, he interrupted me with the words: "I can perfectly well see where all this will end. Over there, in front of the Opera House, under my windows, they will cut off your head, and mine a little while afterwards." . . .

. . . "Yes," I continued, "then we shall be dead; but we must all die sooner or later, and can we perish more honourably? I, fighting for my King's cause, and your Majesty sealing with your own blood your rights as King by the grace of God; whether on the scaffold or the battlefield, makes no difference to the glory of sacrificing life and limb for the rights assigned to you by the grace of God. . . ."

As I continued to speak in this sense, the King grew more and more animated, and began to assume the part of an officer fighting for kingdom and fatherland. In presence of external and personal danger he possessed a rare and absolutely natural fearlessness, whether on the field of battle or in the face of attempts on his life; his attitude in any external danger was elevating and inspiring. The ideal type of the Prussian officer who goes to meet certain death in the service with the simple words, "At your orders," but who, if he has to act on his own responsibility, dreads the criticism of his superior officer or of the world more than death, even to the extent of allowing his energy and correct judgment to be impaired by the fear of blame and reproof—this type was developed in him to the highest degree. . . .

. . . As soon as he regarded his position from the point of view of military honour, it had no more terror for him than the command to defend what might prove a desperate position would have for any ordinary Prussian officer. This raised him above the anxiety about the criticism which public opinion, history, and his wife might pass on his political tactics. He fully entered into the part of the first officer in the Prussian monarchy, for whom death in the service would be an honourable conclusion to the task assigned him. The correctness of my judgment was confirmed by the fact that the King, whom I had found at Jüterbogk weary, depressed, and discouraged, had, even before we arrived at Berlin, developed a cheerful, I might almost say joyous and combative disposition, which was plainly evident to the ministers and officials who received him on his arrival.

Source: Otto, Prince von Bismarck. *Bismarck: The Man and the Statesman, Being the Reflections and Reminiscences of Otto, Prince von Bismarck Written and Dictated by Himself after His Retirement from Office,* vol. 1, pp. 312–316. Trans. A. J. Butler. New York: Harper and Brothers, 1899.

Questions

On the basis of Bismarck's summary of his "blood and iron" speech, how do you expect he planned to unify Germany?

How did Bismarck win William I over to the unification campaign?

What can we learn about Bismarck's diplomatic skills from this anecdote?

9. IMPORTANT HISTORICAL FACTS: STUDY DRILLS

A. Multiple Choice

1. Italian nationalists hoped for a resurgence of Italy, rallying to the cause of
   A. Ausgleich.
   B. the pope.
   C. Renaissance.
   D. Risorgimento.
2. One of several "Pan-German" associations formed in 1858, this was the largest and most influential, and agitated for a constitutional and parliamentary German state:
   A. National Guard (*Landwehr*)
   B. the German Confederation
   C. small German (*Kleindeutsch*)
   D. National Union (*Nationalverein*)
3. Bismarck's policy of pursuing Prussia's self-interest based on a realistic assessment of the costs and consequences of action became known as
   A. *Realpolitik.*
   B. blood and iron.
   C. the balance of power.
   D. neo-absolutism.
4. This territory became a bone of contention, first between Prussia and Denmark, and later between Prussia and Austria:
   A. Alsace and Lorraine
   B. Venetia
   C. Copenhagen
   D. Schleswig and Holstein
5. This battle, fought in July 1866, brought Prussia a dramatic victory against Austria and opened the way for German unification under the leadership of Prussia:
   A. Sedan
   B. Sadowa
   C. Solferino
   D. Magenta

6. The Treaty of Prague of 1866 established
   A. the Confederation of the Rhine.
   B. the North German Confederation.
   C. the German Confederation.
   D. the German Empire.
7. Having lost the Franco-Prussian War to Prussia, France was forced to give up
   A. Alsace and Lorraine.
   B. Nice.
   C. Savoy.
   D. Sedan.
8. The Ringstrasse was
   A. the setting for the declaration of the German Empire in 1871.
   B. Francis Joseph's summer palace.
   C. a broad boulevard built in Vienna in the 1850s and 1860s.
   D. a Pan-German organization established in 1858.
9. The Compromise (*Ausgleich*) of 1867 created
   A. the Dual Monarchy.
   B. the German Parliament.
   C. peaceful relations between Prussia and Austria.
   D. an independent Hungarian state.
10. The Nationality Law of 1868
    A. expelled ethnic minorities from the Austro-Hungarian Empire.
    B. gave ethnic minorities the right to use their own language in schools, churches, and government offices.
    C. gave ethnic minorities in Austria-Hungary a separate political identity.
    D. made all German speakers citizens of the German Empire.

B. Chronological Relationships

1. Make a timeline listing the dates at which each new territory was added to

the unifying Italian and German states. (See Maps 18.1 and 18.2 in text for details.)

2. List the following events in chronological order and identify the date at which they took place:

Victor Emmanuel II makes Cavour prime minister of Piedmont-Sardinia.

The Treaty of Vienna gives Austria and Prussia joint administration of Schleswig and Holstein.

The Italian Parliament reduces the pope's territorial holdings to the Vatican.

The French and the Piedmontese defeat the Austrians at Magenta and Solferino.

Garibaldi and his "red shirts" capture Palermo, on the island of Sicily.

Francis Joseph becomes emperor of Austria.

Cavour signs an agreement with France against Austria at Plombières.

Bismarck becomes chief minister of Prussia.

Austria is defeated by Prussia at the Battle of Sadowa.

A Compromise establishes the Dual Monarchy.

C. Matching Exercise: Historical Actors

_____ Alexander von Bach
_____ Count Camillo di Cavour
_____ Count Otto von Bismarck
_____ Giuseppe Mazzini
_____ Emperor Francis Joseph
_____ Lord Palmerston
_____ Victor Emmanuel II
_____ Napoleon III
_____ William I
_____ Giuseppe Garibaldi

A. As king of Prussia, he furthered the cause of German unification by appointing a formidable chief minister.

B. Having ruled for more than twenty years, he lost his throne and diminished the French Empire at the Battle of Sedan.

C. This republican nationalist was the founder of Young Italy, a secret society intended to mobilize the masses in support of nationalism and democracy.

D. Conservative and intransigent, this political leader was willing to use any means at his disposal to increase the power of Prussia.

E. Having formed an army of "red shirts," this revolutionary republican put his troops at the service of the king of Piedmont-Sardinia.

F. Only eighteen when he took power, this ruler sought throughout his reign to reassert Habsburg power, struggling with the complexities of ruling a multi-ethnic empire.

G. A French speaker by preference, he skillfully manipulated international relations in pursuit of Italian unification under the leadership of Piedmont-Sardinia.

H. Chief architect of Habsburg neo-absolutism, he created a "system" intended to repress liberal and nationalist movements through the centralization and expansion of state power.

I. Ruler of the most prosperous region in Italy, this king wished to unify Italy through a gradual expansion of his power.

J. The only sane man living who understood the problem of Schleswig and Holstein, he had forgotten it.

IMPORTANT HISTORICAL FACTS: STUDY-DRILL ANSWERS

A. Multiple Choice

1. D. Risorgimento.
2. D. National Union (*Nationalverein*)
3. A. *Realpolitik.*
4. D. Schleswig and Holstein
5. B. Sadowa
6. B. the North German Confederation.
7. A. Alsace and Lorraine.
8. C. a broad boulevard built in Vienna in the 1850s and 1860s.
9. A. the Dual Monarchy.
10. B. gave ethnic minorities the right to use their own language in schools.

B. Chronological Relationships

1848 Francis Joseph becomes emperor of Austria.

1852 Victor Emmanuel II makes Cavour prime minister of Piedmont-Sardinia.

1858 Cavour signs an agreement with France against Austria at Plombières.

1859 The French and the Piedmontese defeat the Austrians at Magenta and Solferino.

1861 Garibaldi and his "red shirts" capture Palermo, on the island of Sicily.

1862 Bismarck becomes chief minister of Prussia.

1864 The Treaty of Vienna gives Austria and Prussia joint administration of Schleswig and Holstein.

1866 Austria is defeated by Prussia at the Battle of Sadowa.

1867 A Compromise establishes the Dual Monarchy.

1871 The Italian Parliament reduces the pope's territorial holdings to the Vatican.

C. Matching Exercise: Historical Actors

H. Alexander von Bach

G. Count Camillo di Cavour

D. Count Otto von Bismarck

C. Giuseppe Mazzini

F. Emperor Francis Joseph

J. Lord Palmerston

I. Victor Emmanuel II

B. Napoleon III

A. William I

E. Giuseppe Garibaldi

19 The Dominant Powers in the Age of Liberalism: Britain, France, and Russia

1. CHAPTER OUTLINE

I. VICTORIAN BRITAIN: Ruled over by its respectable queen, Victoria, Britain demonstrated to the world its dedication to the values of Christianity, the constitution, and free trade in the Great Exposition of 1851.

   A. THE VICTORIAN CONSENSUS, formed around the capitalist entrepreneurial ethic and class-based religious affiliations, was a source of great contentment and confidence for the middle classes. In the wake of a religious revival, middle-class Victorians became enthusiastic reformers and undertook a variety of charitable activities.

   B. Britain became involved in THE CRIMEAN WAR (with France and Turkey as its allies) as the result of its refusal to accept Russian expansionism in southeast Europe. The war imposed brutal conditions on all of the troops involved (a situation that Florence Nightingale sought to remedy), but resulted in a decisive defeat for Russia.

   C. THE LIBERAL ERA OF VICTORIAN POLITICS: Under Palmerston and Gladstone, Liberals dominated British politics in the 1850s and 1860s, but Conservatives found a skilled leader in Disraeli.

   D. WORKING-CLASS QUIESCENCE: Unlike their more radical counterparts on the continent, British workers rejected socialism and revolution in favor of self-help and craft-based unionism, confident that gradual improvement in their condition would continue.

   E. THE REFORM BILL OF 1867: Faced with the apparent inevitability of political reform, Conservatives and Liberals finally agreed to extend the suffrage to all male heads of households, thus doubling the electorate.

   F. THE REFORMING STATE: As resistance to state intervention waned, the ruling class came to accept an ever greater role for the government in social and economic life, as evidenced by the passage of public health and education bills.

   G. Under the guidance of Disraeli, a CONSERVATIVE REVIVAL began, resulting in the Conservative Party's return to power in 1874. As a result of new social and economic realities, the party's constituency expanded beyond the landed aristocracy, including wealthy businessmen and a small number of nationalist workers in its membership.

II. TSARIST RUSSIA stood in marked contrast to Victorian Britain. Its autocratic ruler presided over a vast but underdeveloped multinational empire increasingly subject to Western influences.

    A. RUSSIAN BACKWARDNESS AND STIRRINGS OF REFORM: Its population still composed almost entirely of impoverished serfs, Russia lagged behind Western Europe economically and intellectually. The small intelligentsia was very active, but was divided between Westernizers, who urged development along the lines of Western models, and Slavophiles who rejected Western values (and who were themselves divided between traditionalist conservatives and those who saw a revolutionary potential in the Russian peasant village).

    B. THE EMANCIPATION OF THE SERFS was considered a necessary reform by Tsar Alexander, who abolished serfdom in 1861. While former serfs were greatly disappointed in the form their freedom took, emancipation brought a wide range of reforms to the tsarist state (but no lessening of its autocratic character).

    C. THE EXPANSION OF THE RUSSIAN EMPIRE: Russia was frustrated in its attempts to expand to the southeast, but was highly successful in Asia. This eastward growth would generate increasing conflicts between Russia and Britain, China, and Japan.

    D. NIHILISTS AND POPULISTS and anarchists fought amongst themselves but shared a common commitment to overthrowing the tsarist state, forging a distinctively Russian revolutionary tradition. Their options limited by the police state, all three turned to violence as a means of political action.

III. FRANCE'S SECOND EMPIRE brought to power businessmen who flaunted their wealth in ostentatious display. Despite the vulgarity of the Second Empire elite, its prosperity contributed to general improvements in the lives of rich and poor alike.

    A. THE AUTHORITARIAN EMPIRE: Until 1859, Napoleon III reinforced the power of the centralized state and prohibited any expression of political opposition. Winning political backing through patronage and public support through propaganda, the emperor consolidated his regime, but failed to win over French workers.

    B. ECONOMIC GROWTH was dramatic in Second Empire France. An activist state encouraged investment and promoted the growth of the railway system and the rationalization of agricultural production. France's industrial "take off" improved the standard of living of the entire population, as reflected in its more varied diet.

    C. THE REBUILDING OF PARIS was engineered by Haussmann, who cut wide boulevards through the central quarters of the city in the interests of political control, commerce, and sanitation. The wealthy flocked to elegant new apartments and department stores, but workers were forced out into the industrial suburbs.

    D. SCIENCE AND REALISM: Progress in the sciences encouraged philosophers and artists to seek a more "scientific" approach to the study and representation of modern society. Comte's positivism and Courbet's realism reflected a concern with objective observation of social phenomena. Similarly, the poet Baudelaire rejected conventional bourgeois aesthetics in favor of a detached portrayal of the beauties and horrors of modern urban life.

    E. IMPRESSIONISM continued the assault on bourgeois aesthetics begun by realism. Painters such as Manet, Monet, and Degas attempted to paint what they saw, however much it offended traditional middle-class sensibilities. Rebuilt Paris served as the favored setting for painters' portraits of contemporary life, and they painted its boulevards, train stations, and bars.

F. THE "LIBERAL EMPIRE": After 1859 Napoleon III liberalized his regime both economically and politically, but a blundering foreign policy brought international humiliations and a war with Prussia in 1870.

G. THE FRANCO-PRUSSIAN WAR AND THE SIEGE OF PARIS: Prussian troops quickly and decisively defeated French troops and then laid siege to Paris. A republic was proclaimed in France and a provisional government, under the leadership of the very conservative Thiers, negotiated a peace settlement with Germany.

H. Parisian radicals, angered by their government's capitulation to Prussia, rose up in revolt and formed THE PARIS COMMUNE. Thiers sent troops to lay siege to Paris, but the Communards continued to enact a variety of social reforms in the city. In May 1871, the French army entered Paris and fierce fighting ensued between the Communards and government troops, who killed at least 25,000 Parisians and forcefully ended the Commune.

IV. CONCLUSION

2. HISTORICAL GEOGRAPHY

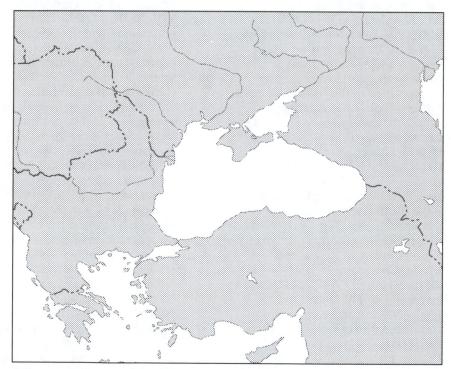

MAP 19.1   THE CRIMEAN WAR

Map Exercises

Familiarize yourself with the maps provided in your text, and then attempt to locate the following places on Blank Maps 19.1 and 19.2.

THE CRIMEAN WAR

Anatolia	Macedonia
Armenia	Moldavia
Austria-Hungary	Odessa
Black Sea	Ottoman
Bulgaria	Empire
Caucasus	Russia
Mountains	Sea of Azov
Crimea	Sebastopol
Gallipoli	Serbia
Greece	Transylvania
Kiev	Wallachia

THE EXPANSION OF RUSSIA

Afghanistan	Arctic Ocean
Aral Sea	Batum
Bering Sea	Mongolia
Bessarabia	Moscow
Caspian Sea	Persia
Finland	Siberia
Japan	St. Petersburg
Kars	Tashkent
Kazakhstan	Turkestan
Manchuria	Vladivostok

Map Questions

How did the Crimean War affect the political boundaries of Southeastern Europe?

In which regions did Russian expansion create conflicts with other European powers?

To what extent did the Franco-Prussian war readjust the borders between France and the German Empire?

3. PEOPLE AND TERMS TO IDENTIFY

Queen Victoria	Slavophiles vs.	First International
Great Exposition of 1851	Westernizers	Crédit Mobilier
Respectability	*Mir*	Suez Canal
Charles Darwin	Alexander Herzen	Baron Georges Haussmann
Crimean War	Tsar Alexander II	Positivism
Florence Nightingale	The emancipation of the	Flâneur
William Gladstone	serfs	Gustave Courbet
Benjamin Disraeli	Nihilists	Impressionism
New model unions	Michael Bakunin	Cobden-Chevalier Treaty
Household suffrage	*Narodniki*	Franco-Prussian War
Education Act of 1870	Napoleon III	Paris Commune

4. STUDY QUESTIONS

1. What was the "Victorian consensus"? How did it shape social relations in mid-nineteenth-century Britain?

2. In what sense was Florence Nightingale a model Victorian?

3. Compare and contrast British Liberals and Conservatives. To what extent did both parties' political agendas and strategies change during the course of the nineteenth century?

4. *Historical Continuities:* Why did British workers reject the socialism and revolutionary action of workers on the continent? How successful was this strategy?

5. Why did state intervention in the economy and in social relations become increasingly acceptable to Britons during this period?

6. What caused the conservative revival of the 1870s in Britain?

7. *Historical Continuities:* Why did Russian development differ from that of Western states like Britain and France?

8. On what points did Westernizers and Slavophiles disagree? On what points

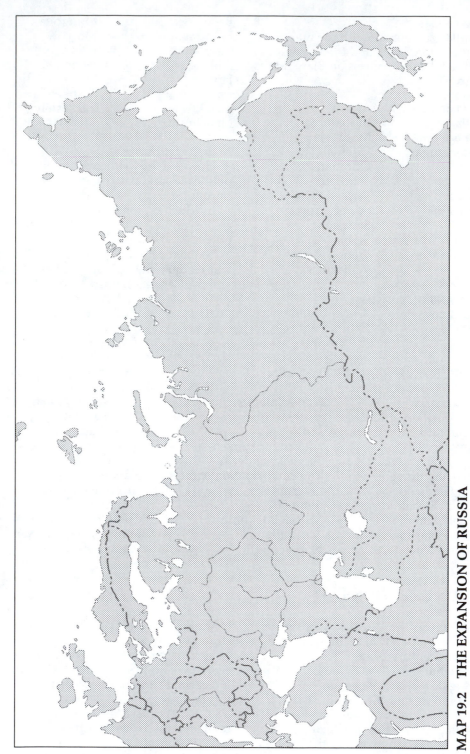

MAP 19.2   THE EXPANSION OF RUSSIA

did these nineteenth-century Russian intellectuals agree?

9. Why did Tsar Alexander II emancipate the Russian serfs? What were the results of this governmental action?

10. What were goals of the Russian nihilists, anarchists, and *narodniki*?

11. *Historical Continuities:* Why had France lagged behind Britain in its industrial development? What caused France's industrial "take off" during the Second Empire?

12. Why did Napoleon III "Haussmannize" Paris?

13. How did the artists of the Second Empire demonstrate their growing concern with "modernity"?

14. Why did Napoleon III liberalize his regime beginning in 1859? What form did this liberalization take?

15. What caused the Franco-Prussian War? Why did France lose?

16. What was the Paris Commune? Why was it forcibly repressed by the French republican government?

5. ANALYZING ART AND ARTIFACTS

What characteristics typify the realist painting of Millet and Courbet and the impressionist painting of Manet and Degas? To what extent was impressionism an outgrowth of realism? How did the two styles differ in subject matter? In technique?

6. TECHNOLOGY AND HISTORY

What sorts of technological innovations were utilized in the construction of the Crystal Palace?

How were cities made healthier places in the second half of the nineteenth century?

7. HISTORICAL ANALYSIS: INTERPRETIVE ESSAYS

1. *Historical Continuities:* Write an essay arguing one of the following points:
   a. That the political organization of Britain, France, and Russia had a determining influence on each country's economic development.
   b. That the economic development of Britain, France, and Russia had a determining influence on each country's political organization.

2. In the mid-nineteenth century, British society was characterized by a considerable degree of social harmony, while Russian society seemed increasingly disharmonious. What factors—whether economic, political, social, or cultural— can explain this difference?

3. Recreate a debate between a Slavophile and a Westernizer. Use examples from British, French, and Russian history in your arguments.

4. What is modernity? How was it expressed in the intellectual and artistic trends of the mid- to late-nineteenth century?

5. *Historical Continuities:* Why did European states go to war in the nineteenth century? To what extent were these grounds for war different from those of the past?

8. HISTORICAL VOICES: THE THEME OF PROGRESS IN THE AGE OF LIBERALISM

A. Evolutionary Theory as a Scientific Confirmation of Progress

Charles Darwin (1809–1882) was born into an affluent and distinguished British family, the grandson of the naturalist Erasmus Darwin and of the successful

potter and businessman Josiah Wedgwood. As a young man, his father pressured him to pursue a respectable career, and Darwin studied first to be a doctor and then to enter the clergy. Disenchanted with both careers, Darwin found his life's calling in 1831, when he took a position as ship's naturalist aboard the H.M.S. Beagle. During the course of his five-year journey to South America and the South Pacific, Darwin made careful observations of plant and animal life; he was especially struck by the distinctive species he encountered on the isolated Galapagos Islands.

Darwin was a painstaking and modest researcher, and spent more than twenty years elaborating the ideas he first developed during the course of his travels. He was only convinced to publish *On the Origin of Species* in 1859 because another researcher, Alfred Russel Wallace, had arrived at virtually the same conclusions and was preparing to publish a manuscript. *On the Origin of Species* had an immediate and profound impact on nineteenth-century scientific thought, and it sparked heated debate. While subsequent scientific research has led to important revisions of certain of Darwin's arguments, his evolutionary theory still stands as one of the most significant breakthroughs in the history of natural science.

However much Darwin thought of himself as a scientist, his theories were deeply influenced by the dominant concerns of the Victorian age. In a Europe typified by economic competition, nationalist rivalries, political clashes, and social conflict, it is not surprising that Darwin predicated a "struggle for survival" as the motive force behind the evolutionary development of life forms. Like his optimistic liberal contemporaries, Darwin posited progress as a fundamental law of the cosmos. However, his theories also had a darker side: Progress was achieved only at the cost of the failure of the "unfit" (later conceived by Social Darwinists as colonized peoples, "inferior races," etc.). Nature, represented as a kindly and beneficent force by Enlightenment thinkers, was now revealed as indifferent or even cruel— "red in tooth and claw," as the poet Alfred Tennyson put it.

And however much Darwin may have wished to deny that his theories contradicted traditional religious thought, his contemporaries recognized that his ideas shook the very foundations of revealed religion. Darwin's theory of evolution flatly contradicted most interpretations of the Book of Genesis, but it did even more than that: it provided the nineteenth century with a scientific explanation of the "descent of man" according to which God was virtually unnecessary. As the Victorians discovered, progress could be a double-edged sword—an increase in human knowledge might only serve to further secularize the modern worldview.

FROM *Origin of Species* by Charles Darwin

. . . Nothing at first can appear more difficult to believe than that the more complex organs and instincts have been perfected, not by means superior to, though analogous with, human reason, but by the accumulation of innumerable slight variations, each good for the individual possessor. Nevertheless, this difficulty, though appearing to our imagination insuperably great, cannot be considered real if we admit the following propositions, namely, that all parts of the organization and instincts offer, at least, individual differences—that there is a struggle for existence leading to the preservation of profitable deviations of structure or instinct—and, lastly, that gradations in the state of perfection of each organ may have existed each good of its kind. The truth of these propositions cannot, I think, be disputed. . . .

. . . In the survival of favored individuals and races, during the constantly-recurrent Struggle for Existence, we see a powerful and ever-acting form of Selection. The struggle for existence inevitably follows from the high geometrical ratio of increase which is common to all organic beings. This high rate of increase is proved by calculation—by the rapid increase of many animals and plants during a succession of peculiar seasons, and when naturalized in new countries. More individuals are born than can possibly survive. A grain in the balance may determine which individuals shall live and which shall die—which variety or species shall increase in number, and which shall decrease, or finally become extinct. As the individuals of the same species come in all respects into the closest competition with each other, the struggle will generally be most severe between them; it will be almost equally severe between the varieties of the same species, and next in severity between the species of the same genus. On the other hand, the struggle will often be severe between beings remote in the scale of nature. The slightest advantage in certain individuals, at any age or during any season, over those with which they come into competition, or better adaptation in however slight a degree to the surrounding physical conditions, will, in the long run, turn the balance.

With animals having separated sexes, there will be in most cases a struggle between the males for the possession of the females. The most vigorous males, or those which have most successively struggled with their conditions of life, will generally leave most progeny. But success will often depend on the males having special weapons, or means of defence, or charms; and a slight advantage will lead to victory. . . .

I see no good reason why the views given in this volume should shock the religious feelings of any one. It is satisfactory, as showing how transient such impressions are, to remember that the greatest discovery ever made by man, namely, the law of the attraction of gravity, was also attacked by Leibnitz, "as subversive of natural, and inferentially of revealed, religion." A celebrated author and divine has written to me that "he has gradually learned to see that it is just as noble a conception of the Deity to believe that He created a few original forms capable of self-development into other and needful forms, as to believe that He required a fresh act of creation to supply the voids caused by the action of His laws." . . .

It is interesting to contemplate a tangled bank, clothed with many plants of many kinds, with birds singing on the bushes, with various insects flitting about, and with worms crawling through the damp earth, and to reflect that these elaborately constructed forms, so different from each other, and dependent upon each other in so complex a manner, have all been produced by laws acting around us. These laws, taken in the largest sense, being Growth with Reproduction; Inheritance which is almost implied by reproduction; Variability from the indirect and direct action of the conditions of life, and from use and disuse: a Ratio of Increase so high as to lead to a Struggle for Life, and as a consequence to Natural Selection, entailing Divergence of Character and the Extinction of less-improved forms. Thus, from the war of nature, from famine and death, the most exalted object which we are capable of conceiving, namely, the production of the higher animals, directly follows. There is grandeur in this view of life, with its several powers, having been originally breathed by the Creator into a few forms or into one; and that, while this planet has gone cycling on according to the fixed law of gravity, from so simple a beginning endless forms most beautiful and most wonderful have been and are being evolved.

Source: Charles Darwin, *Origin of Species By Means of Natural Selection, or the Preservation of Favored Races in the Struggle for Life,* pp. 276–77, 304, 315–16. New York: P. F. Collier & Son, 1901.

Questions

According to Darwin, how does the "Struggle for Existence" produce the evolution of species?

How does Darwin attempt to reconcile traditional religious belief with his theories? How successful is he in this endeavor?

How might evolutionary theory be used (or rather, misapplied) to justify social inequality? Unregulated economic competition? Imperialism? Warfare? The subordination of women?

B. Russian Nihilism Champions Progress in Human Relations

Ideas of progress permeated mid-nineteenth-century European society. In Russia, geographically and culturally distant from Darwin's England, some social theorists argued that their "backward" nation could be led forward into the modern world through a concerted emulation of Western models of political liberalism and social reform. Especially after the emancipation of the serfs in 1861, many educated Russians were hopeful that their society could enter on the path of progress, either through a gradual evolution away from autocratic rule, or through a revolutionary overthrow of the existing system.

The son of a priest, Nikolai Chernyshevsky (1828–1889) studied philology at St. Petersburg University and eventually pursued a career as a journalist. In the early 1860s he sharply criticized the tsarist regime for having forced the Russian peasantry to accept onerous economic conditions in exchange for freedom. In 1862 he was arrested for "plotting the overthrow of the existing order" and was sentenced to deportation. He spent the next twenty years of his life living in exile in Siberia.

While awaiting his trial in a St. Petersburg prison, Chernyshevsky wrote *What's To Be Done?*, a novel that became a sort of guidebook for the radical generation of the 1860s. While the novel advocated a variety of reforms—including the improvement of workers' conditions through cooperative enterprises—the focus, as Chernyshevsky boldly announced, was on love and the relations between men and women. For Chernyshevsky, political, social, and economic change was impossible without a corresponding change of heart. Strongly influenced by Western writers like Fourier, Owen, and John Stuart Mill, Chernyshevsky argued that human relations could only be improved through an improvement in the status of women. Vera Pavlovna, his novel's heroine, is raised in a narrow-minded bourgeois family, but becomes an enlightened social activist through her own intellect and with the help of enlightened and loving men.

In the following brief passages from *What's To Be Done?*, Chernyshevsky exhorts Russians of his generation to seek happiness in the development of their hearts and minds. Similarly, he calls on young men to reject the patriarchalism of the past in favor of "modern" marriages based on mutual respect and equality. In both cases, Chernyshevsky's optimistic belief in the possibility of human progress—maintained even within the walls of a tsarist prison—remains vividly apparent.

FROM *What's To Be Done?* by N. G. Tchernychewsky

Come up from your caves, my friends, ascend! It is not so difficult. Come to the surface of this earth where one is so well situated and the road is easy and attractive! Try it: development! development! Observe, think, read those who tell you of the pure enjoyment of life, of the possible goodness and happiness of man.

Read them, their books delight the heart; observe life,—it is interesting; think,—it is a pleasant occupation. And that is all. Sacrifices are unnecessary, privations are unnecessary, unnecessary. Desire to be happy:

this desire, this desire alone, is indispensable. With this end in view you will work with pleasure for your development, for there lies happiness.

Oh! how great the pleasure enjoyed by a man of developed mind! That which would make another suffer he feels to be a satisfaction, a pleasure, so many are the joys to which his heart is open.

Try it, and you will see how good it is. . . .

. . . Whoever has not felt himself must at least have read that there is a great difference between a simple evening party and one where the object of your love is present. That is well known. But what very few have felt is that the charm which love gives to everything should not be a passing phenomenon in man's life, that this intense gleam of life should not light simply the period of desire, of aspiration, the period called courting, or seeking in marriage; no, this period should be only the ravishing dawn of a day more ravishing yet. Light and heat increase during the greater part of the day; so during the course of life ought love and its delights to increase. Among people of the old society such is not the case; the poetry of love does not survive satisfaction. The contrary is the rule among the people of the new generation whose life I am describing. The longer they live together, the more they are lighted and warmed by the poetry of love, until the time when the care of their growing children absorbs them. Then this care, sweeter than personal enjoyment, becomes uppermost; but until then love grows increasingly. That which the men of former times enjoyed only for a few short months the new men keep for many years.

And why so? It is a secret which I will unveil to you, if you wish. It is a fine secret, one worth having, and it is not difficult. One need have but a pure heart, an upright soul, and that new and just conception of the human being which prompts respect for the liberty of one's life companion. Look upon your wife as you looked upon your sweetheart; remember that she at any moment has the right to say to you: "I am dissatisfied with you; leave me." Do this, and ten years after your marriage she will inspire in you the same enthusiasm that she did when she was your sweetheart, and she will have as much charm for you as then and even more. Recognize her liberty as openly, as explicitly, and with as little reserve, as you recognize the liberty of your friends to be your friends or not, and ten years, twenty years, after marriage you will be as dear to her as when you were her sweetheart. This is the way in which the people of our new generation live. Their condition in this respect is very enviable. Among them husbands and wives are loyal, sincere, and love each other always more and more.

After ten years of marriage they do not exchange false kisses or false words. "A lie was never on his lips; there was no deception in his heart," was said of some one in a certain book. In reading these things we say: The author, when he wrote this book, said to himself that this was a man whom all must admire as one to be celebrated. This author did not foresee that new men would arise, who would not admit among their acquaintances people who had not attained the height of his unparalleled hero, and the readers of the aforesaid book will have difficulty in understanding what I have just said, especially if I add that my heroes do not consider their numerous friends as exceptions, but simply as estimable, though very ordinary, individuals of the new generation.

What a pity that at the present hour there are still more than ten antediluvians for every new man! It is very natural, however. An antediluvian world can have only an antediluvian population.

Source: N. G. Tchernychewsky, *What's To Be Done? A Romance,* 4th ed., pp. 240, 272–273. Trans. Benj. R. Tucker. New York: Manhattan Book Co., 1909.

Questions

According to Chernyshevsky, how can love be sustained in a marriage? How will this benefit the individual? The society?

Is Chernyshevsky a liberal?

How would you expect Chernyshevsky to respond to Darwin's theory of evolution? Which aspects of it might he accept? Which might he reject?

9. IMPORTANT HISTORICAL FACTS: STUDY DRILLS

A. Multiple Choice

1. The enormous glass and iron Crystal Palace was built
   A. as a model factory by Krupp.
   B. for the Great Exposition of 1851.
   C. as a residence for Queen Victoria after the death of Prince Albert.
   D. as an exhibition hall for impressionist painters.

2. As a result of the Crimean War
   A. the British army invaded Afghanistan.
   B. Russia took control of the Straits of Constantinople.
   C. the Black Sea was declared neutral.
   D. France lost Alsace-Lorraine to Prussia.

3. This deeply religious leader of the Liberal Party worked to reduce the role of the monarchy in British government (for which he was loathed by Queen Victoria) and supported expanding the electorate to include the "aristocracy of labor":
   A. William Gladstone
   B. Lord Palmerston
   C. Benjamin Disraeli
   D. Samuel Smiles

4. In nineteenth-century Britain, the term "household suffrage" was used in reference to
   A. a system of taxation based on family income.
   B. a form of domestic service.
   C. an electoral system in which each adult male head of a family had a vote.
   D. the feminist campaign to extend the vote to all married women.

5. In Russia, the word *mir* was used in reference to
   A. a village commune.
   B. a freed serf.
   C. a district assembly.
   D. a member of a terrorist organization.

6. Russian serfs were disappointed by their emancipation in 1861 because
   A. they were forced to pay redemption fees to their former lords.
   B. they would have preferred to remain serfs.
   C. they were forced to relocate to urban areas.
   D. it was granted only after a long period of civil war.

7. Built by Ferdinand de Lesseps, it was opened in 1869 and greatly facilitated international commerce:
   A. The Crédit Mobilier
   B. The Panama Canal
   C. The Suez Canal
   D. The French railway system

8. Wandering through the streets of Paris, this idler observed both its beauty and its horrors, representing the city in poems and paintings that rejected traditional bourgeois aesthetic standards:
   A. The nihilist
   B. The *flâneur*
   C. The positivist
   D. The Barbizon artist

9. Signed in 1860, it represented a rejection of economic protectionism on the part of the French government:

A. The Treaty of Paris
B. The Falloux Law
C. The First International
D. The Cobden-Chevalier Treaty

10. The Paris Commune was established as a result of:
    A. impressionist painters' wish to exhibit paintings rejected by the Salon jury.
    B. French workers' desire to emulate Russian village life.
    C. monarchists' outrage over the creation of a French Republic in 1870.
    D. Parisian radicals' anger over their government's willingness to sign a peace treaty with Prussia.

B. Chronological Relationships

1. List the following events in chronological order and identify the date at which they took place:
   The Treaty of San Stefano makes Bulgaria an independent state.
   A Public Health Act assures Britons a cleaner water supply.
   Outbreak of the Franco-Prussian War.
   The emancipation of the Russian serfs.
   The Great Exposition.
   Jules Verne publishes his best-seller, *Around the World in 80 Days.*
   Napoleon III begins to liberalize his regime.
   Outbreak of the Crimean War.
   Passage of the Second Reform Act in Britain.
   Tsar Alexander II is assassinated by the "People's Will."

2. Nineteenth-Century Political Regimes: Make a chronological list of the governments of Britain, France, and Russia in the years between 1800 and 1875. You may need to refer to previous chapters for information on the first half of the century.

C. Fill in the Blanks

1. Regardless of their class background, most British people were eager to maintain their claim to _____, whether that meant keeping three servants or avoiding a pauper's grave.

2. Rejecting the socialist and revolutionary tendencies of their continental counterparts, the members of the British "aristocracy of labor" joined _____, craft-based organizations emphasizing self-help.

3. The _____ made schooling obligatory for British children younger than age thirteen and attempted to ensure that schools would be built in all areas of the country.

4. _____ argued that Russia should borrow its model of progress from more developed European nations. _____ believed that Russians should reject foreign models and rely on indigenous cultural and social traditions.

5. _____ rejected all dogmas. The more romantic _____ clung to their faith in the Russian rural community and went into the countryside to learn from peasants.

6. The _____ was founded in 1864. It united European workers from a variety of socialist persuasions, but was dominated by Karl Marx and his communist theory.

7. Created with the encouragement of the French state in 1854, the _____ was an investment bank that provided loans to businessmen, financing railroads, mines, and Parisian gas companies.

8. Auguste Comte argued that laws of social development could be discovered through the application of scientific principles to the study of society, a theory that became known as _____.

9. _____ was a modernist artistic movement whose members emphasized the representation of fleeting visual sensations.

10. The _____ had a deep and lasting impact on France. In its immediate aftermath, the French suffered the collapse of the Second Empire, the loss of Alsace and Lorraine, an outbreak of bloody civil war, and the establishment of a conservative republican government.

D. Matching Exercise

Connect the person with the appropriate word or phrase.

1.	Tsar Alexander II	a.	Westernization
2.	Michael Bakunin	b.	Emancipation of the serfs
3.	Gustave Courbet	c.	"Imperial festival"
4.	Charles Darwin	d.	Anarchism
5.	Benjamin Disraeli	e.	Respectability
6.	Baron Georges Haussmann	f.	Rebuilding of Paris
7.	Alexander Herzen	g.	Realism
8.	Napoleon III	h.	Nursing
9.	Florence Nightingale	i.	Evolution
10.	Queen Victoria	j.	Conservative Party

IMPORTANT HISTORICAL FACTS: STUDY-DRILL ANSWERS

A. Multiple Choice

1. B. for the Great Exposition of 1851.
2. C. the Black Sea was declared neutral.
3. A. William Gladstone
4. C. an electoral system in which each adult male head of a family had a vote.
5. A. a village commune.
6. A. they were forced to pay redemption fees to their former lords.
7. C. The Suez Canal
8. B. The *flâneur*
9. D. The Cobden-Chevalier Treaty
10. D. Parisian radicals' anger over their government's willingness to sign a peace treaty with Prussia.

B. Chronological Relationships

1. 1851 The Great Exposition.
   1853 Outbreak of the Crimean War.
   1859 Napoleon III begins to liberalize his regime.
   1861 The emancipation of the Russian serfs.
   1866 A Public Health Act assures Britons a cleaner water supply.
   1867 Passage of the Second Reform Act in Britain.
   1870 Outbreak of the Franco-Prussian War.
   1873 Jules Verne publishes *Around the World in 80 Days*.
   1878 The Treaty of San Stefano makes Bulgaria an independent state.
   1881 Tsar Alexander II is assassinated by the "People's Will."

2. Nineteenth-Century Political Regimes

BRITAIN	RUSSIA	FRANCE
Hanoverian Dynasty:	*Romanov Dynasty:*	*First Empire:*
George III (1760–1820)	Alexander I (1801–1825)	Napoleon I
George IV (1820–1837)	Nicholas I (1825–1855)	(1804–1814/1815)
Victoria (1837–1901)	Alexander II (1855–1881)	*Bourbon Restoration:*
		Louis XVIII
		(1814/1815–1824)
		Charles X (1824–1830)
		July Monarchy:
		Louis-Philippe (1830–1848)
		Second Republic (1848–1852)
		Second Empire
		Napoleon III (1852–1870)
		Third Republic (1870–1939)

C. Fill in the Blanks
1. respectability
2. new model unions
3. Education Act of 1870
4. Westernizers; Slavophiles
5. Nihilists; *narodniki*
6. First International
7. Crédit Mobilier
8. positivism
9. Impressionism
10. Franco-Prussian War

D. Matching Exercise
1. Tsar Alexander II
2. Michael Bakunin
3. Gustave Courbet
4. Charles Darwin
5. Benjamin Disraeli
6. Baron Georges Haussmann
7. Alexander Herzen
8. Napoleon III
9. Florence Nightingale
10. Queen Victoria

b. Emancipation of the serfs
d. Anarchism
g. Realism
i. Evolution
j. Conservative Party
f. Rebuilding of Paris
a. Westernization
c. "Imperial Festival"
h. Nursing
e. Respectability

20 *Rapid Industrialization and Its Challenges, 1870–1914*

1. CHAPTER OUTLINE

I. THE SECOND INDUSTRIAL REVOLUTION began in the 1870s, as new manufacturing processes appeared and "big business" began to replace small-scale production.

   A. NEW TECHNOLOGY AND NEW INDUSTRIES: Major advances in steel production led the way in this renewed burst of industrial development.

   B. THE ELECTRIC REVOLUTION produced new consumer conveniences—electric lighting and tramways, electric household appliances—but also provided heavy industry with an important new source of power.

   C. TRAVEL AND COMMUNICATIONS: A series of technological breakthroughs and manufacturing strategies made possible the mass production of automobiles (and later airplanes), greatly improving transportation and contributing to a rise in tourism. At the same time, the telephone, radio, and silent motion pictures brought a revolution in communications.

   D. REGIONAL VARIATION: A latecomer to industrialization, Germany was the most important industrial power on the continent by the end of the nineteenth century. Britain remained the world's number one economic power, while France and Russia lagged behind, suffering from dual economies in which modern manufacturing coexisted with traditional artisanal and agricultural production.

II. A CHANGING POPULATION: Between 1870 and 1914 Europe experienced rapid population growth and urbanization, and an ever-increasing geographic mobility.

   A. Decreased mortality, even among traditionally vulnerable infants, produced a DEMOGRAPHIC BOOM, although fertility rates had also begun to decline as well. Life expectancy increased with improved nutrition and sanitation, and a concern with limiting family size caused a growing number of Europeans to use artificial contraception.

   B. TEEMING CITIES sprang up as rural Europeans fled the growing unemployment of the countryside. Despite some improvements in urban housing, overcrowding was a serious problem. Social segregation continued to increase, with the poor concentrated in suburbs and slums and the rich in more elegant neighborhoods.

   C. MIGRATION AND EMIGRATION: Migration within Europe was

substantial, especially between rural and urban regions. Similarly, tens of millions of Europeans emigrated from Europe in the late nineteenth and early twentieth centuries, usually to the United States, Canada, or Latin America.

III. SOCIAL CHANGES: Wage labor in factories had become the most common working-class experience by the end of the century.

A. INDUSTRIAL WORKERS: Some factory workers were highly skilled and well paid, but most were proletarians who were dependent on unskilled labor for survival. Working women found jobs in factories—at half men's wages—and in domestic service.

B. INDUSTRIALIZATION AND THE WORKING-CLASS FAMILY: Moralists may have exaggerated the negative impact of factory work on family life, but urban industrial labor did tend to encourage a decline in the extended family and an erosion of parental authority.

C. Many working-class women were forced into PROSTITUTION by adverse economic circumstances, and anxiety over the spread of venereal disease led some governments to attempt to regulate prostitution. Reformers protested the immorality of this state intervention, but attitudes toward prostitution were increasingly determined by public health rather than moral concerns.

D. IMPROVING STANDARDS OF LIVING: Workers' real wages increased and food prices declined during the last quarter of the nineteenth century, especially in Northwestern Europe. Workers consumed more food (although many remained malnourished) and were able to purchase more consumer goods.

E. SOCIAL MOBILITY: Social mobility was more limited than it had been earlier in the nineteenth century, but the ranks of the lower middle class swelled as new white-collar occupations opened up.

IV. MASS CULTURE became an important phenomenon as more people enjoyed improved standards of living and increased leisure time.

A. MASS EDUCATION: European states continued to sponsor education reform measures, and overall literacy rates rose significantly, although certain sectors of the population (women, workers, rural residents, Southern and Eastern Europeans) lagged behind.

B. THE DECLINE OF ORGANIZED RELIGION was uneven across Europe, and some areas even experienced religious revivals in the late nineteenth century. However, the overall trend was toward a general "de-christianization" of the population.

C. LEISURE IN THE BELLE ÉPOQUE: With more free time on their hands, Europeans flocked to dance halls, cafés, and theaters.

D. SPORTS IN MASS SOCIETY: Interest in both participatory and spectator sports was high, both as a result of increased leisure and of anxiety over the softening effects of modern life, especially upon men.

E. CONSUMERISM AND DEPARTMENT STORES: In stores like Paris's Bon Marché, consumers could purchase a vast variety of ready-made consumer goods, and shopping itself emerged as a new leisure activity.

V. RESPONSES TO A RAPIDLY CHANGING WORLD: Improved standards of living did not necessarily guarantee happiness or optimism. The years 1870–1914 witnessed an unprecedented cultural crisis, reflected in nervous disorders, alcoholism, drug use, and persistent expressions of anxiety about the negative impact of modern life.

A. ARTISTS' RESPONSES TO MASS CULTURE AND MASS PRODUCTION: Artists such as

William Morris worried that machine-age culture was eroding standards of quality traditionally associated with artisanal production. Many rejected the ugliness of the industrial landscape.

B. SCIENTISTS' ADVANCES AND UNCERTAINTIES: The work of scientists such as Curie, Planck, and Einstein chipped away at the fundamental premises of Newtonian physics, suggesting that the natural world was less predictable—and less well understood—than had been thought.

C. SOCIAL THEORISTS' ANALYSES OF INDUSTRIAL SOCIETY: Seeking explanations for the "alienation" experienced by the modern individual, sociologists developed "scientific" approaches to the study of social problems.

D. FREUD AND THE STUDY OF THE IRRATIONAL: Using psychoanalysis to plumb the depths of the unconscious mind, Viennese doctor Sigmund Freud pioneered the study of the human psyche, arguing that much human behavior was guided by unavowed irrational impulses.

E. NIETZSCHE'S EMBRACE OF THE IRRATIONAL: Rejecting Enlightenment rationalism and all religious beliefs, the philosopher Friedrich Nietzsche exalted the principles of power and struggle, predicting the coming of a "master race" of "supermen."

F. THE AVANT-GARDE'S BREAK WITH RATIONALISM: Artists too explored the irrational aspects of human experience. The rebellious European avant-garde rejected both mass culture and high culture in favor of a defiant and innovative cultural modernism.

VI. CONCLUSION

2. HISTORICAL GEOGRAPHY

Map Exercises

Familiarize yourself with the map provided in your text, and then attempt to locate the following places on Blank Map 20.1.

AREAS OF INDUSTRIAL CONCENTRATION

Barcelona	Liverpool
Bilbao	Manchester
Birmingham	Milan
Budapest	Moscow
Genoa	Munich
Le Creusot	Oviedo
Limoges	Prague
Ruhr	St. Petersburg
Saar	Turin
St. Étienne	Vienna

Map Questions

What specific factors contributed to the industrialization of the regions listed above?

In a short paragraph, describe the geography of late-nineteenth-century European industrialization. Where was industry most heavily concentrated? Which regions were least affected by industrialization?

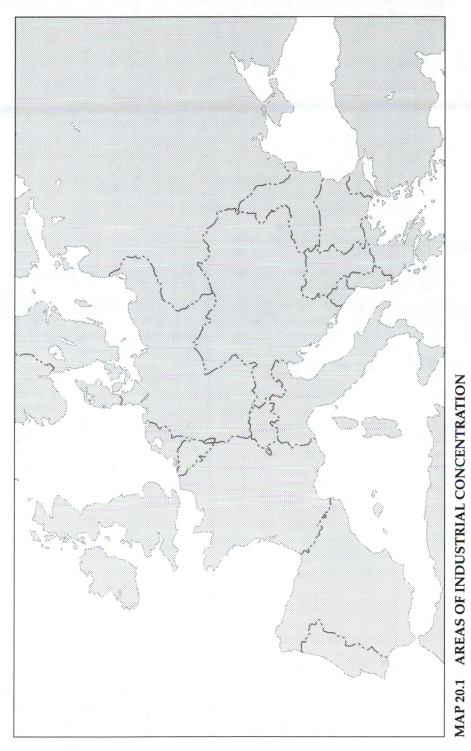

MAP 20.1 AREAS OF INDUSTRIAL CONCENTRATION

3. PEOPLE AND TERMS TO IDENTIFY

Henry Bessemer
Incandescent lamp
Karl Benz
"Kodakers"
Dresdner Bank
Dual economies
Rubber condoms
Pasteurization
London's East End
Urban villages
Emigration

"Farewell to poor old
  Erin's Isle"
Proletarian
Germinal
Contagious Diseases Act
White-collar employees
Ferry Laws
 Lourdes
Sarah Bernhardt
Olympic Games
Bon Marché

Neurasthenia
William Morris
Quantum theory
Albert Einstein
Alienation
Sigmund Freud
Nietzsche's Superman
Rite of Spring
Avant-garde
Pablo Picasso

4. STUDY QUESTIONS

1. *Historical Continuities:* What was the "Second Industrial Revolution"? How did it compare with the first?

2. How did the new technologies of the Second Industrial Revolution affect the lives of ordinary people?

3. Why did Germany take the lead in industrial development in the final quarter of the nineteenth century?

4. Why did mortality and fertility rates decrease between 1870 and 1914?

5. Why did the urban population increase and the rural population decrease in the late nineteenth century?

6. Why did so many Europeans emigrate from Europe during this period? Which Europeans were most likely to leave?

7. What kind of work did working-class women do? How did their work lives affect their personal and family experiences?

8. In what ways did Europeans' standard of living improve between 1870 and 1914? How was this related to new employment patterns?

9. What was the impact of mass literacy?

10. What did Europeans do with their increased earnings and leisure time?

11. What caused the cultural crisis of the late nineteenth century?

12. Why did the Newtonian synthesis collapse in the early twentieth century? In what ways did the work of European scientists both reflect and reinforce the anxieties of the modern age?

13. *Historical Continuities:* To what extent did the work of late-nineteenth-century social scientists, psychologists, and philosophers undermine the rationalist consensus of the previous century and a half?

14. What is the avant-garde? What does its existence tell us about European culture in the years between 1870 and 1914?

15. How was the cultural crisis of the period demonstrated in the visual arts?

5. ANALYZING ART AND ARTIFACTS

What sort of housing was available to the poor—whether they lived in the country or the city—in late-nineteenth-century Europe?

What distinguishes avant-garde painting from earlier European artistic traditions?

Referring to illustrations in the text (pp. 878 and 897), explain how Art Nouveau differs from other styles of the period.

What aspects of late-nineteenth-century culture are expressed in Pablo Picasso's *Les Demoiselles d'Avignon* (p. 899)?

What makes Umberto Boccioni's *Dynamism of a Cyclist* (p. 900) a work of futurist art? Why is its subject especially appropriate as a symbol of late-nineteenth-century modernity?

6. TECHNOLOGY AND HISTORY

What do you think was the *single* most important technological innovation of the late nineteenth century?

Using the photographs of an automobile assembly line (p. 850) and a telephone switchboard (p. 852) in your text, discuss the impact new industrial and communications technologies had on the type of work Europeans did in the *fin de siècle* period.

What practical results might be expected from the discoveries of scientists like Marie Curie and Albert Einstein?

7. HISTORICAL ANALYSIS: INTERPRETIVE ESSAYS

1. *Historical Continuities:* How did the Second Industrial Revolution differ from the first?

2. *Historical Continuities:* Compare and contrast the lives of an average worker living in 1800 and one living in 1900, focusing on social and technological change.

3. Was rapid industrialization a blessing or a curse?

4. Why did Belle Époque artists feel "alienated"? How did they express their alienation?

5. *Historical Continuities:* In what sense might the period between 1870 and 1914 be considered the end of the Enlightenment?

8. HISTORICAL VOICES: REASON AND UNREASON IN THE AGE OF "ALIENATION"

"You see, gentlemen, reason is an excellent thing. There is no doubt about that. But reason is only reason, and it can only satisfy the reasoning ability of man, whereas volition is a manifestation of the whole of life, I mean, of the whole of human life, including reason with all its concomitant head-scratchings."*

Thus, in 1864, did Fyodor Dostoevsky's "Underground Man" attack the reigning positivism of the mid-nineteenth century. In the second half of the century, the limits of reason became the subject of widespread discussion.

A. Freud's Reasoned Analysis of the Unreasonable Dream

Sigmund Freud (1856–1939) developed and promoted a theory of psychology that became one of the leading factors in the collapse of the nineteenth-century rationalist consensus. Yet Freud's "scientific" approach to the analysis of the human mind had deep roots in the Enlightenment: While insisting that unconscious impulses shaped human behavior, Freud remained a positivist in his allegiance to a reasoned analysis of unreason.

For his contemporaries, the most startling, and disturbing, aspect of Freud's theories was their emphasis on the role played by sexual urges in normal psychic development. Sexuality, which was often conceived by Europeans as a base, animal instinct divorced from the higher faculties of man, was now described by Freud and by other "sexologists" such as Richard von Kraft-Ebing and Havelock Ellis as a fundamental, if hidden (in Freudian terms, "repressed") component of all human activity. Indeed, Freud's "pansexual" psychology was based on the premise that supposedly passionless women were fully as lustful as men, and that strong sexual drives were even present in young, innocent children. Furthermore, while Freud argued that healthy adults were those who had learned to "sublimate" their desires—to divert their sexual energies into constructive pursuits such as art and

*Fyodor Dostoevsky, *Notes from the Underground,* trans. David Magarshack, in *Great Short Works of Fyodor Dostoevsky* (New York: Harper & Row, 1968), pp. 285–286.

science—he also insisted that a too-powerful repression of sexual impulses could have damaging consequences, producing hysteria, neurosis, and other mental illness.

In 1901, Freud published *On Dreams,* a short, easily accessible summary of one of his most important works, *The Interpretation of Dreams* (1900). Here, Freud presented his arguments about the operations of the unconscious mind through an analysis of the nature and significance of dreams. Rejecting medical theories that dreams were products of either outside stimuli or internal physiological processes, Freud hypothesized that dreams had a psychological meaning that could be analyzed once it was realized that the apparent absurdity of most dreams masked a deeper truth. In the following passages from *On Dreams,* Freud explains the mechanism through which the "latent content" of the dream—its real meaning—is transformed into the "manifest content"—the dream itself. Freud then argues (in a passage added in 1911) that the latent content of dreams is very often of a sexual nature.

From *On Dreams* by Sigmund Freud

Hitherto philosophers have had no occasion to concern themselves with a psychology of repression. We may therefore be permitted to make a first approach to this hitherto unknown topic by constructing a pictorial image of the course of events in dream formation. It is true that the schematic picture we have arrived at—not only from the study of dreams—is a fairly complicated one; but we cannot manage with anything simpler. Our hypothesis is that in our mental apparatus there are two thought-constructing agencies, of which the second enjoys the privilege of having free access to consciousness for its products, whereas the activity of the first is in itself unconscious and can only reach consciousness by way of the second. On the frontier between the two agencies, where the first passes over to the second, there is a censorship, which only allows what is agreeable to it to pass through and holds back everything else. According to our definition, then, what is rejected by the censorship is in a state of repression. Under certain conditions, of which the state of sleep is one, the relation between the strength of the two agencies is modified in such a way that what is repressed can no longer be held back. In the state of sleep this probably occurs owing to a relaxation of the censorship; when this happens it becomes possible for what has hitherto been repressed to make a path for itself to consciousness. Since, however, the censorship is never completely eliminated but merely reduced, the repressed material must submit to certain alterations which mitigate its offensive features. What becomes conscious in such cases is a compromise between the intentions of one agency and the demands of the other. *Repression—relaxation of the censorship—the formation of a compromise*, this is the fundamental pattern for the generation not only of dreams but of many other psychopathological structures; and in the latter cases, too, we may observe that the formation of compromises is accompanied by processes of condensation and displacement and by the employment of superficial associations, which we have become familiar with in the dream work. . . .

No one* who accepts the view that the censorship is the chief reason for dream distortion will be surprised to learn from the results of dream interpretation that most of the dreams of adults are traced back by analysis to *erotic wishes*. This assertion is not aimed at dreams with an *undisguised* sexual content, which are no doubt familiar to all dreamers from their own experience and are as a rule the only ones to be described

*The whole of this section was added in 1911.

as "sexual dreams." Even dreams of this latter kind offer enough surprises in their choice of the people whom they make into sexual objects, in their disregard of all the limitations which the dreamer imposes in his waking life upon his sexual desires, and by their many strange details, hinting at what are commonly known as "perversions." A great many other dreams, however, which show no sign of being erotic in their manifest content, are revealed by the work of interpretation in analysis as sexual wish fulfillments; and, on the other hand, analysis proves that a great many of the thoughts left over from the activity of waking life as "residues of the previous day" only find their way to representation in dreams through the assistance of repressed erotic wishes.

There is no theoretical necessity why this should be so; but to explain the fact it may be pointed out that no other group of instincts has been submitted to such far-reaching suppression by the demands of cultural education, while at the same time the sexual instincts are also the ones which, in most people, find it easiest to escape from the control of the highest mental agencies. . . . We can thus understand how it is that repressed infantile sexual wishes provide the most frequent and strongest motive forces for the construction of dreams. . . .

Although the study of dream symbols is far from being complete, we are in a position to lay down with certainty a number of general statements and a quantity of special information on the subject. There are some symbols which bear a single meaning almost universally: thus the Emperor and Empress (or the King and Queen) stand for the parents, rooms represent women and their entrances and exits the openings of the body. The majority of dream symbols serve to represent persons, parts of the body and activities invested with erotic interest; in particular, the genitals are represented by a number of often very surprising symbols, and the greatest variety of objects are employed to denote them symbolically. Sharp weapons, long and stiff objects, such as tree trunks and sticks, stand for the male genital; while cupboards, boxes, carriages or ovens may represent the uterus.

Source: Sigmund Freud. *On Dreams*, pp. 93–95, 105–106, 108–109. Trans. James Strachey. New York: W. W. Norton, 1980.

Questions

According to Freud, how does the human mind produce dreams?

Why is the repressed content of a dream so likely to be sexual?

Why would Freud's theories have seemed threatening to his contemporaries? To what extent do Freud's ideas undermine the belief in the rationality of human action?

B. Nietzsche and the "Revaluation of All Values"

Before he descended into total madness in 1889, Friedrich Nietzsche (1844–1900) wrote some of the most influential works of philosophy of the nineteenth century. Unlike Freud, who maintained a consistently professional, even scientific tone in his writings, Nietzsche was an innovative stylist whose works were filled with irony, explosive outbursts of anger, and daringly modern experiments in form and content. Nonetheless, he shared Freud's paradoxical commitment to a reasoned analysis of the limits of human reason, which Nietzsche hoped would lead to a new, more constructive philosophical foundation for human life, to a "revaluation of all values" (the title of his final, unfinished work). In Nietzsche's case, this project began with a rejection of all traditional belief structures, of all of the conceptual "idols" to which Europeans had sacrificed their reason throughout history. "Convictions," Nietzsche announced in one of his early works, "are more dangerous enemies of truth than lies."

Nietzsche favored aphorisms—pithy statements—over extended explanations of his ideas, making it notoriously difficult to pin down his thought. The fragmentary nature of his pronouncements may be read as a product of the collapse of traditional linear exposition in late-nineteenth-century philosophy and literature, but it also meant that Nietzsche's ideas could easily be misread and even abused. Some later enthusiasts, encouraged by his unscrupulous and anti-Semitic younger sister, attempted to transform Nietzsche into a Nazi forerunner, although Nietzsche himself would have abhorred the fascist ideologies of the twentieth century.

One of the most consistent elements in Nietzsche's philosophy was his radical rejection of Christianity, which he perceived as a devaluation of both unrestricted human reason and healthy human passions. This "slave religion" glorified suffering and subjected its followers to a moral and physical emasculation—"castratism," in Nietzsche's terminology.* Nietzsche's critique of organized religion reflected not only the ongoing secularization of European culture, but also a more radical rejection of all mythologies of transcendence, including not only religion, but also nationalism, naive positivism, and the proto-fascist anti-Semitism of the period.

The following fragments from Nietzsche's works provide a taste of his mature style and thought. "Anti-Darwin," from *Twilight of the Gods* (1888) demonstrates Nietzsche's fierce rejection of his contemporaries' unexamined and often complacent belief in the necessity of "evolutionary" progress. In an ironic twist, Nietzsche turns Darwin's thought on its head, arguing that the fittest are not necessarily those who survive. In the second set of excerpts, taken from *The Antichrist* (also 1888), Nietzsche argues that the success of Christianity has resulted in a "devolution" of humanity, due to this religion's tendency to side with the "unfit" over the intellectually and physically strong.

FROM *Twilight of the Idols* and *The Antichrist* by Friedrich Nietzsche

Anti-Darwin. As for the famous "struggle for *existence*," so far it seems to me to be asserted rather than proved. It occurs, but as an exception; the total appearance of life is not the extremity, not starvation, but rather riches, profusion, even absurd squandering—and where there is struggle, it is a struggle for *power.* One should not mistake Malthus for nature.

Assuming, however, that there is such a struggle for existence—and, indeed, it occurs—its result is unfortunately the opposite of what Darwin's school desires and of what one *might* perhaps desire with them—namely, in favor of the strong, the privileged, the fortunate exceptions. The species do *not* grow in perfection: the weak prevail over the strong again and again, for they are the great majority—and they are also more *intelligent.* Darwin forgot the spirit (that is English!); *the weak have more spirit.* . . .

What is good? Everything that heightens the feeling of power in man, the will to power, power itself.

What is bad? Everything that is born of weakness.

What is happiness? The feeling that power is *growing,* that resistance is overcome.

---

*As this phrasing suggests, Nietzsche felt nothing but contempt for women and their effeminate weakness. While Nietzsche's male philosopher could aspire to become a "master" or "overman" (*übermensch*), the best a woman could hope for was to give birth to the "overman."

Not contendedness but more power; not peace but war; not virtue but fitness (Renaissance virtue, *virtù*, virtue that is moraline-free).

The weak and the failures shall perish: first principle of *our* love of man. And they shall even be given every possible assistance.

What is more harmful than any vice? Active pity for all the failures and all the weak: Christianity.

The problem I thus pose is not what shall succeed mankind in the sequence of living beings (man is an *end*), but what type of man shall be *bred*, shall be *willed*, for being higher in value, worthier of life, more certain of a future.

Even in the past this higher type has appeared often—but as a fortunate accident, as an exception, never as something *willed*. In fact, this has been the type most dreaded—almost *the* dreadful—and from dread the opposite type was willed, bred, and *attained*: the domestic animal, the herd animal, the sick human animal—the Christian.

Mankind does *not* represent a development toward something better or stronger or higher in the sense accepted today. "Progress" is merely a modern idea, that is, a false idea. The European of today is vastly inferior in value to the European of the Renaissance: further development is altogether *not* according to any necessity in the direction of elevation, enhancement, or strength.

In another sense, success in individual cases is constantly encountered in the most widely different places and cultures: here we really do find a *higher type*, which is, in relation to mankind as a whole, a kind of overman. Such fortunate accidents of great success have always been possible and *will* perhaps always be possible. And even whole families, tribes, or peoples may occasionally represent such a *bull's-eye*.

Christianity should not be beautified and embellished: it has waged deadly war against this higher type of man; it has placed all the basic instincts of this type under the ban; and out of these instincts it has distilled evil and the Evil One: the strong man as the typically reprehensible man, the "reprobate." Christianity has sided with all that is weak and base, with all failures . . .

Source: Friedrich Nietzsche. *Twilight of the Idols or, How One Philosophizes with a Hammer,* and *First Book: The Antichrist.* In *The Portable Nietzsche,* pp. 522–523, 570–571. Ed. Walter Kaufmann. New York: Viking Press, 1954.

Questions

In what sense is Nietzsche "anti-Darwin"? What aspects of evolutionary theory does he reject? Why?

Why is Nietzsche so critical of Christianity?

What sort of a person would Nietzsche's "higher type" or "overman" be?

9. IMPORTANT HISTORICAL FACTS: STUDY DRILLS

A. Multiple Choice

1. The investment capital that fueled the German industrial boom of the second half of the nineteenth century was supplied by institutions which also acted as industrial entrepreneurs. An example is

A. the Dresdner Bank.
B. Mercedes-Benz.
C. the Crédit Mobilier.
D. *Wandervogel.*

2. Greatly improved by new industrial technologies, it was too expensive for most Europeans to use regularly, but contributed to the declining fertility rate:
   A. Coitus interruptus
   B. Famine
   C. The incandescent lamp
   D. The rubber condom

3. It was known for its docks and its slum housing, and its "outcast" residents often spoke with a cockney accent the upper classes found difficult to understand:
   A. London's East End
   B. Vienna's Ringstrasse
   C. The factory town of Saint-Étienne
   D. Paris's Bois de Boulogne

4. They were likely to sing "Farewell to poor old Erin's Isle" as they emigrated from their homeland:
   A. Italian "swallows" on their way to Argentina
   B. Polish Jews on their way to New York's Lower East Side
   C. Irish rural laborers on their way to Boston
   D. The Russian peasants of St. Petersburg

5. Émile Zola's 1885 novel about life in the coal mines of northern France depicted the hard physical labor performed by young girls in the mine shafts. Its title was
   A. *The Rite of Spring.*
   B. *Germinal.*
   C. *King Ubu.*
   D. *Community and Society.*

6. British reformer Josephine Butler led a determined campaign against this state-sponsored attempt to regulate prostitution:
   A. The Ferry Laws
   B. The Contagious Diseases Act
   C. The Temperance Movement
   D. The Protestant Ethic

7. The Ferry Laws
   A. improved waterway transportation in Britain.
   B. returned control of French education to the Catholic Church.

C. required that all British children attend school up to the age of ten.
D. made primary schools free, obligatory, and secular in France.

8. The Bon Marché was
   A. a Parisian department store.
   B. a French sporting club.
   C. a Montmartre cabaret.
   D. an upper-class neighborhood in Western Paris.

9. In the early twentieth century, Max Planck, a German scientist, demonstrated that radiant energy is emitted not in a steady stream but in discrete units, challenging accepted scientific thought about energy. His discovery was known as
   A. quantum theory.
   B. Newtonian physics.
   C. the General Theory of Relativity.
   D. alienation.

10. Performed in 1913, this ballet created an uproar. Traditionalists were outraged by its unconventional choreography and jarring music, but the avant-garde cheered:
    A. *King Ubu*
    B. *Swan Lake*
    C. *The Rite of Spring*
    D. *Tour de France*

B. Chronological Relationships

1. Population Growth: Using the figures provided in Table 20.2, draw a line or bar graph comparing the different nations' population growth rates between 1871 and 1911. How had the size of these populations changed during this period? Which nations experienced the most dramatic growth?

   Historical Continuities: Compare these figures with those provided in Chapter 16 (Table 16.1, p. 672).

2. List the following events in the history of technology in chronological order and identify the date at which they took place:

   Benz invents the internal combustion machine.

   The Paris Métro (subway) opens on Bastille Day (July 14th).

   Bessemer develops a new steel-production process.

Diesel invents the kerosene- or pure-oil-fueled engine.

A silent motion picture is first shown.

Edison invents the incandescent lamp.

Ford starts a car company in Detroit.

Bell invents the telephone.

Kodak introduces a lightweight camera for use by the general public.

Siemens invents the electric dynamo.

C. Fill in the Blanks

1. Electricity was little more than a scientific curiosity until the American Thomas Edison invented the _____, which made electric lighting a practical reality.

2. The industrial development of France and Russia was constrained by their _____, which combined modern manufacturing sectors with traditional handicraft and agricultural production.

3. _____ made milk safe to drink, bringing a decline in cases of tuberculosis and contributing to longer life expectancy.

4. Social theorists worried that urbanization created uprooted and lawless populations, but the chain migration of friends and family members to specific city neighborhoods created _____, which provided community support for recent immigrants.

5. In the second half of the nineteenth century a large percentage of workers had become _____, unskilled industrial laborers with a growing sense of class consciousness.

6. Despite the "de-christianization" of the European population, the late nineteenth century saw a revival of popular religion and a growing cult of miracles. In France, Catholic pilgrims flocked to _____, seeking a miraculous cure for their illnesses and diseases.

7. In 1896, Baron Pierre de Coubertin staged the first modern _____ in Athens, hoping to revive the moral and physical vitality of French men through athletic competition.

8. If you were overly sensitive to noise and light, were always tired and anxious, and had an upset stomach, you were probably suffering from _____, a nervous disorder apparently caused by the complexities of modern life.

9. On the other hand, if you were haunted by thoughts of suicide and and had fallen into a state of disorganization and maniacal agitation, you were probably suffering from _____, the result of the social and moral disintegration experienced by those lost in a faceless urban and industrial world.

10. The European _____, an elite minority of artists and intellectuals who saw themselves as being at the forefront of artistic expression and achievement, was defiantly modern and rejected rationalism as an objective standard.

D. Matching Exercise: Historical Actors

_____ William Morris

_____ Albert Einstein

_____ Sarah Bernhardt

_____ Pablo Picasso

_____ Superman

_____ Karl Benz

_____ Henry Bessemer

_____ Sigmund Freud

_____ "Kodaker"

_____ White-collar employee

A. A German engineer who invented the gas-powered internal combustion engine.

B. A world-famous theater performer whose dramatic gestures included being photographed in a coffin.

C. This unassuming patent examiner postulated the equivalence of mass and energy in the famous equation: $E = mc^2$.

D. A draftsman, accountant, bookkeeper, subway agent, tax collector, postal worker, etc.

E. A Viennese doctor who explored the deepest recesses of the human psyche and formulated a theory of the unconscious.

F. An English inventor who developed a new method for forging high quality steel more cheaply and in greater quantities.

G. A tourist who visited scenic Brittany, camera in hand.

H. An English craftsman and designer who led an "arts and crafts" movement against the "age of shoddy" ushered in by defiling capitalism.

I. This Spanish artist painted in a "cubist" style and is often considered to be the first painter of the modernist movement.

J. A hero of natural nobility who would come forward to rule the "slave races," at least according to Nietzsche.

E. Post-Impressionist Art
   Write a one-sentence definition of each of the following styles of post-impressionist art.

Art Nouveau	futurism
cubism	pointillism
expressionism	secessionism
fauvism	

IMPORTANT HISTORICAL FACTS: STUDY-DRILL ANSWERS

A. Multiple Choice

1. A. the Dresdner Bank.
2. D. The rubber condom
3. A. London's East End
4. C. Irish rural laborers on their way to Boston
5. B. *Germinal.*
6. B. The Contagious Diseases Act
7. D. made primary schools free, obligatory, and secular in France.
8. A. a Parisian department store.
9. A. quantum theory.
10. C. *The Rite of Spring*

B. Chronological Relationships
1. Population Growth Bar Graph

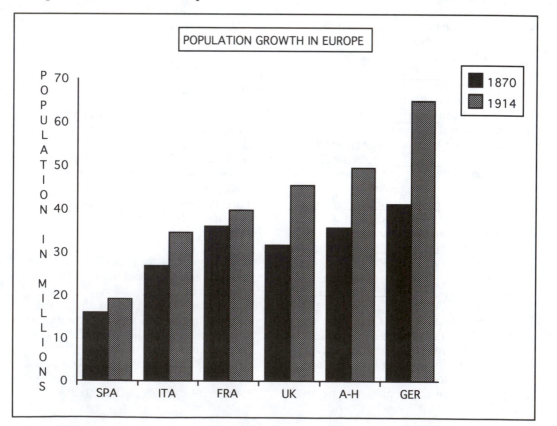

2. 1856 Bessemer develops a new steel-production process.
   1867 Siemens invents the electric dynamo.
   1876 Bell invents the telephone.
   1879 Edison invents the incandescent lamp.
   1885 Benz invents the internal combustion machine.
   1888 Kodak introduces a lightweight camera for use by the general public.
   1895 A silent motion picture is first shown.
   1897 Diesel invents the kerosene- or pure-oil-fueled engine.
   1900 The Paris Métro (subway) opens on Bastille Day (July 14th).
   1903 Ford starts a car company in Detroit.

C. Fill in the Blanks
1. incandescent lamp
2. dual economies
3. Pasteurization
4. urban villages
5. proletarians
6. Lourdes
7. Olympic Games
8. neurasthenia
9. alienation
10. avant-garde

D. Matching Exercise: Historical Actors
H. William Morris
C. Albert Einstein
B. Sarah Bernhardt
I. Pablo Picasso
J. Superman
A. Karl Benz
F. Henry Bessemer
E. Sigmund Freud
G. "Kodaker"
D. White-collar employee

21 *Mass Politics and Nationalism*

1. CHAPTER OUTLINE

I. FROM LIBERALISM TO NATIONALISM: The expansion of the electorate, mass literacy, and the popular press all brought more Europeans into political life. Between 1880 and 1914, liberalism declined in strength and nationalism became an increasingly important force in political culture.

  A. THE WANING OF THE LIBERAL ERA: In the political arena, liberals' insistence that voting privileges be granted only to those with sufficient private property gave way to the gradual implementation of universal manhood suffrage. In the economic sector, the traditional liberal allegiance to free trade policies was undermined by the hardships of the long depression (which encouraged governments to impose protective tariffs) and the cartelization of industry.

  B. THE NEW NATIONALISM was more aggressive and exclusionary than earlier liberal nationalism, and it merged easily with anti-Semitism and imperialism. Largely upper and middle class in its appeal, strident nationalism emerged in part as an anxious response to the internationalism of the activist left.

II. The hardships of working-class life, aggravated by the long depression, brought calls for SOCIAL REFORM from many quarters.

  A. Throughout industrialized Europe, millions of workers joined THE TRADE UNION MOVEMENT, and unionized workers went on strike to protect their interests and to protest labor conditions. Despite the successes of the unions, many workers—and especially women workers—remained unorganized.

  B. STATE SOCIAL REFORM: By the end of the nineteenth century, growing numbers of social reformers and politicians had come to accept the necessity of implementing the social welfare policies demanded by workers. In many European states, laws were passed providing unemployment compensation, old-age pensions, health insurance, and other benefits.

  C. WOMEN'S SUFFRAGE: Some "new women" agitated in favor of increasing women's political rights, but most European political parties rejected this idea out of hand. In Britain, "suffragettes" engaged in dramatic protests against women's political disenfranchisement.

III. In the late nineteenth century, CHALLENGERS TO THE NATION-STATE on both the left and the right agitated for sweeping change or revolution.

    A. THE CATHOLIC CHURCH tended to oppose liberalism and nationalism as threats to papal authority, but Pope Leo XIII put an end to this refusal to accept the modern age, unintentionally lending support to Christian Socialist movements.

    B. THE SOCIALISTS gained increasing power in the industrialized nations of Northern Europe. Internally divided between revolutionary and reformist wings, the socialist movement nonetheless became an important force for social and political change, opposing laissez-faire capitalism and nationalism.

    C. THE ANARCHISTS opposed the state itself, many believing that terrorist action—"propaganda by the deed"—would spark revolution and bring an end to government. A minority movement, anarchism nevertheless received widespread attention as the result of successful bombings and assassinations.

    D. Like the anarchists, THE SYNDICALISTS rejected politics in favor of direct action by unionized workers, hoping to bring capitalism and the state to their knees through a "general strike."

IV. CHANGES AND CONTINUITIES IN BRITISH POLITICAL LIFE: During Victoria's long and stable reign, Conservative and Liberal political leaders responded to universal manhood suffrage with new political strategies.

    A. IRISH HOME RULE: Faced with an increasingly militant Irish nationalist movement, which drew its support from Irish Catholic tenant farmers, the British Liberal Party supported increased (but not total) independence for Ireland. "Home Rule" bills met with opposition from Conservatives and Irish Protestant landowners.

    B. NEW CONTOURS IN BRITISH POLITICAL LIFE: Frustrated by the anti-labor policies of the Conservative government and employers' union-busting, workers—and especially unskilled workers—engaged in a "new unionism," going on strike in record numbers and supporting the creation of a new Labour Party. A split over protective tariff policies brought an end to Conservative rule in 1905, and Liberals moved to reestablish their power by wooing workers' votes. The Parliament Act of 1911 brought an end to the disproportionate power of the nobles in the House of Lords, permitting the Liberal government to support pro-labor policies and enabling the passage of an Irish Home Rule bill.

V. REPUBLICAN FRANCE: In the years following the Franco-Prussian War and the Commune, France wavered between moderate republicanism and a monarchist restoration.

    A. MONARCHISTS AND REPUBLICANS struggled for control of France in the 1870s. Despite voting procedures heavily weighted in favor of monarchist candidates, voters continued to elect republicans to the National Assembly. In 1877, Marshal MacMahon, the monarchist president, provoked a governmental crisis by attempting to replace the republican premier with a monarchist, but new elections returned a republican majority and MacMahon resigned.

    B. THE THIRD REPUBLIC was dominated by centrist "opportunists" who sought to navigate between the extremes of right-wing monarchism and left-wing socialism.

C. GENERAL BOULANGER AND CAPTAIN DREYFUS: Beginning in the 1880s, a series of crises—an attempted coup d'état by the supporters of Boulanger, the Panama Canal scandal, the Dreyfus Affair—disrupted French political life, pitting left-leaning liberals and socialists against a new nationalist and anti-Semitic right wing.

D. THE RADICAL REPUBLIC: The pardon of Dreyfus in 1899 stabilized the republic and helped bring the Radical Party to power. Uniting nationalism with anti-clericalism, leaders like Clemenceau and Poincaré battled anti-militarist internationalism on the left (gaining the support of the military) and conservative Catholicism on the right.

VI. TSARIST RUSSIA: After the assassination of Alexander II in 1881, the tsarist government became even more resistant to criticism and less willing to contemplate liberalization.

A. In the interest of unifying his empire, Alexander III ordered a RUSSIFICATION campaign, forcing non-Russians to learn Russian and strongly encouraging them to join the Russian Orthodox Church. This policy created considerable hostility to the tsar's regime among the non-Russian population of the Russian Empire.

B. THE RUSSO-JAPANESE WAR (1904–1905): Russia and Japan came into conflict over territory on the East Asian mainland. The tiny Asian nation defeated the large Russian Empire, revealing both the weaknesses of the tsar's army and the strengths of Japan.

VII. ITALY: Despite unification, many Italians remained more loyal to local institutions and the Catholic Church than to the central government.

A. RESISTANCE TO THE STATE came from both the impoverished south and the unreconciled Catholic hierarchy.

B. CENTRALIZED AUTHORITY was weak in Italy, and the government came to rely on shifting political alliances and outright corruption to implement its policies.

C. THE RISE OF ITALIAN NATIONALISM: An aggressive nationalism served as a unifying force in divided Italy, inspiring several not-very-successful military adventures.

VIII. AUSTRIA-HUNGARY presented the anomaly of a multinational empire in an increasingly nationalist Europe.

A. ETHNIC TENSIONS IN THE DUAL MONARCHY divided the empire's population into competing national groups. Hungary's "Magyarization" policy was especially disruptive.

B. FORCES OF COHESION: Ethnic divisions were counterbalanced by Francis Joseph's personal prestige, and by unifying institutions like the Catholic Church, the imperial bureaucracy, and the military.

C. NATIONALIST MOVEMENTS developed especially among subject Poles and Serbians, exacerbating preexisting ethnic divisions.

IX. THE GERMAN EMPIRE, dominated by the conservative Prussian nobility, remained aggressive, nationalistic, and authoritarian.

A. NATIONALIST VERSUS INTERNATIONALIST MOVEMENTS: Bismarck strongly opposed the internationalism of both the Catholic Center Party and the German socialists. However, after the chancellor decided that he might need the support of Catholics against the socialists, he ended the *Kulturkampf* and concentrated on repressing left-wing political activism.

B. WILLIAM II AND GERMAN NATIONALISM: The inept William II eventually drove Bismarck from office, and proceeded to antagonize Germany's rivals with his support for a naval build-up and the expansionist aspirations of nationalist leagues.

X. CONCLUSION

2. HISTORICAL GEOGRAPHY

Map Review

   Familiarize yourself with the borders separating the European nations in the late nineteenth century. Be able to name the nations bordering the major Europeans powers (Austria-Hungary, Great Britain, France, Germany, Italy, and Russia).

3. PEOPLE AND TERMS TO IDENTIFY

Universal manhood suffrage
Long Depression
Cartels
Zionism
French General Confederation of Labor (C.G.T.)
Taylorism
German Sickness Insurance Law of 1883
New Woman
Emmeline Pankhurst
Rerum Novarum

Second International
German Social Democratic Party (S.P.D.)
Jean Jaurès
Prince Peter Kropotkin
Propaganda by the deed
General Strike
Joseph Chamberlain
Irish Home Rule
British dockworkers' strike of 1889
British Labour Party
Parliament Act of 1911
Marshal MacMahon

French Third Republic
General Georges Boulanger
The Dreyfus Affair
Georges Clemenceau
Russo-Japanese War
Trasformismo
Italia Irredenta
Magyarization
Francis Joseph
Greater Serbia
German Catholic Center Party
Kulturkampf
William II

4. STUDY QUESTIONS

   1. What caused the decline of liberalism in the late nineteenth century? What replaced it?

   2. *Historical Continuities:* How was the nationalism of the late nineteenth century different from that of the early nineteenth century?

   3. Why did unions attract so many workers in the late nineteenth century? What factors limited the effectiveness of the unions?

   4. *Historical Continuities:* Why did European governments begin to sponsor social reform initiatives in the late nineteenth century? What changes in European politics and the economy made this reversal of earlier policies possible?

   5. Why was women's suffrage almost universally rejected in late-nineteenth-century Europe?

   6. Why did socialism become such an important force in late-nineteenth-century Europe? How did revolutionary socialism differ from reform socialism?

   7. What are the similarities between anarchism and syndicalism? The differences? Why did members of both movements reject involvement in parliamentary politics?

   8. Why did Irish Home Rule become such an important political concern in late-nineteenth-century Britain?

   9. Why was the British Labour Party created?

   10. What was the significance of the Parliament Act of 1911?

   11. Why did right-wing conservatives fail to establish a monarchy in France after 1870?

12. Why did the Dreyfus Affair have such a profound impact on French society in the 1890s?

13. What was "Russification"? Why was this policy pursued by the tsarist state?

14. How did northern Italy differ from southern Italy in the late nineteenth century?

15. What held the patchwork quilt of Austria-Hungary together?

16. Why did Bismarck resign as chancellor of Germany? What effect did his resignation have on international relations?

5. ANALYZING ART AND ARTIFACTS

How might political images like those reproduced in the text (pp. 923, 929, 940, 941, 946, and 955) have been used to influence public opinion during this period? Why would political cartoons be an especially appropriate form of propaganda in an era of "mass" politics?

6. TECHNOLOGY AND HISTORY

To what extent might modern communications and transportation technologies have contributed to the rise of nationalism *and* internationalism between 1880 and 1914?

7. HISTORICAL ANALYSIS: INTERPRETIVE ESSAYS

1. *Historical Continuities:* How did the gradual implementation of universal manhood suffrage, begun in the late eighteenth century and continuing into the twentieth century, transform the political systems of Western Europe?

2. What caused the rise of right-wing nationalism and left-wing internationalism between 1880 and 1914? How did the two movements differ? What concerns did they share?

3. Which of the European Great Powers was most successful in resolving its internal conflicts in the years prior to

World War I? Which was least successful? What can explain the differences between these two nations' experiences?

4. *Historical Continuities:* Why was nationalism a source of instability in Eastern Europe throughout the nineteenth century?

5. Write a speech explaining to the German Reichstag why you, Otto von Bismarck, support state-sponsored social welfare initiatives. Be sure to situate your remarks within both a national and international context.

8. HISTORICAL VOICES: CHANGING RESPONSES TO ECONOMIC AND POLITICAL INEQUALITY

A. The Catholic Church Comes to Terms with "New Things"

Throughout much of the nineteenth century the Catholic Church remained strongly committed to reactionary and anti-modern policies. However, the election of Pope Leo XIII (Vicenzo Gioacchino Pecci, 1810–1903) in 1878 signalled an important reversal of this trend, perhaps to the surprise of the College of Cardinals, which had not expected the delicate sixty-eight-year-old

to lead the Church for the next quarter century. While Pope Leo was by no stretch of the imagination a liberal, he recognized that the Church would continue to lose adherents—especially among the increasingly secular working class—if it failed to demonstrate sympathy for the concerns of industrial laborers.

Pope Leo began his tenure in a traditional vein, criticizing "the evils affecting modern society"—including secular education, political liberalism, and socialism—in no uncertain terms. But having confirmed the papacy's commitment to the fundamentals of orthodox Catholicism, Leo then sought to demonstrate that the Church was capable of attuning itself to the realities of modern life. While insisting, for example, that education must have a Christian basis, he also argued that the Church must abandon its perennial hostility toward science and "favor the wise cultivation of the mind." In the political realm, Leo broke with the Church's long-standing tendency to support only autocratic regimes, acknowledging the validity of a Christian democracy "built . . . on the basic principles of divine faith."

Most significantly, Leo argued that, although economic inequality was condoned by Scripture, the industrial working class had a right to protest unjust treatment by the rich. In the encyclical *Rerum Novarum* ("Of New Things"; May 15, 1891), Leo condemned socialist efforts to end class differences through the abolition of private property, but he also censured unbridled capitalism as irreligious and immoral. The poor must accept their lot in life in a spirit of humility and resignation, but the rich must recognize that it is their responsibility to share their wealth through acts of Christian charity.

FROM *The Condition of the Working Classes. Encyclical Letter Rerum Novarum, May 15, 1891,* by Pope Leo XIII

The great mistake made in regard to the matter now under consideration is to take up with the notion that class is naturally hostile to class, and that the wealthy and the workingmen are intended by nature to live in mutual conflict. . . . Religion teaches the wealthy owner and the employer that their work-people are not to be accounted their bondsmen; that in every man they must respect his dignity and worth as a man and as a Christian; that labor is not a thing to be ashamed of, if we lend ear to right reason and to Christian philosophy, but is an honorable calling, enabling a man to sustain his life in a way upright and creditable; and that it is shameful and inhuman to treat men like chattels to make money by, or to look upon them merely as so much muscle or physical power. Again, therefore, the Church teaches that, as Religion and things spiritual and mental are among the workingman's main concerns, the employer is bound to see that the worker has time for his religious duties; that he be not exposed to corrupting influences and dangerous occasions; and that he be not led away to neglect his home and family, or to squander his earnings. Furthermore, the employer must never tax his work-people beyond their strength, or employ them in work unsuited to their sex or age. His great and principal duty is to give every one a fair wage. Doubtless, before deciding whether wages are adequate, many things have to be considered; but wealthy owners and all masters of labor should be mindful of this—that to exercise pressure upon the indigent and the destitute for the sake of gain, and to gather one's profit out of the need of another, is condemned by all laws, human and divine. To defraud any one of wages that are his due is a crime which cries to the avenging anger of Heaven. *Behold, the hire of the laborers . . . which by fraud hath been kept back by you, crieth aloud; and the cry of them hath entered into the ears of the Lord of Sabaoth.** Lastly, the rich must religiously refrain from cutting down the workmen's earnings, whether by force, by fraud, or by usurious dealing; and with all the greater reason because the laboring man is, as a rule, weak and unprotected, and because his slender means should in proportion to their scantiness be accounted sacred.

*St. James v. 4.

Were these precepts carefully obeyed and followed out, would they not be sufficient of themselves to keep under all strife and all its causes? . . .

. . . Private ownership, as we have seen, is the natural right of man; and to exercise that right, especially as members of society, is not only lawful, but absolutely necessary. . . . But when what necessity demands has been supplied, and one's standing fairly taken thought for, it becomes a duty to give to the indigent out of what remains over. *Of that which remaineth, give alms.** . . .

Let it be then taken for granted that workman and employer should, as a rule, make free agreements, and in particular should agree freely as to the wages; nevertheless, there underlies a dictate of natural justice more imperious and ancient than any bargain between man and man, namely, that remuneration ought to be sufficient to support a frugal and well-behaved wage-earner. If through necessity or fear of a worse evil the workman accept harder conditions because an employer or contractor will afford him no better, he is made the victim of force and injustice. . . .

Associations of every kind, and especially those of workingmen, are now far more common than heretofore. . . . There is a good deal of evidence . . . which goes to prove that many of these societies are in the hands of secret leaders, and are managed on principles ill-according with Christianity and the public well-being; . . .

. . . We may lay it down as a general and lasting law, that workingmen's associations should be so organized and governed as to furnish the best and most suitable means for attaining what is aimed at; that is to say, for helping each individual member to better his condition to the utmost in body, mind, and property. It is clear that they must pay special and chief attention to the duties of religion and morality, and that their internal discipline must be guided very strictly by these weighty considerations; otherwise they would lose wholly their special character, and end by becoming little better than those societies which take no account whatever of religion. . . .

*St. Luke xi. 41.

Source: Pope Leo XIII. The Condition of the Working Classes. Encyclical Letter Rerum Novarum, May 15, 1891. In *The Great Encyclical Letters of Pope Leo XIII,* 2nd ed., pp. 218, 219–220, 221, 222, 236, 241, 243–244. New York: Benziger Bros., 1903.

Questions

According to Pope Leo XIII, how should Catholic factory owners treat their employees? To what extent do the pope's injunctions place restrictions on laissez-faire capitalism?

How do Pope Leo's arguments about class relations differ from those of Karl Marx (see pp. 182–184)? How can this difference be explained?

Imagine that you are a member of one of the Catholic trade unions envisioned by Pope Leo. How might you ask your employer for a wage increase?

B. Anarchists Call for Emancipation from Capital, State, and Church

If the late-nineteenth-century Catholic Church proclaimed a Christian morality that transcended (but did not abolish) class divisions and national borders, anarchists promoted an internationalism based on an absolute rejection of private property, the nation-state, and organized religion. Anarchists who advocated violence as a means of bringing down established political regimes gained considerable notoriety in the late nineteenth century, but others, such as Peter Kropotkin (1842–1921) and his followers, promoted a more peaceable and voluntary transformation of existing economic, political, and social relations. Kropotkin supported "propaganda by the deed," especially in his early years as a political activist, but he also came to believe that a balanced physical and intellectual education was the best hope for the eventual transition to the stateless society of his dreams. Anarchism remained a minor political movement, but theorists such as Kropotkin were influential insofar as they provided an alternative to the otherwise general consensus in favor of increasing the powers of the modern nation-state.

Like other socialists, Kropotkin condemned private property as a violation of the natural rights of all human beings. But he parted with mainstream socialist schools in his rejection of representative government and state bureaucracies.

Instead of guaranteeing "liberty, equality, and fraternity," Kropotkin insisted, the structures of the state place undue restrictions on individual liberty while at the same time "freeing" the individual from personal responsibility for the healthy functioning of the community. Kropotkin's experiences as a political activist only reinforced his distrust of state authority: having escaped a tsarist prison in 1876, he was again imprisoned for his political beliefs in 1886 in republican France.

As a political activist, Kropotkin was eager to distinguish anarchism from other forms of socialism. In the short pamphlet, *The Place of Anarchism in Socialistic Evolution* (1886), he presented a clear formulation of the fundamental tenets of his political theory. As the following excerpts from this pamphlet demonstrate, Kropotkin was firmly convinced that, freed from the oppression of industrial capitalism, the state, and the church, human beings would return to a natural state in which free and independent individuals cooperated with one another to form harmonious social organizations.

FROM *The Place of Anarchism in Socialistic Evolution* by Peter Kropotkin

All things belong to all, and provided that men and women contribute their share of labour for the production of necessary objects, they are entitled to their share of all that is produced by the community at large. "But this is Communism," you may say. Yes, it is Communism, but it is the Communism which no longer speaks in the name of religion or of the state, but in the name of the people. During the past fifty years a great awakening of the working-class has taken place: the prejudice in favour of private property is passing away. The worker grows more and more accustomed to regard the factory, the railway, or the mine, not as a feudal castle belonging to a lord, but as an institution of public utility which the public has the right to control. The idea of possession in common has not been worked out from the slow deductions of some thinker buried in his private study, it is a thought which is germinating in the brains of the working masses, and when the revolution, which the close of this century has in store for us, shall have hurled confusion into the camp of our exploiters, you will see that the mass of the people will demand Expropriation, and will proclaim its right to the factory, the locomotive, and the steamship. . . .

But it is not enough to argue about, "Communism" and "Expropriation;" it is furthermore necessary to know who should have the management of the common patrimony, and it is especially on this question that different schools of Socialists are opposed to one another, some desiring authoritarian Communism, and others, like ourselves, declaring unreservedly in favour of anarchist Communism. . . .

Do we require a government to educate our children? Only let the worker have leisure to instruct himself, and you will see that, through the free initiative of parents and of persons fond of tuition, thousands of educational societies and schools of all kinds will spring up, rivalling one another in the excellence of their teaching. If we were not crushed by taxation and exploited by employers, as we now are, could we not ourselves do much better than is now done for us? The great centres would initiate progress and set the example, and you may be sure that the progress realised would be incomparably superior to what we now attain through our ministeries.—Is the State even necessary for the defence of a territory? If armed brigands attack a people, is not that same people, armed with good weapons, the surest rampart to oppose to the foreign aggressor? Standing armies are always beaten by invaders, and history teaches that the latter are to be repulsed by a popular rising alone.—While Government is an excellent machine to protect monopoly, has it ever been able to protect us against ill-disposed persons? Does it not, by creating misery, increase the number of crimes instead of diminishing them? In establishing prisons into which multitudes of men, women, and children are thrown for a time in order to come forth infinitely worse than when they went in, does not the State maintain nurseries of vice at the expense of the tax-payers? In obliging us to commit to others the care of our affairs, does it not create the most terrible vice of societies—indifference to public matters? . . .

[PART III]

. . . There is no more room for doubting that religions are going; the nineteenth century has given them their death blow. . . . But when we throw religions overboard or store them among our public records as historical curiosities, shall we also relegate to museums the moral principles which they contain? . . .

. . . The whole anarchist morality is . . . the morality of a people which does not look for the sun at midnight—a morality without compulsion or authority, a morality of habit. Let us create circumstances in which man shall not be led to deceive nor exploit others, and then by the very force of things the moral level of humanity will rise to a height hitherto unknown. Men are certainly not to be moralised by teaching them a moral catechism: tribunals and prisons do not diminish vice; they pour it over society in floods. Men are to be moralised only by placing them in a position which shall contribute to develop in them those habits which are social, and to weaken those which are not so. A morality which has become instinctive is the true morality, the only morality which endures while religions and systems of philosophy pass away.

Let us now combine the three preceding elements, and we shall have Anarchy and its place in Socialistic Evolution.

Emancipation of the producer from the yoke of capital; production in common and free consumption of all the products of the common labour.

Emancipation from the governmental yoke; free development of individuals in groups and federations; free organisation ascending from the simple to the complex, according to mutual needs and tendencies.

Emancipation from religious morality; free morality, without compulsion or authority, developing itself from social life and becoming habitual.

Source: Peter Kropotkin. *The Place of Anarchism in Socialistic Evolution,* pp. 6–7, 8, 9–10, 12, 14. Trans. Henry Glasse. London: William Reeves, [n. d.; 1886?].

Questions

Why is the state unnecessary, according to Kropotkin?

In the absence of religion and government, what provides the basis for anarchist morality?

How do you think Kropotkin would have responded to Pope Leo's XIII encyclical, *Rerum Novarum*? Aside from the obvious differences between Kropotkin and Leo, what ideas and beliefs do they share?

9. IMPORTANT HISTORICAL FACTS: STUDY DRILLS

A. Multiple Choice

1. By 1914, universal manhood suffrage had been granted everywhere *except*
   A. Britain.
   B. France.
   C. Russia.
   D. Italy.

2. Cartels were formed in order to
   A. allow big businesses to limit competition.
   B. give workers more say in the organization of production.
   C. bring the collapse of capitalism.
   D. provide price supports for small businesses.

3. All of the following individuals might be considered "new women," *except*
   A. Emmeline Pankhurst.
   B. Maria Montessori.
   C. Queen Victoria.
   D. Marie Curie.

4. Advocacy of the "general strike" is most closely associated with
   A. anarchism.
   B. syndicalism.
   C. the International Women's Suffrage Alliance.
   D. the Russification campaign.

5. Irish Home Rule was opposed by
   A. William Gladstone.
   B. most Irish Catholics.
   C. most Irish Protestants.
   D. Charles Stewart Parnell.

6. Founded after the anti-union Taff Vale decision, it was intended to provide political representation for workers and won twenty-nine parliamentary seats in the 1906 elections:
   A. German Social Democratic Party
   B. French Section of the Working-Class International
   C. Italian Socialist Party
   D. British Labour Party

7. Accused of having sold French military secrets to the Germans in 1894, this Jewish officer was not fully exonerated until 1906:
   A. Alfred Dreyfus
   B. Georges Boulanger
   C. Émile Zola
   D. Édouard Drumont

8. The Austrian territory claimed by Italian nationalists was known as
   A. *Trasformismo.*
   B. *Italia Irredenta.*
   C. *Tripolitania.*
   D. *Ausgleich.*

9. The program of Magyarization was imposed throughout
   A. Greater Serbia.
   B. Hungary.
   C. the Dual Monarchy.
   D. the Balkans.

10. Bismarck abandoned the *Kulturkampf* because he believed that he might need this group's support against the German left-wing
    A. Social Democratic Party
    B. Second International
    C. Bundesrat
    D. Catholic Center Party

B. Chronological Relationships

1. List the following events in chronological order and identify the dates at which they took place:
   Bismarck resigns as chancellor to William II.
   Outbreak of the Russo-Japanese War.
   Founding of the German Social Democratic Party.
   In an Act of Parliament, the British House of Lords eliminates its constitutional veto.
   Bismarck launches the *Kulturkampf.*
   British dockworkers' strike.

Emmeline Pankhurst founds the
Women's Social and Political Union.

The founding of the French General
Confederation of Labor.

Umberto I of Italy falls victim to
"propaganda by the deed."

German Sickness Insurance Law.

2. What was the historical significance of
each of the events listed above?

C. Matching Exercise: Historical Actors

_____ General Georges Boulanger
_____ Joseph Chamberlain
_____ Francis Joseph
_____ Theodor Herzl
_____ Jean Jaurès
_____ Prince Peter Kropotkin
_____ Pope Leo XIII
_____ Marshal MacMahon
_____ Frederick Taylor
_____ William II

A. His encyclical, *Rerum Novarum*,
demonstrated a new willingness on the
part of the Catholic Church to accept
the modern age and called attention to
the injustices suffered by workers.

B. Having rejected the hope of full Jewish
assimilation in an increasingly anti-
Semitic Europe, he founded a Zionist
movement for the establishment of a
Jewish homeland in Palestine.

C. A dashing military man, he served as
the figurehead for a right-wing
attempt to overthrow the French Third
Republic in 1889. Having let his
moment of opportunity pass, he
committed suicide on his dead
mistress's grave.

D. A successful British manufacturer and
professional politician, he broke with
the Liberal Party over Irish Home
Rule, which he opposed out of fear it
would lead to the collapse of the
British Empire.

E. An impulsive and weak-willed
German ruler, he drove Bismarck to
resign in 1890 and proceeded to
antagonize Germany's rivals with his
ill-conceived policies.

F. Unlike those who advocated a violent
overthrow of the state, this Russian
geographer advocated a gentle and
voluntary transition to anarchist
communism.

G. This American engineer developed
techniques of "scientific management"
for factory production, which
increased pressure on workers to be
more productive.

H. Although he favored a monarchist
restoration, this French president was
unable to put together a royalist
majority in the Chamber of Deputies
and resigned in 1879, ensuring the
survival of the Third Republic.

I. As the emperor of Austria and the king
of Hungary, this long-lived monarch
helped to hold together the patchwork
Austro-Hungarian Empire through his
personal prestige and cautious ruling
style.

J. A former philosophy professor, he
united reformist and revolutionary
French socialists in the French Section
of the Working-Class International.

IMPORTANT HISTORICAL FACTS: STUDY-DRILL ANSWERS

A. Multiple Choice
1. C. Russia.
2. A. allow big businesses to limit
   competition.
3. C. Queen Victoria.
4. B. syndicalism.
5. C. most Irish Protestants.
6. D. British Labour Party
7. A. Alfred Dreyfus
8. B. *Italia Irredenta.*

9. B. Hungary.
10. D. Catholic Center Party

B. Chronological Relationships
1873 Bismarck launches the
Kulturkampf.
1875 Founding of the German Social
Democratic Party.
1883 German Sickness Insurance Law.
1889 British dockworkers' strike.

1890 Bismarck resigns as chancellor to William II.

1895 The founding of the French General Confederation of Labor.

1900 Umberto I of Italy falls victim to "propaganda by the deed."

1903 Emmeline Pankhurst founds the Women's Social and Political Union.

1904 Outbreak of the Russo-Japanese War.

1911 In an Act of Parliament, the British House of Lords eliminates its constitutional veto.

C. Matching Exercise: Historical Actors

C. General Georges Boulanger

D. Joseph Chamberlain

I. Francis Joseph

B. Theodor Herzl

J. Jean Jaurès

F. Prince Peter Kropotkin

A. Pope Leo XIII

H. Marshal MacMahon

G. Frederick Taylor

E. William II

22 The Age of European Imperialism

1. CHAPTER OUTLINE

I. FROM COLONIALISM TO IMPERIALISM: Europeans had colonized other parts of the globe since the time of Columbus, but many of these colonies had since gained their independence. By the mid-nineteenth century, only Britain was still in possession of a large colonial empire.

II. THE "NEW IMPERIALISM" AND THE SCRAMBLE FOR AFRICA: Fueled by competitive nationalism, the European powers began to vie with one another for imperial control of the African continent after 1880.

  A. BRITISH AND FRENCH IMPERIAL RIVALRY: The French seized territory in northwest Africa, while the British sought to control the Suez Canal through a protectorate over Egypt. Competing claims in northern Africa created growing tension between the two powers.

  B. GERMANY AND ITALY JOIN THE RACE: At first hesitant to embroil Germany in imperial adventures, Bismarck eventually decided to join the "scramble" in Africa and called the Berlin Conference in 1884. Italy also sought territory in Africa, with little success.

  C. STANDOFF IN THE SUDAN: THE FASHODA AFFAIR: When French and British troops finally confronted one another on the Upper Nile, their governments reached a compromise agreement.

  D. THE BRITISH IN SOUTH AFRICA AND THE BOER WAR: In the south, conflict between British imperialists and Dutch settlers resulted in the Boer War and subsequent British domination of South Africa.

III. THE EUROPEAN POWERS IN ASIA: Moved by the same imperialist spirit as in Africa, the European powers also expanded their empires in Asia.

  A. INDIA, SOUTHEAST ASIA, AND CHINA: The British government took over formal control of India in 1858, and forcibly asserted its trading rights in China. The Dutch expanded their dominion over Indonesia, while the French consolidated their Southeast Asian holdings as French Indochina.

  B. JAPAN AND CHINA: CONTRASTING EXPERIENCES: In response to Western imperialist pressures, Japan successfully "westernized," becoming an imperial power in its own right. The weak Chinese government, on the other hand, failed to develop an adequate response to Western demands and found itself forced to make humiliating concessions.

  C. THE UNITED STATES IN ASIA: The United States made the Philippines an American territory, but insisted on an "open door" for all nations wishing to engage in trade with China.

IV. DOMINATION OF INDIGENOUS PEOPLES: European imperialism found intellectual support in arguments that Europeans were superior to non-Western peoples.

A. SOCIAL DARWINISM: Europeans used pseudo-scientific evolutionary theories to prove the "natural" inferiority of non-Westerners. As a result of these attitudes, the lives of indigenous peoples were readily sacrificed to imperial interests, as in the massacre of the Herero of German Southwest Africa.

B. TECHNOLOGICAL DOMINATION AND INDIGENOUS SUBVERSION: Industrial technologies facilitated imperial expansion, but indigenous peoples continued to resist military and cultural subjugation by Western powers.

C. IMPERIAL ECONOMIES: European imperialists "plundered" their colonies, appropriating the land of indigenous peoples, imposing taxation upon them, and forcing them to work in the interests of the Western economies.

D. COLONIAL ADMINISTRATIONS: Some European nations exercised formal control over their colonies, while others relied on informal economic or military domination.

V. ASSESSING THE GOALS OF EUROPEAN IMPERIALISM: Was the dominant impulse behind European imperialism religious, moral, economic, or cultural?

A. THE "CIVILIZING MISSION": Missionaries and other reformers sought to Christianize or "civilize" non-Westerners, arguing that Europeans had an obligation to bring cultural and economic progress to backward peoples.

B. THE ECONOMIC RATIONALE: Some Europeans argued that colonies offered substantial economic benefits to private investors and to the imperial power as a whole, but imperialism was not always profitable.

C. IMPERIALISM AND NATIONALISM: The "new imperialism" developed in the context of growing rivalries between the European powers and the rise of aggressive nationalism. Even when colonies brought little or no profit, strategic concerns and popular enthusiasm supported the extension of European imperial domination.

VI. CONCLUSION

2. HISTORICAL GEOGRAPHY

Map Exercises

Familiarize yourself with the maps provided in your text, and then attempt to locate the following places on Blank Maps 22.1 and 22.2.

EUROPEAN IMPERIALISM IN AFRICA

Abyssinia (Ethiopia)
Algeria
Anglo-Egyptian Sudan
Angola
Bechuanaland
British East Africa (Kenya)
Cameroons
Congo Free State (Belgian Congo)
Egypt
Fashoda
French West Africa
German East Africa (Tanganyika)
Liberia
Libya
Morocco
Mozambique
Nigeria
Rhodesia
Suez Canal
Union of South Africa

EUROPEAN IMPERIALISM IN ASIA

Annam
Bangkok
Borneo
Burma
Cambodia
China
Dutch East Indies
Guam
Hong Kong
India

MAP 22.1   EUROPEAN IMPERIALISM IN AFRICA

Indochina	Saigon
Java	Siam
Malaya	Singapore
Manila	Sumatra
Philippines	Taiwan (Formosa)

Map Questions

Compare European colonial holdings prior to 1880 (Map 22.1 on p. 960 of the text) with the empires built between 1880 and 1914 (Map 22.2 on p. 966 and Map 22.4 on p. 978).

How did colonial settlement patterns in South Africa change between 1800 and 1910 (Map 22.3 on p. 975 of the text)?

Why was Fashoda the logical location for a confrontation between France and Great Britain over the issue of African colonial holdings?

In what sense might British colonial holdings be described as an international "network"?

MAP 22.2   EUROPEAN IMPERIALISM IN ASIA

3. PEOPLE AND TERMS TO IDENTIFY

King Leopold II
Imperialism
"Scramble for Africa"
Suez Canal
Berlin Conference
Fashoda Affair
Boer War
Opium War

Sepoy Mutiny
Meiji Restoration
Boxer Rebellion
Open-door policy
Social Darwinism
Herero
Dum-dum bullet
Plunder economies

Formal vs. informal
  imperialism
"Civilizing mission"
Dual mandate
J. A. Hobson
Jingoism

4. STUDY QUESTIONS

1. *Historical Continuities:* What is the difference between the "new" European imperialism and the old European colonialism?

2. What specific colonial interests brought France and Britain into conflict in Africa? How and why did the two nations settle their differences?

3. Why did Bismarck resist German imperial expansion? Why did he finally come to accept it?

4. What caused the "scramble for Africa"?

5. *Historical Continuities:* How did Great Britain acquire and consolidate control over the Indian subcontinent?

6. Why was Japan able to maintain its independence? Why was China forced to make concessions to the Western powers?

7. What cultural and intellectual theories were used to justify European imperialism?

8. How did new technologies—the fruits of the Industrial Revolution—support the European states in their empire-building?

9. How and why did indigenous peoples resist European imperialism? What factors served to limit the success of this resistance?

10. Describe British colonial culture. How did it differ from the French model of imperial administration?

11. To what extent were colonial holdings economically beneficial to the European imperial powers?

12. Of "Christianity, commerce, and civilization," which do you think was the most important stimulus to late-nineteenth-century imperialism?

5. ANALYZING ART AND ARTIFACTS

How were non-Western peoples portrayed in Western photographs and cartoons? How did these images serve to reinforce Westerners' belief in their own superiority?

6. TECHNOLOGY AND HISTORY

Why did Europeans find it relatively easy to establish military control over African and Asian territories?

To what extent was the administration of colonial holdings facilitated by new transportation and communications technologies?

7. HISTORICAL ANALYSIS: INTERPRETIVE ESSAYS

1. *Historical Continuities:* "In 1500, the European powers controlled about 7 percent of the globe's land; . . . in 1914, they controlled 84 percent." What long-term trends in Western history can explain this dramatic expansion of European domination?

2. In what ways might the new imperialism be considered a predictable result of the post-1870 European Great-Power system?

3. Imagine that you are the leader of an African people resisting imperial rule. If you could give a speech at the Berlin Conference, what would you say?

4. Why was the British Empire the envy of all other European imperial powers?

8. HISTORICAL VOICES: CONTRASTING EUROPEAN PERSPECTIVES ON THE "CIVILIZING MISSION"

A. Rudyard Kipling and "The White Man's Burden"

Rudyard Kipling (1865–1936), one of the most popular British authors of the late nineteenth century, was a quintessential product of imperialism. Born to British parents in Bombay, India, Kipling spent much of his childhood in England, but returned to India as a young man, where he earned a living as a journalist. In the late 1880s he began to publish poems and short stories, many of which dealt with colonial subjects, and these works earned him great international acclaim. Although his mature short fiction demonstrates considerable sophistication, Kipling is best known for his children's stories—including *Kim* and *The Jungle Book*—and for his energetic if hackneyed verse, which often reproduced the colloquial speech of the soldiers who defended the British Empire.

Kipling's contemporary success—and the subsequent decline in his popularity in the later twentieth century—was a product of his ability to lend cultural legitimacy to British imperialism. An inveterate traveller within the British Empire, Kipling lived during different periods of his life in England, India, South Africa, and the United States (still something of a colonial outpost in the late nineteenth century, at least in the British imagination), and he drew on his experiences to produce a body of literature that emphasized the triumphant, if sometimes slow, progress of British culture and values throughout the "uncivilized" world. His colorful portraits of colonial societies and his sentimentalized descriptions of relations between colonizers and the colonized helped to engender among ordinary Britons an emotional commitment to ongoing imperial conquest.

For all his sympathy toward the Asian and African subjects of Western rule, Kipling remained convinced that they were "backward" peoples and that it was the duty of enlightened Europeans to civilize them. This paternalism is clearly evident in "The White Man's Burden," one of the most famous of Kipling's poems. Published in 1899, it was written in response to the American takeover of the Philippines after the Spanish-American War of 1898. While the poem was specifically intended to encourage the United States to join the other Western nations in shouldering the imperial burden, it was read, then as now, as a ringing celebration of the "civilizing mission" in general.

From "The White Man's Burden" by Rudyard Kipling

Take up the White Man's burden—
  Send forth the best ye breed—
Go bind your sons to exile
  To serve your captives' need;
To wait in heavy harness,
  On fluttered folk and wild—
Your new-caught, sullen peoples,
  Half-devil and half child.

Take up the White Man's burden—
　In patience to abide,
To veil the threat of terror
　And check the show of pride;
By open speech and simple,
　An hundred times made plain,
To seek another's profit,
　And work another's gain.

Take up the White Man's burden—
　The savage wars of peace—
Fill full the mouth of Famine
　And bid the sickness cease;
And when your goal is nearest
　The end for others sought,
Watch Sloth and heathen Folly
　Bring all your hope to naught.

Take up the White Man's burden—
　No tawdry rule of kings,
But toil of serf and sweeper—
　The tale of common things.
The ports ye shall not enter,
　The roads ye shall not tread,
Go make them with your living,
　And mark them with your dead.

Take up the White Man's burden—
　And reap his old reward;
The blame of those ye better,
　The hate of those ye guard—
The cry of hosts ye humour
　(Ah, slowly!) toward the light:—
"Why brought ye us from bondage,
　Our loved Egyptian night?"

Take up the White Man's burden—
　Ye dare not stoop to less—
Nor call too loud on Freedom
　To cloak your weariness;
By all ye cry or whisper,
　By all ye leave or do,
The silent, sullen peoples
　Shall weigh your Gods and you.

Take up the White Man's burden—
　Have done with childish days—
The lightly proffered laurel
　The easy, ungrudged praise.
Comes now, to search your manhood
　Through all the thankless years,
Cold, edged with dear-bought wisdom,
　The judgment of your peers!

Source: Rudyard Kipling. "The White Man's Burden." In *Kipling Stories and Poems Every Child Should Know,* vol. 2, pp. 359–361. Boston: Houghton Mifflin, 1909.

Questions

What makes imperial rule such a thankless task, according to Kipling? If it is such a "burden," why should Americans and Europeans accept this duty?

To what extent was this poem written as a justification for imperialism?

How are those peoples subject to imperial domination depicted by Kipling? Do you find any evidence of Social Darwinism in Kipling's description of the "captives" of empire?

B. Joseph Conrad and the Heart of Darkness

Like Kipling, Joseph Conrad (1857–1924) had considerable personal experience of the workings of empire. Born Józef Teodor Konrad Korzeniowski in a Polish region of Russia, Conrad left Eastern Europe as a young man for a life at sea. In between stints in the British merchant marine, he began to write novels and short stories based on his travels. In 1889, Conrad sailed to the Congo Free State for a Belgian firm. He contracted a tropical fever during this journey and returned to Europe a broken man. He retired from the merchant marine in the mid-1890s and dedicated himself to a full-time career as an author. Although he had not learned English until he was already in his twenties, Conrad came to be considered one of the great English-language stylists of the modern period.

If Kipling and Conrad shared a familiarity with the far-flung reaches of empire, they differed in their evaluation of the imperial venture. Conrad's depiction of European domination of non-Europeans is complex, somber, and deeply ambivalent. While his contemporaries read his novels for their "exotic" characters and settings, Conrad himself was primarily interested in analyzing the more mundane reality of evil in human experience. His works are highly nuanced and ambiguous, reflecting a distinctively modern concern with the fragility of individual identity and with the unconscious impulses shaping human behavior. Conrad was drawn to the sea and to the "uncivilized" regions of the world because he conceived of them as environments in which human beings were exposed to both physical and psychological extremes, driving them to confront their deepest fears and impulses—often learning that European "civilization" was slight protection against the "primitive" self lurking deep within the individual.

The short story "Heart of Darkness," published in 1902, is a fictionalized account of Conrad's experiences in the Congo Free State. Other authors had written journalistic exposés of the atrocities committed in this personal holding of Belgium's King Leopold, but Conrad's story transformed the raw materials of his own personal experiences into a brilliant—and deeply disturbing—meditation on the darkness at the heart of the human spirit. Controversial to this day, the work maintains a perennial fascination, both because of its dazzling literary qualities and its complex meditation on imperialism as a historical endeavor and as a state of mind. Its mythic vitality was demonstrated in Francis Ford Coppola's 1979 film, *Apocalypse Now,* a retelling of "Heart of Darkness" set in the war-torn Vietnam of the 1960s.

Before Marlow, the story's narrator, leaves for Africa, his elderly aunt congratulates him for taking up the challenge of "weaning [the] ignorant millions from their horrid ways." Marlow reminds his aunt that imperialism also has a profit motive. In the following passages from "Heart of Darkness," Conrad describes Marlow's first encounter with colonized Africa in a narrative deeply marked by the tension between the civilizing impulse and the reality of economic exploitation.

From *Heart of Darkness* by Joseph Conrad

". . . A rocky cliff appeared, mounds of turned-up earth by the shore, houses on a hill, others with iron roofs, amongst a waste of excavations, or hanging to the declivity. A continuous noise of the rapids above hovered over this scene of inhabited devastation. A lot of people, mostly black and naked, moved about like ants. A jetty projected into the river. A blinding sunlight drowned all this at times in a sudden recrudescence of glare.

. . . "I came upon a boiler wallowing in the grass, then found a path leading up the hill. It turned aside for the boulders, and also for an undersized railway-truck lying there on its back with its wheels in the air. One was off. The thing looked as dead as the carcass of some animal. I came upon more pieces of decaying machinery, a stack of rusty rails. To the left a clump of trees made a shady spot, where dark things seemed to stir feebly. I blinked, the path was steep. A horn tooted to the right, and I saw the black people run. A heavy and dull detonation shook the ground, a puff of smoke came out of the cliff, and that was all. No change appeared on the face of the rock. They were building a railway. The cliff was not in the way or anything; but this objectless blasting was all the work going on.

"A slight clinking behind me made me turn my head. Six black men advanced in a file, toiling up the path. They walked erect and slow, balancing small baskets full of earth on their heads, and the clink kept time with their footsteps. Black rags were wound round their loins, and the short ends behind waggled to and fro like tails. I could see every rib, the joints of their limbs were like knots in a rope; each had an iron collar on his neck, and all were connected together with a chain whose bights swung between them, rhythmically clinking. Another report from the cliff made me think suddenly of that ship of war I had seen firing into a continent. It was the same kind of ominous voice; but these men could by no stretch of imagination be called enemies. They were called criminals, and the outraged law, like the bursting shells, had come to them, an insoluble mystery from the sea. All their meagre breasts panted together, the violently dilated nostrils quivered, the eyes stared stonily uphill. They passed me within six inches, without a glance, with that complete, deathlike indifference of unhappy savages. Behind this raw matter one of the reclaimed, the product of the new forces at work, strolled despondently, carrying a rifle by its middle. He had a uniform jacket with one button off, and seeing a white man on the path, hoisted his weapon to his shoulder with alacrity. This was simple prudence, white men being so much alike at a distance that he could not tell who I might be. He was speedily reassured, and with a large, white, rascally grin, and a glance at his charge, seemed to take me into partnership in his exalted trust. After all, I also was a part of the great cause of these high and just proceedings.

"Instead of going up, I turned and descended to the left. My idea was to let that chain-gang get out of sight before I climbed the hill. . . . I've seen the devil of violence, and the devil of greed, and the devil of hot desire; but, by all the stars! these were strong, lusty, red-eyed devils, that swayed and drove men—men, I tell you. But as I stood on this hillside, I foresaw that in the blinding sunshine of that land I would become acquainted with a flabby, pretending, weak-eyed devil of a rapacious and pitiless folly. How insidious he could be, too, I was only to find out several months later and a thousand miles farther. For a moment I stood appalled, as though by a warning. Finally I descended the hill, obliquely, towards the trees I had seen.

"I avoided a vast artificial hole somebody had been digging on the slope, the purpose of which I found it impossible to divine. It wasn't a quarry or a sandpit, anyhow. It was just a hole. It might have been connected with the philanthropic desire of giving the criminals something to do. I don't know. Then I nearly fell into a very narrow ravine, almost no more than a scar in the hillside. I discovered that a lot of imported drainage-pipes for the settlement had been tumbled in there. There wasn't one that was not broken. It was a wanton smash-up. At last I got under the trees. My purpose was to stroll into the shade for a moment; but no sooner within than it seemed to me I had stepped into the gloomy circle of some Inferno. The rapids were near, and an uninterrupted, uniform, headlong, rushing noise filled the mournful stillness of the grove, where not a breath stirred, not a leaf moved, with a mysterious sound— as though the tearing pace of the launched earth had suddenly become audible.

"Black shapes crouched, lay, sat between the trees leaning against the trunks, clinging to the earth, half coming out, half effaced within the dim light, in all the attitudes of pain, abandonment, and despair. Another mine on the cliff went off, followed by a slight shudder of the soil under my feet. The work was going on. The work! And this was the place where some of the helpers had withdrawn to die.

"They were dying slowly—it was very clear. They were not enemies, they were not criminals, they were nothing earthly now—nothing but black shadows of disease and starvation, lying confusedly in the greenish gloom. Brought from all the recesses of the coast in all the legality of time contracts, lost in uncongenial surroundings, fed on unfamiliar food, they sickened, became inefficient, and were then allowed to crawl away and rest. These moribund shapes were free as air—and nearly as thin. I began to distinguish the gleam of the eyes under the trees. Then, glancing down, I saw a face near my hand. The black bones reclined at full length with one shoulder against the tree, and slowly the eyelids rose and the sunken eyes looked up at me, enormous and vacant, a kind of blind, white flicker in the depths of the orbs, which died out slowly. The man seemed young—almost a boy—but you know with them it's hard to tell. I found nothing else to do but to offer him one of my good Swede's ship's biscuits I had in my pocket. The fingers closed slowly on it and held—there was no other movement and no other glance. He had tied a bit of white worsted round his neck—Why? Where did he get it? Was it a badge—an ornament—a charm—a propitiatory act? Was there any idea at all connected with it? It looked startling round his black neck, this bit of white thread from beyond the seas.

"Near the same tree two more bundles of acute angles sat with their legs drawn up. One, with his chin propped on his knees, stared at nothing, in an intolerable and appalling manner: his brother phantom rested its forehead, as if overcome with a great weariness; and all about others were scattered in every pose of contorted collapse, as in some picture of a massacre or a pestilence. While I stood horror-struck, one of these creatures rose to his hands and knees, and went off on all-fours towards the river to drink. He lapped out of his hand, then sat up in the sunlight, crossing his shins in front of him, and after a time let his woolly head fall on his breastbone.

"I didn't want any more loitering in the shade, and I made haste towards the station. When near the buildings I met a white man, in such an unexpected elegance of get-up that in the first moment I took him for a sort of vision. I saw a high starched collar, white cuffs, a light alpaca jacket, snowy trousers, a clean necktie, and varnished boots. No hat. Hair parted, brushed, oiled, under a green-lined parasol held in a big white hand. He was amazing, and had a penholder behind his ear.

. . . I respected the fellow. Yes; I respected his collars, his vast cuffs, his brushed hair. His appearance was certainly that of a hairdresser's dummy; but in the great demoralization of the land he kept up his appearance. That's backbone. His starched collars and got-up shirt-fronts were achievements of character. . . .

"Everything else in the station was in a muddle—heads, things, buildings. Strings of dusty niggers with splay feet arrived and departed; a stream of manufactured goods, rubbishy cottons, beads, and brass-wire set into the depths of darkness, and in return came a precious trickle of ivory."

Source: Joseph Conrad. *Heart of Darkness.* 1902.

Questions
How "civilized" was European treatment of Africans, according to Conrad?

What meanings do the terms "black" and "white" take on in the context of this passage? To what extent does Conrad's use of black/white imagery play against established European symbolism?

Conrad has been called a racist by the Nigerian author Chinua Achebe. Would you agree with this appraisal? Why or why not?

9. IMPORTANT HISTORICAL FACTS: STUDY DRILLS

A. Multiple Choice

1. The "scramble for Africa" began as the result of
   A. European interest in African cultures.
   B. the discovery of gold in South Africa.
   C. the disappearance of David Livingstone.
   D. colonial rivalries between the European Great Powers.

2. Bismarck called the Berlin Conference in order to
   A. stop the "scramble for Africa."
   B. settle territorial claims in the Congo.
   C. keep Germany out of the race for colonies.
   D. deprive Leopold II of the Congo Free State.

3. The Boer War was fought between
   A. France and Britain on the Upper Nile.
   B. Britain and Dutch settlers in South Africa.
   C. Germany and the Herero people in German Southwest Africa.
   D. the United States and the Philippines.

4. Britain won the Opium War through the use of
   A. dum-dum bullets.
   B. gunboat diplomacy.
   C. the Gatling gun.
   D. a negotiated settlement, ratified at the Berlin Conference.

5. In 1900, a Chinese secret society led an attack on European and American "foreign devils" resident in Northern China. This was known as
   A. the Boxer Rebellion.
   B. the Sepoy Mutiny.
   C. the Meiji Restoration.
   D. the Mahdist Revolt.

6. Social Darwinism—which posited the natural superiority of Europeans over

other "backward" peoples—was
popularized by
A. Charles Darwin.
B. Queen Victoria.
C. Herbert Spencer.
D. V. I. Lenin.

7. In 1903, Germans in German
Southwest Africa slaughtered
approximately 55,000 Africans. These
people were known as
A. the Sepoy.
B. the Herero.
C. the Ashanti.
D. the Mahdists.

8. The "plunder economies" established
by European imperial powers were
characterized by all of the following
except
A. expropriation of land.
B. forced labor.
C. taxation.
D. social welfare benefits.

9. Lord Frederick Lugard popularized
the idea that European imperialists
were responsible for improving the
moral and material conditions of
indigenous peoples. This concept was
known as
A. the "white man's burden."
B. the civilizing mission.
C. the dual mandate.
D. the open-door policy.

10. In 1902, J. A. Hobson argued that
imperialism was caused by
A. missionaries' religious fervor.
B. nationalist expansionism.
C. businessmen's need for an
outlet for excess manufactured
goods.
D. European governments' desire
to acquire strategic military
outposts.

B. Chronological Relationships

1. List the following events in
chronological order and identify the
dates at which they took place:
Opium War
Battle of Adowa
Boer War
Boxer Rebellion
Battle of Omdurman
Leopold II sends Henry Stanley to the
Congo.
Completion of the Suez Canal
Meiji Restoration
Berlin Conference
Sepoy Mutiny

2. How did each of the events listed above
shape the history of European
imperialism?

C. Fill in the Blanks

1. As the owner of the Congo Free State,
_____ established a colonial
regime typified by brutal exploitation
of the indigenous population in the
pursuit of profits derived from ivory
and rubber.

2. After the opening of the _____,
the British became extremely
concerned with maintaining access to
India via the eastern Mediterranean
and established a protectorate over
Egypt.

3. In 1898, French and British troops met
on the Upper Nile in the Sudan.
Recognizing Britain's prior claim to
the region, the French government
backed down, averting war between
the two European powers. This event
was known as the _____.

4. In 1857, Indian troops in the British
army rose in revolt, protesting a
variety of British colonial policies.
After this outbreak of rebellion,
known as the _____, the British
government took formal control of the
Indian subcontinent.

5. In 1868, as a result of the _____,
the Japanese began to "westernize"
their economy, making it possible for
Japan to emerge as a world power in
the early twentieth century.

6. As a result of the United States'
support for an _____, all of the
European Great Powers were allowed
to trade freely with China.

7. Designed to explode upon impact, the
_____ was developed in India
and was intended for use in colonial
military engagements.

8. Historians distinguish between two
types of colonial administration:
_____, which involves direct
administration of a territory given the
status of a "protectorate," and
_____, which involves indirect
control through economic and
military domination.

9. Europeans' belief that they had a duty to Christianize non-Western peoples and to bring their "inferior" cultures up to "superior" European standards was known as the _____.
10. In Britain, fervent nationalism was popularly known as _____.

D. Imperial Powers and Colonial Holdings
Name the key African and Asian holding(s) of the following European nations:
1. Belgium
2. Britain
3. France
4. Germany
5. Holland
6. Italy
7. Portugal
8. Spain

IMPORTANT HISTORICAL FACTS: STUDY-DRILL ANSWERS

A. Multiple Choice
1. D. Colonial rivalries between the European Great Powers.
2. B. settle territorial claims in the Congo.
3. B. Britain and Dutch settlers in South Africa.
4. B. gunboat diplomacy.
5. A. the Boxer Rebellion.
6. C. Herbert Spencer.
7. B. the Herero.
8. D. social welfare benefits.
9. C. the dual mandate.
10. C. businessmen's need for an outlet for excess manufactured goods.

B. Chronological Relationships
1839	Opium War
1857	Sepoy Mutiny
1868	Meiji Restoration
1869	Completion of the Suez Canal
1879	Leopold II sends Henry Stanley to the Congo.
1884–1885	Berlin Conference
1896	Battle of Adowa
1898	Battle of Omdurman
1899	Boxer Rebellion
1899–1902	Boer War

C. Fill in the Blanks
1. King Leopold II
2. Suez Canal
3. Fashoda Affair
4. Sepoy Mutiny
5. Meiji Restoration
6. open-door policy
7. dum-dum bullet
8. formal imperialism; informal imperialism
9. "civilizing mission"
10. jingoism

D. Imperial Powers and Colonial Holdings

	AFRICA	ASIA
1. Belgium	Belgian Congo	
2. Britain	Bechuanaland	British North Borneo
	British East Africa	Burma
	British Somaliland	India
	Egypt	Malay States
	Gambia	
	Gold Coast	
	Nigeria	
	Nyasaland	
	Sarawak	
	Sierra Leone	
	Sudan	
	Uganda	
	Union of South Africa	

		AFRICA	ASIA
3.	France	Algeria French Equatorial Africa French Somaliland French West Africa Madagascar Morocco Tunisia	Indochina
4.	Germany	Cameroons German East Africa German Southwest Africa Togoland	
5.	Netherlands		Dutch East Indies
6.	Italy	Eritrea Italian Somaliland Libya	
7.	Portugal	Angola Mozambique Portuguese Guinea	
8.	Spain	Rio Muni Rio de Oro	

23 *The Origins of the Great War*

1. CHAPTER OUTLINE

I. By 1914, ENTANGLING ALLIANCES had divided Europe into two opposing camps, pitting the Triple Alliance (Austria-Hungary, Germany, and Italy) against the Triple Entente (Britain, France, and Russia).

A. IRRECONCILABLE HATREDS: After 1870, Alsace and Lorraine and colonial rivalries pitted France and Germany against one another; Austria-Hungary was internally divided, and at odds with Russia in the Balkans; and tensions existed between Britain and Russia over control of the eastern Mediterranean.

B. THE ALLIANCE SYSTEM that developed out of these antagonisms was created by diplomats (many of whom were nobles) who negotiated secret treaties in the hopes of procuring a favorable balance of power for their respective nations.

C. GERMANY AND AUSTRIA-HUNGARY AGAINST RUSSIA: Bismarck sought to unite the three autocratic empires of Eastern Europe in a defensive alliance, but tensions between Austria-Hungary and Russia rendered this difficult. As an alternative, Bismarck negotiated a Triple Alliance of Central European powers.

D. GERMANY ENCIRCLED: RUSSIA AND FRANCE ALLY: Brought together by mutual isolation and growing financial ties, France and Russia formed a Dual Alliance in 1894.

E. ANGLO-GERMAN RIVALRY: German criticism of Britain's war with the Boers and competition between the two nations' navies drove a wedge between Britain and Germany.

F. BRITISH-FRENCH RAPPROCHEMENT, reflecting Britain's desire to end its diplomatic isolation, resulted in the Entente Cordiale of 1904.

G. THE FIRST MOROCCAN CRISIS demonstrated the solidity of the Entente Cordiale, and resulted in a treaty agreement between Britain and Russia.

II. THE EUROPE OF TWO ARMED CAMPS, 1905–1914: With Britain, France, and Russia now united as the Triple Entente, and Italy only loosely tied to the Triple Alliance, Germany found itself isolated and dangerously bound to its weaker partner, Austria-Hungary.

A. THE BALKAN TINDERBOX AND UNREST IN THE OTTOMAN EMPIRE: Serbian nationalism and governmental crises in the Ottoman Empire created a highly unstable situation in the Balkans.

B. THE BOSNIAN CRISIS OF 1908: An international crisis was provoked when Austria-Hungary unilaterally annexed Bosnia-

Herzegovina, but Russia backed down and war was averted.

C. THE SECOND MOROCCAN CRISIS: Germany again provoked a crisis over Morocco, which only served to further cement the Anglo-French alliance.

D. THE BALKAN WARS broke out when Serbia, Bulgaria, Montenegro, and Greece sought to seize additional territory from the weak Ottoman Empire and then fought amongst themselves over the spoils.

III. BALANCING THE CAUSES OF THE GREAT WAR: The Great War was caused by a combination of factors, including entangling alliances, nationalism, military planning, Social Darwinist beliefs, and domestic politics.

A. MILITARY PLANNING in all countries placed a premium on rapid mobilization and a powerful offense, putting pressure on political leaders to make hasty decisions in crisis situations.

B. DOMESTIC POLITICS: The specific concerns of the populations of the different Great Power states shaped responses to international relations, as did the personalities of their political leaders.

IV. THE FINAL CRISIS: Once the European states were divided into opposing armed camps, war became likely. The assassination of Archduke Francis Ferdinand, heir to the Habsburg empire, was the spark that set off the powderkeg.

A. ASSASSINATION IN SARAJEVO: The archduke was killed by a member of a Serbian nationalist group on June 28, 1914.

B. THE ULTIMATUM: Austria-Hungary, given a "blank check" by Germany, sent a harshly worded ultimatum to Serbia. The British attempted to engineer a peaceful settlement to the crisis, but the continental powers all refused to back down.

C. "A JOLLY LITTLE WAR": Austria declared war on Serbia on July 28. German leaders decided to implement the Schlieffen Plan, and declared war on Russia on August 1st, and on France on August 3rd. After German troops violated Belgian neutrality, Britain declared war on Germany on August 4th.

2. HISTORICAL GEOGRAPHY

Map Exercises

Familiarize yourself with the maps provided in your text, and then attempt to locate the following places on Blank Map 23.1.

WESTERN EUROPE IN 1914

Algeciras	Luxembourg
Alsace	The Netherlands
Belgium	Norway
Denmark	Portugal
East Prussia	Southern Tyrol
France	Spanish Morocco
Germany	Spain
Great Britain	Sweden
Italy	Switzerland
Lorraine	Trieste

EASTERN EUROPE IN 1914

Albania	Macedonia
Athens	Montenegro
Austria-Hungary	Ottoman Empire
Belgrade	Poland
Bosnia	Romania
Bucharest	Russia
Bulgaria	Sarajevo
Croatia-Slavonia	Serbia
Greece	Sofia
Herzegovina	Tirana

MAP 23.1   EUROPE IN 1914

Map Questions

Why were France and Italy discontented with the territorial status quo of 1914?

How did the ongoing collapse of the Ottoman Empire affect the balance of power in the Balkans? In Europe?

How were the borders of the Balkan states changed by the Balkan Wars of 1912–1913?

Why was Belgian neutrality of so much concern to Great Britain?

3. PEOPLE AND TERMS TO IDENTIFY

Alsace and Lorraine
Pan Slav nationalism
The Three Emperors' League
Triple Alliance
Anglo-German naval rivalry
Entente Cordiale

Triple Entente
"Pig War"
Young Turks
Bosnian Crisis of 1908
Archduke Francis Ferdinand
Moroccan Crises
Balkan Wars

Élan
Gavrilo Princip
"Blank check"
The Austro-Hungarian ultimatum
General Alfred von Schlieffen

4. STUDY QUESTIONS

1. *Historical Continuities:* What were the long-term origins of the "irreconcilable" differences between the various European Great Powers in the years after 1870?

2. Why wasn't Bismarck able to maintain an alliance between Austria-Hungary, Germany, and Russia? Why did he negotiate the Triple Alliance?

3. What brought republican France and tsarist Russia together in an alliance?

4. Why did Britain agree to ally with France in 1904?

5. What made the Balkans a "tinderbox" in the years before 1914? How did developments in the Balkans affect relations between Austria-Hungary and Russia?

6. *Historical Continuities:* How did outstanding colonial tensions affect the relations between the European Great Powers in the years prior to 1914?

7. In what sense can military planning be considered one of the causes of the Great War?

8. How did domestic politics influence the international relations of the various Great Powers in the years leading up to 1914?

9. Outline the chain of events that took place from the assassination of Archduke Francis Ferdinand on June 28 to the general outbreak of war by August 4.

10. What kind of war did Europeans expect in August 1914?

5. ANALYZING ART AND ARTIFACTS

How are the different European nations personified in political cartoons (see pp. 1004, 1005, 1007, 1015, 1022, 1023 of the textbook) of the period? What particular characteristics are used to typify each of the powers?

6. TECHNOLOGY AND HISTORY

How did technologies like the railroad affect the speed and efficiency of military mobilization in the years prior to 1914? How did they influence military planning?

How did technological developments influence Europeans' beliefs about the nature and likely outcomes of war in the late nineteenth and early twentieth centuries?

7. HISTORICAL ANALYSIS: INTERPRETIVE ESSAYS

1. How did the European Great Powers come to be arrayed in two opposing sets of alliances by 1914?

2. *Historical Continuities:* What long-term developments in European history caused the outbreak of the Great War?

3. Why did the assassination of the Archduke Francis Ferdinand set off a world war?

4. Knowing what Europeans knew in the summer of 1914, how might war have been avoided?

8. HISTORICAL VOICES: HEADLINE NEWS, 1914: THE *LONDON TIMES* REPORTS ON THE "LOWERING CLOUDS" OF WAR

On June 27, 1914, the *London Times* published a letter from one of its readers in the sports pages under the headline: "Anti-Golf. . . . Protest From Oxford." In this correspondence, the writer, "Ohe Jam Satis,"* complained about a recent spate of letters to the sports editor debating the virtues of golf:

> . . . Sir, I, in common with all those of your readers who are not wholly absorbed in politics, finance, or feminism, consider your sporting page to be one of the most valuable of your pages; yet the daily stream of letters on "Anti-golf" or "Pro-golf"—for by this time the two are the same, and it does not matter a straw which is which—has positively got on my nerves. Sir, it has become a downright obsession. Stop it, I beg you, before we are compelled to stop reading your paper.

Satis requested that the *Times* take "a little mercy on your less subtle readers, who dearly love to ponder over a good account of the last put [sic]on the last green."

On the day following the publication of this letter, Gavrilo Princip assassinated the Archduke Francis Ferdinand. As storm clouds gathered over the Balkans and then broke across Europe, it became increasingly difficult for ordinary Britons to selectively ignore "hard news" in favor of the sports pages or other topics of specialized interest.

In 1914, the *London Times* was—as it still is—one of the most important newspapers in Europe. Having commenced publication in 1785 (as the *Daily Universal Register*), the *Times* had established itself as a highly respected daily paper by the mid-nineteenth century. It was widely read, especially by the more affluent and educated sector of the British population.

The international crisis set off by the assassination of the archduke now seems to us of overwhelming importance as a historical event, but it was only one news story among many in the summer of 1914. In the balmy weeks of June, British newspaper readers' attention was drawn especially to the Irish Home Rule debates agitating Parliament. The forced-feeding of imprisoned "suffragettes" also received considerable coverage. And for a diversion from the serious internal tensions that seemed to be tearing British society apart at the seams, readers might turn to the many columns of print reporting on the juicily scandalous trial of French finance Minister Joseph Caillaux's wife, Henriette, for the murder of a Parisian newspaper editor.

The following news items, published in the *Times* between June 29 and August 5, chart the progress of the developing Balkan crisis, from initial reports on the archduke's assassination to the British declaration of war.

On Monday, June 29, the *Times* gave extensive coverage to events in Sarajevo. One short item posted from the paper's German correspondent commented on the German response to the assassination of the heir to the Austro-Hungarian throne and his dearly beloved wife:

*A pseudonym. In Latin it means, roughly, "I've had enough!"

Heroism of the Duchess

Berlin, June 28

The news of the assassination of the Archduke Francis Ferdinand and the Duchess of Hohenberg was made known here by extra editions of the newspapers at about 5 o'clock this evening. The version published here states that the Duchess attempted to shield her husband by throwing her own body in the way of the assassin's bullets.

The utmost horror and consternation have been aroused by the crime, which is a terrible blow to the ally of the Dual Monarchy. No one has yet attempted to gauge its possible effect upon the stability of Europe, and the diplomatic world is almost stunned.

On the following day (Tuesday, June 30), reports on reactions in Russia, France, and the British financial community appeared.

Russian Reflections

St. Petersburg, June 29

The feelings of Russians have been stirred by the Sarajevo tragedy. Horror at the crime vies with pity for the aged Emperor. But the organs of public opinion feel bound to add that the dead archduke was no friend of Russia, and if his demise is likely to affect the relations between the two Empires this influence is likely to be favorable rather than other. . . .

Contending French Sympathies

Paris, June 29

. . . Abbé Leblond, Vicar-General of Versailles, and a personal friend of the archduke, is . . . at pains to correct the impression that [the Archduke]was not a friendly supporter of [France]. [Leblond] represents him, not as a man of war, but as the moderator of the Triple Alliance, and states that last September, when he was staying with the Archduke in Tirol, the Archduke said to him:—"We have passed through anxious moments and the peace of Europe has been endangered. Thanks to God, the Emperor and I

have been able to stay a movement which was pushing us to war."

Stock Exchange— Effect of the Austrian Tragedy

The Stock Markets opened in a somewhat hesitating mood yesterday morning, it being feared that the murder of the Archduke Francis Ferdinand and his Consort would have a bad effect on the Bourses [Stock Exchanges] of Vienna and other places on the continent. Prices were accordingly inclined to be weak, and in a number of cases declined a little. Before very long, however, it was found that on the continent the Bourses were displaying fair strength and that no large amounts of stock were being offered; and the tendency became quite firm, though there was no increase in the volume of business. . . .

Throughout much of July, the growing tensions between Austria-Hungary and Serbia were followed closely in the *Times*, but news stories on this topic did not seem to suggest that disaster was imminent. Life—and reporting—went on as before, although even events as innocuous as a literary festival carried reminders that events in the Balkans might well serve to activate the alliances between the Great Powers.

An "Entente" Festival Victor Hugo Celebrations in Guernsey

St. Peterport, July 8

Vive l'Entente Cordiale has been the predominant note in the concluding part of the Victor Hugo fêtes at Guernsey. The French military band sounded it first yesterday when marching up the hill to its position behind the Victor Hugo statue. It played loudly "The Death of Nelson," a singular choice, perhaps, but one designed as a compliment to the representatives of Great Britain.

Everywhere the French Tricolor and the Union Jack fly side by side. Everywhere also French sailors and English sailors have been fraternizing. . . .

Late in July, the crisis deepened, creating a greater sense of impending doom. The editorial page of the *Times* began to warn that war might be imminent, as, for example, in the following items from the July 22 and 25 editions.

A Danger to Europe

The growing tension between Austria-Hungary and Servia [Serbia] has created a situation in European politics too serious to be ignored, even amongst the deep anxieties which weigh upon us at home. We have no wish to exaggerate the dangers which exist. A cool perception of their greatness may enable the Powers to conjure them before it is too late. There is no time to lose. Italy has suddenly recalled over 70,000 men to the colours; incidents are occurring daily between certain of the Balkan States; Albania appears to be in a process of dissolution; "important negotiations," we are told, are pending between Austria-Hungary, Bulgaria, and Turkey. The Governments of the Dual Monarchy have not yet spoken, but the belief is general that, when the inquiry into the Sarajevo murders is complete they will present certain demands to Servia of a peremptory kind. . . .

What chance is there . . . of "localizing" a war between German and Slav, between a Roman Catholic and an Orthodox Power in the Balkans; what prospect that such a war would end without disaster to the Dual Monarchy? It is impossible that these reflections are not present to the mind of FRANCIS JOSEPH. It is incredible that they will not confirm the determination, underlying his proclamations, to judge the outrage committed against him and his state with the justice and the moderation that are his own.

Europe and the Crisis

England cannot suffer the fresh burden which the failure of the Home Rule Conference casts upon her to divert her attention from the grave crisis that has arisen in Europe within the last thirty-six hours. All who have the general peace at heart must earnestly hope that Austria-Hungary has not spoken her last word in the Note to Servia to which she requires a reply to-night. If she has, we stand upon the edge of war, and of a war fraught with dangers that are incalculable to all the Great Powers. . . .

The result of [fixing a limit of forty-eight hours for the reply] is that Austria-Hungary leaves a small and excitable Balkan kingdom to decide at a few hours' notice whether there is, or is not, to be a third Balkan war, and a Balkan war, this time, in which one of the Great Powers will be involved as a principal from the first. That hardly seems statesmanlike, whatever may be [Austria-Hungary's] grievances against her neighbor. . . . She might easily find, were complications to follow, that in order to save herself from a danger which can be met in other ways she has placed the very existence of the Monarchy at stake. No effort should be spared to save her and to save Europe from so grievous a mistake.

By Monday, July 27, an even greater sense of urgency made itself felt. Bold headlines identified the Balkan Crisis as the big news story for the day.

Peace in the Balance
Austrian Minister Leaves Belgrade
The Servian Reply
Removal of the Seat of Government
Hurried Mobilizations
A Movement for Mediation

The possibility of maintaining peace has not entirely vanished. War is not yet declared, and a faint hope still persists that it may be avoided. But Austro-Servian diplomatic relations are broken off. The Austro-Hungarian Army is partially, and the Servian Army wholly, mobilised. The Servian Government and Court have abandoned Belgrade, and proceeded to Kraguievatz, a fortified town 60 miles south of the capital.

A certain optimism about ongoing diplomatic negotiations made itself felt the following day, but reports that "matters appear to have become somewhat calmer," as an article entitled "Assurances to Russia" noted, did not convince the financial world.

Nervousness on the Stock Exchange

Fear of European complications continued to dominate the London Stock Exchange yesterday, but the net result of the movement in prices was less unsatisfactory than on Saturday. At the outset quotations suffered a further collapse under renewed pressure to sell, partly on Continental account. Dealers became very nervous and excited, and promptly marked down prices, especially of the inter-bourse securities. Many jobbers declined to deal, except as a result of negotiations, while others quoted prices so wide as almost to prohibit the transaction of business.

On the 29th, bold headlines announced that Austria had declared war on Serbia. A *Times* editorial called on Britons to bury their differences in the face of war.

Close the Ranks

This morning's news opens up the gravest possibilities for the whole of Europe. It also imposes an instant duty upon political parties in this country. Now that issue has been joined on the Danube, no man can foresee how far the conflict may spread. It is therefore imperative that we should patch up our domestic differences without delay, in order that the whole nation may present a united front in this threatening international crisis. With the best will in the world we cannot, of course, expect to find a real solution to the Irish problem. . . . All we can hope to do is to agree upon some device which will temporarily close our ranks and leave the Government free to turn their attention to the greater issues abroad. We press these considerations in the interests of European peace not less than of national security. The Government should be able at this moment to devote all their energies to the difficult task of joining with other Powers in limiting the area of war . . . in all the circumstances we prefer to see SIR EDWARD GRAY continue at his post at the Foreign Office. No one else in Parliament can now equal his intimate knowledge of the present tendencies of European politics. He enjoys the respect and esteem of Continental statesmen, and his skill and patience in composing international differences have already been amply tested. . . .

In the following days, headlines emphasized the seriousness of the expanding crisis, proclaiming: "The Arming of Europe. 'A Situation of Extreme Gravity.' Call to War"; "A Gloomy Outlook. Great Britain the Deciding Factor"; "Lowering Clouds"; and "Waning Hopes." On the 31st, the *Times* published an appeal from religious leaders, who called on Britons to seek aid from a higher authority.

Prayers for Peace
The Archbishops and the Church's Duty

The following appeal for suitable prayer during the European crisis has been issued by the Archbishops of Canterbury and York:

"At a time of quite unusual anxiety, perplexity, and strain, both at home and abroad, when 'wars and rumours of war' are hourly in the thoughts and on the lips of our people, it is necessary above all things that we should remind ourselves of Him Who is not only 'the King of all the earth,' but is also 'a very present help in trouble.' For such prayers, special opportunity, suggestion, and leadership ought everywhere to be given to those who meet in the public services of the Church, as well as in quieter and less formal gatherings.

"To issue special and distinctive Collects [short prayers] appropriate to the hour is unsuitable, or indeed impossible, while the situation is literally changing from day to day. Rather we would urge upon the clergy the duty and privilege of 'bidding' the people to prayer, by the use of a few words of invitation and suggestion at particular points in the conduct of the Divine Service and by making a pause after or before petitions which bear upon the desire of our hearts for 'unity, peace, and concord,' both in Europe and in our own country. . . .

". . . The Prayer book is rich in prayers for peace, and with a little care, people can at such a time be made to feel afresh the living significance and point of familiar words.

"We are sure that at this grave hour all Christian citizens will be at one in the fellowship of prayer."

In the first days of August, the general outbreak of war became the central focus of the news. German and Russian mobilization were major stories, as was the assassination of French Socialist Jean Jaurès. In a special Sunday news edition on the 2nd, the *Times* warned its readers that demand for the paper had increased so greatly that they should take the precaution of reserving a daily copy from their news agent. More importantly, the paper also announced that Germany had launched an assault on Luxembourg.

The Beginning of War
Invasion of Luxembourg
Conflict on the Russian Border
British Responsibilities

. . . In virtue of the Treaty of London signed on May 11, 1867, the Grand Duchy of Luxembourg was neutralized under the collective guarantee of the signatory Powers. The signatories also bound themselves to respect its neutrality (Article II). The signatory Powers were Great Britain, France, Russia, the Netherlands, Belgium, Italy, Prussia, and Austria-Hungary.

The invasion of Luxembourg is a violation of this Treaty, which Great Britain, in common with France, Russia, and the Netherlands is pledged to uphold.

On August 5th, a military recruiting advertisement figured prominently in the paper, and the *Times* announced that Britain had declared war on Germany.

War Declared
Note Rejected by Germany
British Ambassador to Leave Berlin
Rival Navies in the North Sea
British Army Mobilizing
Government Control of Railways

The following statement was issued from the Foreign Office at 12:15 this morning:—

"Owing to the summary rejection by the German Government of the request made by his Majesty's Government for assurances that the neutrality of Belgium will be respected, his Majesty's Ambassador at Berlin has received his passports and his Majesty's Government have declared to the German Government that a state of war exists between Great Britain and Germany as from 11 p.m. on August 4."

Awaiting the Declaration
The Scene at the Foreign Office
Patriotic Demonstrations

A large crowd gathered at the entrance to Downing street [site of the British Government's offices] last evening to await the first news of the German reply to the British ultimatum. As the evening wore on, the crowd became denser, and excitement grew. . . .

As the news of the declaration of war reached the street, the crowd expressed its feelings in loud cheering. It left the precincts of Downing street and gathered in front of the War Office, where patriotic demonstrations continued until an early hour this morning.

Source: [London] Times. Excerpts taken from the following 1914 editions (listed in order of appearance): "Anti-Golf," (June 27); "Heroism of the Duchess" (June 29); "Russian Reflections," "Contending French Sympathies," "Stock Exchange" (June 30); "An 'Entente' Festival" (July 9); "A Danger to Europe" (July 22); "Europe and the Crisis" (July 25); "Peace in the Balance" (July 27); "Nervousness on the Stock Exchange" (July 28); "Close the Ranks" (July 29); "Prayers for Peace" (July 31); "The Beginning of War" (August 2); "War Declared," "Awaiting the Declaration" (August 5).

Questions

How would you characterize the *London Times'* coverage of the events leading up to the outbreak of World War I? Does it differ from the way in which you might expect a contemporary paper to report on this sort of crisis?

How do you expect the average British newspaper reader—"Ohe Jam Satis," perhaps—responded to these articles?

What does the archbishops' call to prayer tell you about public responses to the imminent outbreak of war?

9. IMPORTANT HISTORICAL FACTS: STUDY DRILLS

A. Multiple Choice

1. Identify the foreign ministers of each of the following countries in the years immediately prior to the outbreak of the Great War:
   A. Austria-Hungary   Leopold Berchtold
   B. Britain   Theobald von Bethmann-Hollweg
   C. Germany   Sir Edward Grey
   D. Russia   Sergei Sazonov

2. Following 1870, relations between France and Germany were embittered by France's loss of
   A. Alsace and Lorraine.
   B. Indochina.
   C. Morocco.
   D. Nice and Savoy.

3. The Triple Alliance united
   A. Austria-Hungary, Germany, and Italy.
   B. Austria-Hungary, Germany, and Russia.
   C. Britain, France, and Russia.
   D. Bulgaria, Greece, and Serbia.

4. Anglo-German naval rivalry resulted in
   A. the reduction of German naval expenditures.
   B. the arrival of the gunboat *Panther* in Agadir.
   C. William II's yacht trip to Morocco.
   D. the building of Dreadnought-class battleships by Britain and Germany.

5. The Triple Entente was the result of three separate agreements linking Britain, France, and Russia. They were signed in
   A. 1873, 1881, 1887.
   B. 1894, 1904, 1907.
   C. 1905, 1906, 1911.
   D. 1914.

6. The Bosnian Crisis of 1908 was the direct result of
   A. the Algeciras Conference.
   B. the Tripoli War.
   C. Serbian support for the "Black Hand."
   D. Austrian annexation of Bosnia-Herzegovina.

7. The Moroccan Crises of 1906 and 1911 had the effect of
   A. driving a wedge between Britain and France.
   B. strengthening Germany's position in Africa.
   C. further cementing the alliance between Britain and France.
   D. winning Germany a port on the North African coast.

8. Albania was created at the conclusion of the Second Balkan War because
   A. Serbia wanted an independent Albania as its ally in the Balkans.
   B. Austria-Hungary wished to deprive Serbia of an Adriatic port.
   C. Albanian nationalists staged a revolt.
   D. the defeated Turks wished to deprive Serbia of territory populated by Muslims.

9. The Austrian response to the assassination of Archduke Francis Ferdinand was to
   A. declare war on Serbia.
   B. request that Germany declare war on Serbia.
   C. send Serbia an ultimatum.
   D. call an international conference to settle the conflict in the Balkans.

10. Europeans expected a "jolly little war" in August of 1914 for all of the following reasons *except* that they thought
    A. it would be over by Christmas of 1914.
    B. it would be fought only in the Balkans.
    C. it would demonstrate their own nation's superiority.
    D. war was inevitable and they wanted to get it over with.

B. Chronological Relationships

1. Entangling Alliances: Arrange the following events in chronological order under the most appropriate heading, and give the date of each.
   Franco-Russian Dual Alliance
   Austro-German Dual Alliance
   Three Emperors' League revived

   Anglo-Japanese Alliance
   Triple Alliance
   Anglo-French Entente Cordiale
   Three Emperors' League
   Anglo-Russian Agreement over Persia and Afghanistan
   Reinsurance Treaty

DATE	TRIPLE ALLIANCE	TRIPLE ENTENTE
1.		
2.		
3.		
4.		
5.		
6.		
7.		
8.		
9.		

2. Origins of the First World War: List the following events in chronological order, identify the dates at which they took place, and briefly explain their role in the outbreak of the Great War.
   Algeciras Conference
   Assassination of the Archduke Francis Ferdinand
   Bosnian Crisis
   First Balkan War
   First Moroccan Crisis
   Pig War
   Second Moroccan Crisis
   Treaty of London
   Tripoli War
   Young Turk Revolt

C. Fill in the Blanks

1. Much of the nationalist agitation in the Balkans was motivated by _____, a belief that all peoples of a common Slavic origin should be united in their own nation-state under the guidance of Russia.

2. In an attempt to unite the autocratic monarchies of Eastern Europe, Bismarck negotiated the _____ between Austria-Hungary, Germany, and Russia in 1873.

3. The friendly agreement reached between Britain and France in 1904 was known as the _____.

4. The 1906 _____, an Austro-Hungarian boycott of Serbian agricultural goods, increased tensions between the two nations.

5. In 1908, the brutal Ottoman Sultan Abdul-Hamid II was forced to restore the constitution of 1876 and was later deposed by the _____.

6. Heir to the Austro-Hungarian throne, _____ was relatively anti-German and was sympathetic to the plight of the South Slavs (which did not save him from being assassinated by Serbian nationalists in 1914).

7. French military planners expected to win an eventual war with Germany through _____, an all-out offensive attack fueled by patriotic energy.

8. Having been expelled from school for his anti-Austrian sentiments, _____, a youthful member of the

"Black Hand," assassinated the Archduke Francis Ferdinand and the archduke's wife in 1914.

9. When Austria-Hungary consulted with Germany over the appropriate response to the assassination of the Archduke Francis Ferdinand, the German government wrote Austria a _____, offering full support should Austria declare war on Serbia.

10. In his attempt to solve the problem of a two-front war with France and Russia, the military planner _____ proposed that Germany first attack France via Belgium and, following the rapid defeat of France, then quickly turn around to take out Russia.

IMPORTANT HISTORICAL FACTS: STUDY-DRILL ANSWERS

A. Multiple Choice

1. A. Austria-Hungary: Leopold Berchtold
   B. Britain: Sir Edward Grey
   C. Germany: Theobald von Bethmann-Hollweg
   D. Russia: Sergei Sazonov
2. A. Alsace and Lorraine.
3. A. Austria-Hungary, Germany, and Italy.
4. D. the building of Dreadnought-class battleships by Britain and Germany.

5. B. 1894, 1904, 1907.
6. D. Austrian annexation of Bosnia-Herzegovina.
7. C. further cementing the alliance between Britain and France.
8. B. Austria-Hungary wished to deprive Serbia of an Adriatic port.
9. C. send Serbia an ultimatum.
10. B. it would be fought only in the Balkans.

B. Chronological Relationships

1.

DATE	TRIPLE ALLIANCE	TRIPLE ENTENTE
1873	Three Emperors' League	
1879	Austro-German Dual Alliance	
1881	Three Emperors' League revived	
1882	Triple Alliance	
1887	Reinsurance Treaty	
1894		Franco-Russian Dual Alliance
1902		Anglo-Japanese Alliance
1904		Anglo-French Entente Cordiale
1907		Anglo-Russian Agreement

2. 1905 First Moroccan Crisis
   1906 Algeciras Conference
   1906 The Pig War
   1908 Young Turk Revolt
   1908 Bosnian Crisis
   1911 Second Moroccan Crisis
   1911 Tripoli War
   1912 First Balkan War
   1913 Treaty of London
   1914 Assassination of the Archduke Francis Ferdinand

C. Fill in the Blanks

1. Pan Slav nationalism
2. Three Emperors' League
3. Entente Cordiale
4. "Pig War"
5. Young Turks
6. Archduke Francis Ferdinand
7. élan
8. Gavrilo Princip
9. "blank check"
10. General Alfred von Schlieffen

24 *The Great War*

1. CHAPTER OUTLINE

I. THE OUTBREAK OF WAR: Believing that victory would go to the army that moved most rapidly, Germany hastened to attack France.
  A. THE SCHLIEFFEN PLAN had been formulated as a solution to the problem of a two-front war and required that Germany violate Belgian neutrality (inevitably bringing Britain into the war) in the interest of a rapid assault on France. French military planners had responded with Plan XVII, which underestimated German troop strength and speed of attack.
  B. OPENING HOSTILITIES: German General von Moltke modified Schlieffen's original plan, fatally weakening the German assault. At the Battle of the Marne, French and British troops turned back the German offensive, at great cost to both sides.

II. THE CHANGING NATURE OF WAR: Allied and German troops were now frozen into defensive positions, confronting one another across a long line of trenches on the western front. This new form of warfare relied on new weapons and on the total mobilization of the home front.
  A. TRENCH WARFARE was physically and mentally devastating to soldiers, who suffered both from wretched living conditions and deadly but inconclusive attempts to break through enemy lines.
  B. WAR IN THE AIR AND ON THE SEAS: Airplanes were initially used for reconnaissance, but later for bombing raids on military and civilian targets. Few major sea battles were fought, but the German strategy of unrestricted submarine warfare eventually brought the United States into the war.
  C. SUPPORT FROM THE HOME FRONT was essential to the war effort, which could not be continued without a sustained effort on the part of the civilian population. Men enlisted in the military in unprecedented numbers, while women took men's places in factories and offices.

III. THE WAR RAGES ON: As casualties mounted on both sides, more countries joined what was rapidly becoming a world war.
  A. THE EASTERN FRONT: Despite its many weaknesses, the Russian army proved surprisingly effective, especially against Austro-Hungarian troops.
  B. WAR IN THE MIDDLE EAST, AFRICA, AND THE FAR EAST: The British launched an assault on Turkey in 1915, but suffered a devastating defeat at Gallipoli. Fighting also spread to the Balkans, Africa, and Asia.
  C. After Gallipoli, the British again focused their attention on THE WESTERN FRONT. At Verdun and the Somme, the Allies and the Germans attempted to "bleed [one another] white" in a war of attrition.

D. FUTILITY AND STALEMATE: The war ground on with no end in sight. A few tentative peace proposals were made but a compromise settlement was not acceptable to most participants, especially the French.

E. SOLDIERS AND CIVILIANS: While some civilians were little affected by the war, it soon became impossible for most people to ignore its rising cost. Soldiers themselves were alienated from the home front, but deeply attached to their comrades in arms. Protest against the war—on both the home front and the battle front—remained uncommon, although opposition increased as the war dragged on.

IV. THE FINAL STAGES OF THE WAR: In 1917 the United States joined the war and revolution broke out in Russia. French divisions began to mutiny and the Germans prepared a final offensive.

A. THE UNITED STATES ENTERS THE WAR: Taking a calculated risk, the Germans resumed unrestricted submarine warfare, bringing the U.S. into the war on the Allied side.

B. RUSSIA WITHDRAWS FROM THE WAR: As a result of the Bolshevik takeover of the Russian government, and in the face of military collapse, Russia signed a separate peace with Germany, ending the two-front war.

C. OFFENSIVES AND MUTINIES: New and fruitless Allied offensives on the western front produced mutinies among soldiers, while civilians also gave signs of an increasing war weariness. Allied initiatives in the Middle East were more successful.

D. THE GERMAN SPRING OFFENSIVE: In a final "victory drive," the Germans broke through the Allied lines, but were eventually pushed back by the Allies, with the help of newly arrived American troops. Germany sued for peace, and Austria-Hungary withdrew from the war.

E. THE FOURTEEN POINTS AND PEACE: As Austria-Hungary and Germany collapsed under the strain of defeat, they sought to negotiate on the basis of Woodrow Wilson's Fourteen Points, but they were forced to accept unconditional surrender.

V. THE IMPACT OF THE WAR: As a result of the Great War, Europe suffered a devastating loss of lives and property, and an equally severe loss of idealism, both of which would haunt the world in the post-war period.

2. HISTORICAL GEOGRAPHY

Map Exercises

Familiarize yourself with the maps provided in your text, and then attempt to locate the following places on Blank Maps 24.1 and 24.2.

THE WESTERN FRONT

Alsace	Marne River
Ardennes	Metz
Belgium	Netherlands
Brussels	Somme River
Dunkirk	Strait of Dover
Flanders	Verdun
Lorraine	Vosges Mountains
Luxembourg	

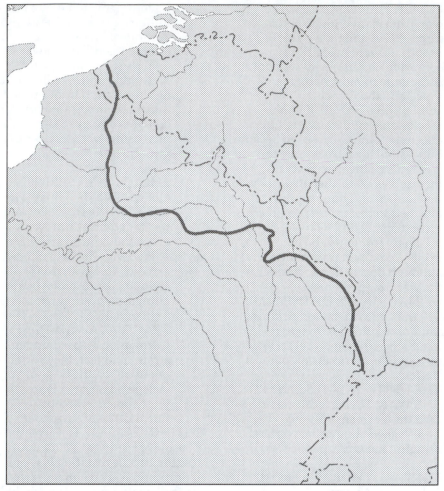

MAP 24.1   THE WESTERN FRONT

Map Questions

Diagram the Schlieffen Plan as originally conceived and as implemented by Moltke in 1914.

Why was the Battle of the Marne of crucial importance to the outcome of the war?

Explain the reasoning behind the Gallipoli campaign.

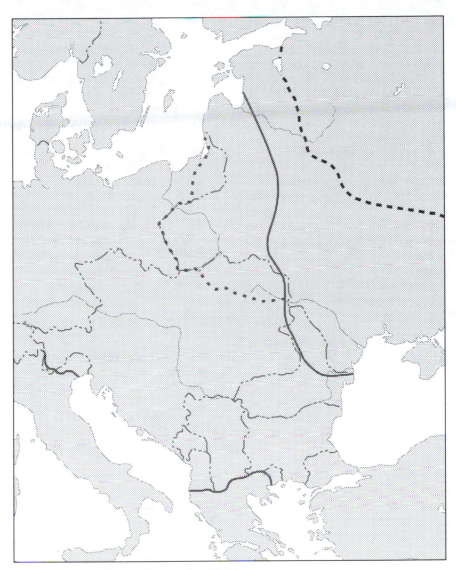

MAP 24.2   THE EASTERN FRONT

3. PEOPLE AND TERMS TO IDENTIFY

Schlieffen Plan
Plan XVII
Battle of the Marne
Trench warfare
Mustard gas
Red Baron Manfred von
    Richthofen
Home front
"Shells made by a wife may
    save a husband's life."

Treaty of London
Gallipoli
War of attrition
Battle of the Somme
"A queer sardonic rat"
Clara Zetkin
Siegfried Sassoon
"He kept us out of war."
Unrestricted submarine
    warfare

"Peace, land, and bread"
Treaty of Brest-Litovsk
Nivelle Offensive
Balfour Declaration
Fourteen Points

4. STUDY QUESTIONS

1. *Historical Continuities:* What long-term considerations produced the German Schlieffen Plan and France's Plan XVII?
2. Why did the Schlieffen Plan fail?
3. Why did the western front "freeze" into a static line of trenches? What was trench warfare like?
4. How was life on the home front affected by the war?
5. Why, despite its many weaknesses, was the Russian army initially successful in the east?
6. Why did some British leaders favor an attack on the periphery of Europe? Why did French military planners reject this strategy?
7. Why were the military engagements on both the western and eastern fronts so deadly?

8. How was civilian morale maintained in the face of "total war"?
9. Why did the United States enter the war? What impact would this have on the outcome of the war?
10. How did the Russian Revolution affect the war?
11. Why did the German spring offensive of 1918 fail?
12. What happened to the German and Austro-Hungarian governments at the end of the war?
13. What impact did the war have on the size of the European population? *Historical Continuities:* How might you expect this catastrophic loss of life to affect post-war society?

5. ANALYZING ART AND ARTIFACTS

If Paul Nash (the painter of *We Are Making a New World*, p. 1044) had been a writer, how would he have described the landscape around Ypres?

Imagine you are a British man of draft age. Explain why you were convinced to enlist in the military by the Lord Kitchener recruiting poster (p. 1052)?

What does the "Women of Britain" poster (p. 1052) tell you about cultural understandings of masculinity and femininity in the early twentieth century?

6. TECHNOLOGY AND HISTORY

Make a list of all of the new military technologies utilized during the war.

Historical Continuities: In light of previous discussions of warfare, explain how these innovations transformed the waging of war.

7. HISTORICAL ANALYSIS: INTERPRETIVE ESSAYS

1. What is "total war"? What made this new form of warfare possible in 1914?
2. In what sense was the Great War a "moral, spiritual and physical catastrophe" for all Europeans?
3. Imagine you are a Great War veteran, writing in 1919. Describe your experiences as a soldier, and explain how they have changed your understanding of the world and your future plans.

4. *Historical Continuities:* It is 1919 and you are a British diplomat. Prepare a report on the transformation of the international balance of power between 1914 and 1919. Your report will presumably reflect your British perspective, but it should include comments on general changes in the Great Power system.

8. HISTORICAL VOICES: LOST GENERATIONS

When the British veteran Charles Edmund Carrington published his World War I memoirs in 1929, he complained that well-known fictionalized accounts of the war, such as Henri Barbusse's *Fire* (1916) and Erich Maria Remarque's *All Quiet on the Western Front* (1929), misrepresented the real wartime experiences of less articulate combatants:

> The typical soldier has held his tongue, vaguely disliking the character that has been thrust on him. He was not at all like the jaded individualist described in the works of the school of disillusion. He was a social animal undergoing a particular social experience. However, the unhappy individualists got the publicity.

Whether or not Carrington's own account of his wartime experiences is more "representative" than Barbusse's or Remarque's, his larger point is well taken. While it is the historian's job to generalize about major events like the Great War, individual historical actors always experience such events in their own distinctive manners. The following brief excerpts from wartime memoirs and poetry collections illustrate certain general themes—initial enthusiasm about the war, the physical and psychological trauma of trench warfare, the camaraderie born of these hardships, the perception of the war as a crucial watershed in personal and national histories, etc.—but they also introduce us to a handful of unique individuals whose lives were forever transformed by this great cataclysm.

In August 1914, many Europeans greeted the war with overwhelming excitement—the young men who would do the actual fighting not least among them. British soldier-poet Rupert Brooke's "Peace," taken from a set of sonnets entitled "1914," is one of the most famous expressions of this sentiment. Brooke, who had just turned twenty-seven when the war was declared, served with the British Mediterranean Expeditionary Force and died in the Aegean in April 1915.

"Peace" by Rupert Brooke

Now, God be thanked Who has matched us with His hour,
  And caught our youth, and wakened us from sleeping,
With hand made sure, clear eye, and sharpened power,
  To turn, as swimmers into cleanness leaping,
Glad from a world grown old and cold and weary,
  Leave the sick hearts that honour could not move,
And half-men, and their dirty songs and dreary,
  And all the little emptiness of love!

Oh! we, who have known shame, we have found release
      there,
  Where there's no ill, no grief, but sleep has mending,
    Naught broken save this body, lost but breath;
Nothing to shake the laughing heart's long peace there
  But only agony, and that has ending;
    And the worst friend and enemy is but Death.

Like Brooke, young men throughout Europe hastened to join the battle, which so many expected to be over before Christmas. Charles Edmonds (Charles Edmund Carrington) was only seventeen when war was declared, but he enlisted almost immediately. Due to his extreme youth, he was not sent to the front until January 1916. Up to that point, the war had seemed like a "picnic" to him, certainly no worse than a visit to the dentist.

FROM *A Subaltern's War* by Charles Edmonds

. . . Only on rare occasions did the comedy turn to tragedy, for to the bitter end of the war it remained the greatest wonder that so much ammunition could be expended without hurting anyone but the taxpayer.

The first of these catastrophes which I saw gave me a truer impression of the danger. After two or three weeks at the front I was watching, as orderly officer, the giving out of tea from a great cauldron, or "dixie," to a queue of men standing in the sunken road. Without warning a whizz-bang pitched on the bank and burst among us flinging tea and men in all directions. In an instant there was a scramble for the dugout. Some men staggered and fell. Dizzy and scratched, but not hurt, I found myself holding a big sergeant who was hit in the thigh, and was collapsing in my arms. Behind us on the ground a man lay groaning, but it was some seconds before I dared turn and look, afraid of what horror I should see. I busied myself dragging into shelter and bandaging the serjeant, while others attended to the groaning man. In two minutes there was no sign of the disaster; in twenty all the men off duty were lounging again in the lane, cleaning rifles, picking the lice off their shirts, laughing and joking, just as before. But I never knew the same carefree feeling in the sunken road again. I found myself inclined to cock an eye or an ear perpetually in the direction whence that shell had come.

At the front or behind the lines, many soldiers filled their free moments writing verse, not only to pass the time, but also to help them make sense of their ordeal. Poetry published during the war reached a large audience and boosted civilian and military morale by offering comfort to grieving loved ones and by upholding the spiritual values that were felt to give meaning and value to the "war to end all wars." Like the following two poems from a British collection of "songs by fighting men," much of this verse commemorated dearly beloved comrades fallen in battle or meditated on the paradoxical persistence of religious faith in the face of the harsh realities of war.

"Requiescat" by Corporal Martin Hill

How young and bright he was, and when he laughed
The air around seemed sharing in his joy;
Fair was the world to him, nor spot nor stain
Of all its hidden ugliness had laid
A mark upon his face (that mark that sears
And brands the souls that know it but too well);
But all that's lovely in it lay beneath
The wonder that shone shyly in his eyes.
A child of Nature he, of woods and sunlit ways,
Of rolling meadows where the air was sweet
With new-born blossoms and the scent of hay;
Of hills and valleys, laughing streams and lakes
Where rustling reeds their whispered secrets told.
All these he knew and loved, they were his friends,
His sole companions, and through them he learnt
To know his mother Nature; all her moods
Diverse and strange he learnt them one by one;
Her summer laughter and her autumn tears,
Her seeming winter harshness and the sweet

Serene repentance of her early spring.
Life was his love, and in her warm soft arms
He freedom found from care, repose and peace,
And finding knew that it sufficed.

And then came War to claim him, dragged him forth,
Forth from his quiet world, and flung him down
Bewildered and amazed, yet unafraid,
The merest cypher in that crowded train.
So hour by hour the meanness of War,
And all its horrors, petty hates and sins
Raged round his struggling head, until the day
A wandering bullet found him, and Death took
Unto himself what Life once held so dear.

His face was smiling when they picked him up
As though he'd learnt his Mother's last great secret
And in learning found all well.

No. 7 Stationary Hospital, B.E.F., France.

"Easter Day, 1917—The Eve of the Battle" by Captain John Eugene Crombie*

I rose and watched the eternal giant of fire
Renew his struggle with the grey monk Dawn,
Slowly supreme, though broadening streaks of blood
Besmirch the threadbare cloak, and pour his flood
Of life and strength on our yet sleeping choir,
As I went out to church on Easter morn.

Returning with the song of birds and men
Acclaiming victory of throbbing life,
I saw the fairies of the morning shower
Giving to drink each waking blade and flower,
I saw the new world take Communion then—
And now 'tis night and we return to strife.

Hutts, France, April 1917.

Turkish Lieutenant Mehmet Arif Ölçen was not a poet, but he did keep a diary during the two years he spent in Russia as a prisoner of war. In February 1916, he was captured by Russian troops during the Battle of Erzurum. A fierce snowstorm had been raging for two days, and Ölçen and his men were dressed in thin uniforms and had not eaten a warm meal in many days. The young officer was pleasantly surprised by the hospitality offered by his Russian captors, and he made note of their obvious discontent with the tsar's regime.

FROM *Vetluga Memoir* by Mehmet Arif Ölçen

FRIENDSHIP FROM AN ENEMY

In the distance, smoke was rising from the snow. There was probably a shelter, underground bunker, or cabin there. We went toward the place from which the smoke rose. The soldiers stopped before a bunker buried in the snow. Over the door was stretched a tent canvas. The soldiers motioned for me to enter. When I poked my head inside, two Russian offi-

*Crombie was killed in action in 1917.

cers looked at me. One of them was young. The other was about forty-five years old.

"*Pozhaluista* [Please]!" they said, wanting me to enter.

I went inside. We looked at each other. I sat where they indicated. They did not understand what I said nor did I understand them. They summoned a soldier from Kazan. This soldier was going to translate.

"*Kakoy chin* [What is your rank]?" asked the older officer.

"*Poruchik* [Lieutenant]."

"How old are you?"

"Twenty-three."

"Are you happy to be a prisoner?"

"No," I said. How could I be happy? This morning I was a company commander. Now I'm a prisoner.

"If a man's life were saved, wouldn't he be glad? At twenty-three, don't you want to enjoy life? We would certainly prefer to be prisoners if we could."

. . . The young Russian officer who appeared to be a lieutenant interrupted. "You captured this place and then we captured this place. Is there any sense in shedding each other's blood? Russia is a very large country. Even if it wins the war, will the captured lands be given to the Russian villagers? It will become part of the estates of the nobility from the czar's family. Russia is shedding blood for their pleasure. A great many officers think the way I do."

I drank tea while answering their questions. They offered çörek and pastry. A friendship began to develop, and they continued to speak frankly. There were other officers in the Russian army who thought like them. At the first opportunity on the front, they apparently wanted to go over to the Turkish side. They took from their pockets notebooks in which they had kept a daily record of events. Captured Turkish officers had written statements in these notebooks. The Russian officers had them read out and translated into Russian. One of the Turks had written, "I truly have great sorrow for the Russian officer who will lose his life to a bullet tomorrow." They wanted me to write something as well. I wrote the following: "When I was captured, I was treated with great kindness by this officer. If he is captured by our army, I hope my brothers-in-arms will protect him." They were pleased. Then I added, "A Turkish regiment is facing you. They surely will not fail to respect you."

Ölçen's memoirs highlight the often friendly relations between Turkish prisoners of war and their Russian hosts, providing evidence of the soldierly solidarity commented upon by many other World War I soldiers. On the other hand, Princess Evelyn Blücher, who lived in Germany throughout the length of the war, experienced intense personal conflict as a result of nationalist hostilities further magnified by the war. As the English wife of a German nobleman, she found herself trapped between two sets of competing loyalties.

FROM *An English Wife in Berlin* by Evelyn, Princess Blücher

Not only has the great conflict swept away kingdoms and empires, undone a whole code of civilization, and destroyed innumerable forces of ethical and aesthetic value in every country, but it has also loosened or torn asunder all those finer ties which bound the members of different countries in friendship and kindly intercourse with one another.

Instead of a courteous friendliness we were accustomed to meet from acquaintances and friends in former times, we English or Americans who happen to have alien husbands are subject to mistrust and suspicion everywhere. Instead of our position being alleviated by the end of actual hostilities, we shall be treated as pariahs and outsiders in every country.

From the very outbreak of the war our position was difficult, and the more conscientiously we tried to act up to our feeling of duty to both countries, the more keenly did we feel the slights and insults we often had to bear. Destiny devolved upon us the task of trying to be impartial (as far as this was possible) to both countries, and of endeavouring to keep up some shred of courteous feeling between them.

It was not an easy moment for many of us, when, loving our country and our families with every fibre of our being, we followed our husbands abroad into their own land, urged by loyalty to them to try and be just in our opinions, at a moment when our relatives were falling at their hands, and all the evil spirits of hatred and resentment were let loose on the world.

. . . everywhere we feel banished and in exile, and long for a time when a more charitable feeling shall prevail in the world. . . . There is indeed no place under the sun for us, and absolutely no laws to protect us and our property. One lesson which I hope and believe all women in the same position as myself will have learnt is, that it is our imperative duty to try and restore friendship and confidence as far as possible between the inimical nations, and that we ought all to unite in this common task.

Sources: Rupert Brooke. "1914. I. Peace." In *1914 and Other Poems*, p. 11. London: Sidgwick and Jackson, 1919.

Charles Edmonds [Charles Edmund Carrington]. *A Subaltern's War*, pp. 21–22. New York: Arno Press, 1972.

Corporal Martin Hill. "Requiescat." In *More Songs by the Fighting Men*, pp. 71–72. London: Erskine Macdonald, 1917.

Captain John Eugene Crombie. "Easter Day, 1917—The Eve of the Battle." In *More Songs by the Fighting Men*, p. 50. London: Erskine Macdonald, 1917.

Mehmet Arif Ölçen. *Vetluga Memoir: A Turkish Prisoner of War in Russia, 1916–1918*, pp. 37–38. Trans. Gary Leiser. Gainesville, FL: University Press of Florida, 1995.

Evelyn, Princess Blücher. *An English Wife in Berlin: A Private Memoir of Events, Politics, and Daily Life in Germany Throughout the War and the Social Revolution of 1918*, pp. 328–329. London: Constable & Co., 1920.

Questions

If Brooke's sonnet is a "pro-war" poem, why is it entitled "Peace"?

Was the war a "picnic" for soldiers? What was the psychological impact of trench warfare?

Why, despite the hardships of war, might veterans look back on their years of service with fondness?

Imagine you are founding an international anti-war organization in 1920. Use evidence from the documents presented here (and in your text) to write an essay in support of your pacifist beliefs.

9. IMPORTANT HISTORICAL FACTS: STUDY DRILLS

A. Multiple Choice

1. Europeans greeted the outbreak of war with
   A. indifference.
   B. enthusiastic celebration.
   C. dread.
   D. violent anti-war protests.

2. The Schlieffen Plan consisted of
   A. a simultaneous attack on France and Russia.
   B. an attack on Turkey via the Dardanelles Straits.
   C. a rapid offensive against France, followed by an attack on Russia.
   D. a rapid offensive against Russia, followed by an attack on France.

3. A decisive battle in the early stages of the war, it saved France from the German offensive:
   A. Gallipoli
   B. The Battle of the Marne
   C. The Battle of the Somme
   D. The Battle of Verdun

4. The incapacitating psychological trauma suffered by many soldiers fighting in the trenches was known as
   A. mustard gas poisoning.
   B. venereal disease.
   C. creeping barrages.
   D. shell shock.

5. In Britain, the morale of home front industrial workers was kept up with slogans like
   A. "Peace, land, and bread."
   B. "He kept us out of war."
   C. "Shells made by a wife may save a husband's life."
   D. "Peace without victory."

6. Under the terms of the Treaty of London
   A. Italy entered the war on the side of the Allied Powers.
   B. Italy entered the war on the side of the Central Powers.
   C. Austria-Hungary ceded Trieste to Italy.
   D. Italy renounced its claim to the "unredeemed lands."

7. The United States entered the war on the side of the Allied Powers because
   A. American public opinion had long supported U.S. intervention.
   B. U.S. bankers hoped to profit from arms sales.
   C. Woodrow Wilson feared a German attack on Texas.
   D. Germany resumed unrestricted submarine warfare.

8. The Balfour Declaration of 1917 expressed Britain's willingness to support
   A. the creation of a "national home" for Jews in Palestine.
   B. the creation of British and French "zones of influence" in Syria.
   C. the new Bolshevik government in Russia.
   D. the strategic bombing of Turkish railroads.

9. Russia's new Bolshevik government signed the Treaty of Brest-Litovsk in 1918 because
   A. it wanted the Allied Powers to lose the war.
   B. the war was unpopular among all sectors of the Russian population.
   C. it hoped to acquire territory from Germany.
   D. it saw the war as a capitalist plot.

10. The blueprint for permanent peace President Wilson proposed as the grounds for an armistice settlement is known as
    A. the Fourteen Points.
    B. Plan XVII.
    C. the Zimmermann Telegram.
    D. the Victory Drive.

B. Chronological Relationships

Arrange the following events (you can use the key words shown with capital letters) in chronological order in the spaces provided below. When listed in the correct order, each set of two events will form a matched pair linked by a causal relationship. Explain this relationship.

Communist Russia signs a SEPARATE PEACE with Germany.

The GALLIPOLI Campaign begins.

The Battle of the SOMME takes place.

The RACE for the sea occurs.

The Battle of the MARNE is fought.

AMERICAN TROOPS engage in their first sustained action in Europe.

The UNITED STATES enters the war.
The BOLSHEVIKS overthrow the
provisional government of Russia.
Germany resumes unrestricted
SUBMARINE WARFARE.
The Germans launch their "VICTORY
DRIVE."

1. _____
2. _____
Relationship:

3. _____
4. _____
Relationship:

5. _____
6. _____
Relationship:

7. _____
8. _____
Relationship:

9. _____
10. _____
Relationship:

C. Matching Exercise: Historical Actors

_____ Winston Churchill
_____ Erich von Falkenhayn
_____ Vladimir Lenin
_____ Helmuth von Moltke
_____ Philippe Pétain
_____ A queer sardonic rat
_____ Manfred von Richthofen
_____ Siegfried Sassoon
_____ Woodrow Wilson
_____ Clara Zetkin

A. This Bolshevik leader called for an
armistice and then took Russia out of
the war by signing the Treaty of Brest-
Litovsk with Germany.

B. This First Lord of the Admiralty
helped to plan the British attack on
Turkey, which ended after the
disastrous Gallipoli Campaign.

C. This constant companion of the
soldiers in the trenches was known for
his "cosmopolitan sympathies,"
visiting Germans as well as Britons.

D. The successor of Alfred von Schlieffen,
this German general revised
Schlieffen's plan for an offensive
against France by reducing the
strength of the attacking force.

E. This political leader had campaigned
for office with the slogan: "He kept us
out of war," but he soon brought his
country into the Great War on the
Allied side.

F. A dashing and courageous flying
"ace," also known as the "Red Baron."

G. This general led the French to a costly
victory at Verdun. Later in the war he
ended the Nivelle Offensive and
attempted to improve the living
condition of mutinous soldiers.

H. This British poet fought in the Great
War, was wounded twice at the front
and also spent time in a mental asylum
during the war. In poems like "The
Hero," he attempted to provide a
realistic picture of death in the
trenches.

I. This German socialist was jailed for
denouncing the war as a struggle
between capitalist states, which pitted
workers against one another.

J. This German general decided that
victory could come only through a war
of attrition that would "bleed France
white."

IMPORTANT HISTORICAL FACTS: STUDY-DRILL ANSWERS

A. Multiple Choice

1. B. enthusiastic celebration.
2. C. a rapid offensive against France,
   followed by an attack on Russia.
3. B. The Battle of the Marne
4. D. shell shock.
5. C. "Shells made by a wife may save a
   husband's life."
6. A. Italy entered the war on the side of
   the Allied Powers.
7. D. Germany resumed unrestricted
   submarine warfare.

8. A. the creation of a "national home" for Jews in Palestine.
9. B. the war was unpopular among all sectors of the Russian population.
10. A. the Fourteen Points.

B. Chronological Relationships
1. MARNE [September 1914]
2. RACE [September, October 1914]
3. GALLIPOLI [March 1915]
4. SOMME [July 1, 1916]
5. SUBMARINE WARFARE [February 1, 1917]
6. UNITED STATES [April 6, 1917]
7. BOLSHEVIKS [November 6, 1917]
8. SEPARATE PEACE [March 3, 1918]
9. VICTORY DRIVE [Spring, 1918]
10. AMERICAN TROOPS [May, 1918].

C. Matching Exercise: Historical Actors
B. Winston Churchill
J. Erich von Falkenhayn
A. Vladimir Lenin
D. Helmuth von Moltke
G. Philippe Pétain
C. A queer sardonic rat
F. Manfred von Richthofen
H. Siegfried Sassoon
E. Woodrow Wilson
I. Clara Zetkin

25 Revolutionary Russia and the Soviet Union

1. CHAPTER OUTLINE

I. UNREST, REFORM, AND REVOLUTION: Despite a backward, largely agricultural economy, Russia began to industrialize between 1890 and 1914, sparking calls both for reform and revolution.
    A. INDUSTRIALIZATION AND THE MOVEMENT FOR REFORM: Russian industrial development created a potentially disruptive urban working class and also contributed to the rise of a liberal constitutionalist movement among the growing middle class.
    B. ENEMIES OF AUTOCRACY: Liberals called for reform of the tsarist state, but revolutionary populists and socialists sought to overthrow it. Marxist socialists were divided over whether or not a democratic revolution had to be preceded by a bourgeois revolution.
    C. LENIN AND THE BOLSHEVIKS argued that a small, tightly organized secret organization of workers and intellectuals could lead a successful proletarian revolution in Russia.
    D. THE REVOLUTION OF 1905: When the Russian army was defeated by Japan in 1905, liberals and many socialists demanded more say in the government, and many workers went on strike. The tsar acquiesced and established the Duma, a national representative assembly, but implemented counter-revolutionary measures shortly thereafter. Harsh repression silenced opponents of tsarist autocracy, but the years 1912 to 1914 saw a new surge of strikes and peasant violence.

II. WAR AND REVOLUTION: Lenin viewed the outbreak of the Great War as evidence that international capitalism was on the verge of collapse and he argued that a revolution begun in Russia would quickly spread to other countries.
    A. RUSSIA AT WAR: Russians greeted the Great War with an outburst of patriotic enthusiasm, but inept military leadership again produced unrest and demands for liberal reform. The political influence of Tsarina Alexandra was especially resented.
    B. THE PROGRESSIVE BLOC, formed by liberals in the Duma, sought to work with the tsar in the interest of reform, but the tsar's resistance limited its effectiveness. Food shortages produced strikes among increasingly organized urban workers.
    C. THE FEBRUARY REVOLUTION: In February 1917, a general strike broke out in Petrograd, followed by revolution. Many soldiers went over to the side of the revolutionaries, and the Duma organized a provisional

government. In the absence of support from his generals, Nicholas abdicated in early March.

D. **THE PROVISIONAL GOVERNMENT AND THE SOVIET:** In the vacuum created by the collapse of the tsarist regime, a Duma-appointed provisional government and the Petrograd Soviet formed an uneasy alliance. Fearing counter-revolution, the radical Soviet initially supported the more moderate provisional government.

E. **THE ARMY** was quickly being democratized by the Revolution, but the eastern front did not collapse, despite increasing desertion.

F. **THE REVOLUTION SPREADS:** As news of the Revolution spread throughout Russia, nationalist movements sprang up and peasants took land reform into their own hands. The provisional government pledged to keep Russia in the war, but only in support of a "peace without annexations."

G. **LENIN'S RETURN:** Back in Russia from exile, Lenin rallied the Bolsheviks, promoting a policy of withdrawal from the war, opposition to the provisional government, and land reform. Arguing that Russia was ripe for proletarian revolution, Lenin won the support of radical workers and soldiers.

H. **THE JULY DAYS:** Encouraged by ongoing agrarian revolution and popular hostility to the war, the Bolsheviks staged an insurrection in July 1917, but it was quickly crushed, forcing Lenin to flee to Finland.

I. **THE KORNILOV AFFAIR:** Conservatives and liberals, concerned about the Bolshevik threat and peasant land seizures, looked to General Kornilov to restore order through the establishment of a military

government, but no coup d'état took place.

III. **THE OCTOBER REVOLUTION:** Organized workers, seeking improved working conditions and an end to the war, lent their support to the Bolsheviks, who now seemed like the only viable alternative to the apparently powerless provisional government.

A. **THE BOLSHEVIKS SEIZE POWER:** Under the military leadership of Leon Trotsky, the Bolsheviks successfully overturned the provisional government, and quickly moved to impose their rule over all of Russia. The Cheka rounded up the Bolsheviks' opponents, and the democratically elected constituent assembly was forced to adjourn.

B. **THE PEACE OF BREST-LITOVSK:** In order to preserve the Revolution, the Bolsheviks accepted Germany's harsh peace terms, removing Russia from the war at the cost of substantial territorial losses.

IV. The **CIVIL WAR:** In 1918 a fierce and often brutal civil war broke out between the "Reds"—the Bolsheviks and their supporters—and the "Whites"—a disparate collection of conservative, liberal, socialist, and nationalist armies united only in their opposition to the Reds. Despite military support from the Allies, the Whites were decisively defeated by 1920.

V. **THE SOVIET UNION:** Having established military control over what had become known as the Union of Soviet Socialist Republics, the Bolsheviks created a "dictatorship of the proletariat." However, instead of "withering," the Bolshevik-controlled state exercised increasingly exclusive command over the Russian people.

A. **DEMOCRATIC CENTRALISM:** The Bolsheviks' Communist Party was authoritarian and repressive, and rejected ethnic minorities' calls for rights and workers' desire for self-management.

B. THE NEW ECONOMIC POLICY: In 1921, recognizing that the abolition of private ownership was not feasible in existing circumstances, Lenin allowed peasants and some merchants and factory-owners to engage in private enterprise on a small scale—but only as a temporary concession.

C. THE RISE OF STALIN: Joseph Stalin, a Georgian Bolshevik, was a skillful politician who climbed to power after the death of Lenin. Espousing "socialism in one country," he engineered the expulsion of internationalists such as Trotsky from the Communist Party, and assumed dictatorial powers in the late 1920s.

D. FIVE-YEAR PLANS: Stalin imposed collectivization on the Russian peasantry with the goal of accelerating Soviet industrialization. While the first Five-Year Plan resulted in untold suffering for the population, it was successful in spurring industrial development.

E. SOVIET CULTURE: In its early stages, the Revolution encouraged avant-garde artistic expression, but under Stalin artists were expected to conform to the conventions of "socialist realism." Stalinist conservatism was also expressed in the reassertion of traditional moral values and the rejection of equal opportunity for women.

F. "DARKNESS AT NOON": STALIN'S PURGES: In the late 1930s, an increasingly paranoid Stalin "purged" the Communist Party of anyone he suspected might pose a threat to his power. He also authorized the arrest of millions of so-called "terrorists," many hundreds of thousands of whom were later executed.

VI. CONCLUSION

2. HISTORICAL GEOGRAPHY

Map Exercises

Familiarize yourself with the maps provided in your text, and then attempt to locate the following places on Blank Maps 25.1 and 25.2.

THE RUSSIAN EMPIRE

Baku	Kiev
Baltic Sea	Minsk
Barents Sea	Moscow
Black Sea	Poland
Caspian Sea	St. Petersburg
Caucasus	(Petrograd)
Mountains	Ukraine
Estonia	Ural Mountains
Finland	Warsaw

THE SOVIET SOCIALIST REPUBLICS

Armenian SSR	Russian SFSR
Azerbaijan SSR	Tadzhik SSR
Byelorussian SSR	Turkmen SSR
Georgian SSR	Ukrainian SSR
Kazakh SSR	Uzbek SSR
Kirghiz SSR	

Map Questions

Where was most industry in the Russian Empire concentrated in the years between 1870 and 1914? Why?

What regions of the Russian Empire supported the Revolution of 1917? To what extent did the geographic distribution of the Revolution overlap with industrialization?

What territories were lost to the Soviet Union as a result of the signing of the Treaty of Brest-Litovsk?

During the Russian Civil War which territories came under the control of the White armies? Of the Red Army?

MAP 25.1   THE RUSSIAN EMPIRE

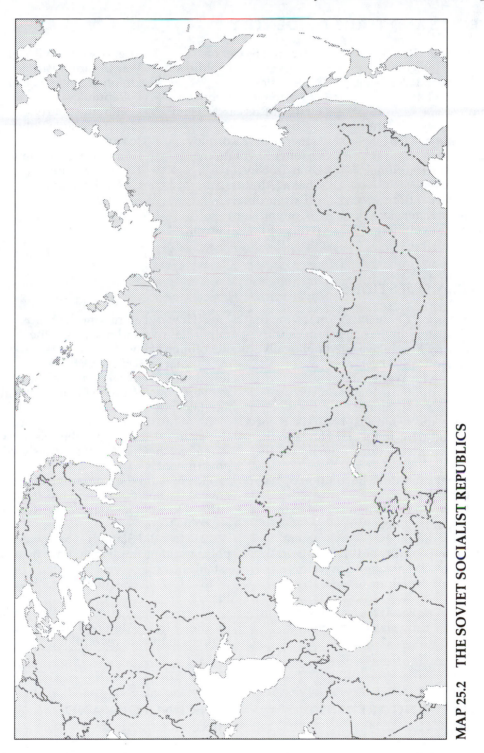

MAP 25.2   THE SOVIET SOCIALIST REPUBLICS

3. PEOPLE AND TERMS TO IDENTIFY

Tsar Nicholas II
Zemstvos
Russian Social Democratic
  Workers' Party
Lenin
Bolsheviks vs. Mensheviks
Revolution of 1905
Duma
Kadets (Constitutional
  Democrats)
Tsarina Alexandra
Alexander Kerensky
February Revolution

Petrograd Soviet of
  Workers' and Soldiers'
  Deputies
Provisional government
First All-Russian Muslim
  Congress
General Lavr Kornilov
October Revolution
Leon Trotsky
Cheka (All Russian
  Extraordinary
  Commission)
Treaty of Brest-Litovsk

The Russian Civil War
War Communism
Union of Soviet Socialist
  Republics
Communist Party
New Economic Policy
Joseph Stalin
Communist International
Five-Year Plans
Collectivization
Stakhanovite

4. STUDY QUESTIONS

1. *Historical Continuities:* Reviewing the nation's history in the nineteenth century, explain why Russia remained politically and economically "backward" as compared with Western Europe.

2. How did industrialization change Russia's social structure?

3. How did Lenin adapt Marxist theory to suit conditions in Russia? How did this "Bolshevik" theory differ from that of the Mensheviks?

4. What caused the Revolution of 1905? Why did it fail?

5. How did Russians respond to the outbreak of the Great War?

6. Why did the tsar's government collapse in February of 1917? *Historical Continuities:* What long-term factors can explain the failure of the tsarist state?

7. What replaced the tsarist regime in early 1917? How viable was the new government?

8. How did ethnic and religious minorities respond to news of the Revolution? How did peasants respond?

9. What caused the October Revolution? Why were the Bolsheviks able to overthrow the provisional government and take power?

10. Why did a civil war break out in Russia in 1918? How did the Russian Civil War affect the policies of the Bolshevik government?

11. How did the Communist Party govern the Soviet Union in the early 1920s? How did it organize the Russian economy?

12. How did Stalin rise to power? What policies did he implement once he had established his power?

13. How successful were the Five-Year Plans?

14. *Historical Continuities:* Was Stalin's dictatorship any different from the tsarist regimes of the pre-revolutionary period?

5. ANALYZING ART AND ARTIFACTS

Would Stalin have approved of the artistic style of *Fighting Lazy Workers* (p. 1135 in the textbook)? Why or why not?

6. TECHNOLOGY AND HISTORY

Historical Continuities: Compare Soviet industrialization under Stalin with the industrialization of Britain in the late eighteenth and early nineteenth centuries.

7. HISTORICAL ANALYSIS: INTERPRETIVE ESSAYS

1. *Historical Continuities:* Compare and contrast the political and economic policies of the pre-1917 tsarist state and the post-1917 Soviet state.

2. How did the February Revolution differ from the October Revolution? Why did the former fail and the latter succeed?

3. Write the biography of the life of a Russian peasant in the years between 1914 and 1939.

4. *Historical Continuities:* What impact was the Soviet Revolution likely to have on international Great Power relations?

8. HISTORICAL VOICES: WORKERS AND WORKER-SOLDIERS OF THE WORLD UNITE!

A. Lenin on War and the Workers' Revolution

In the years prior to the outbreak of the Russian Revolution, many Russian socialists accepted the "revisionist" Marxism that had become increasingly popular among European leftists in general. Russian revisionists argued that industrial capitalism and political liberalism must be allowed to develop in Russia prior to the establishment of a Communist society. Many of these Russian socialists, who were known as Mensheviks after 1903, also hoped that communism might be achieved without recourse to violent revolution—that the democratic principles of liberal, parliamentary political structures might permit a broad-based socialist movement to take power not by force, but through the ballot box.

Lenin, on the other hand, was a fierce opponent of the gradualist approach of the Mensheviks. As the leader of the Bolshevik faction, he argued that capitalism could be "leapfrogged"—that Russia could move directly from "feudalism" to communism—if a small, tightly-organized "vanguard" of professional revolutionaries would lead both industrial laborers and peasants in violent revolution against the autocratic state.

During the course of World War I, many European socialists embraced pacifism, rejecting absolutely the violent militarism that they believed lay at the root of the cataclysmic Great War. Lenin saw a direct link between this rejection of war in any form and the revisionists' rejection of immediate (and violent) revolution. In 1916, he wrote "The Military Programme of the Proletarian Revolution," which appeared in the German Socialist Youth journal *Jugend-Internationale* shortly before the October Revolution. In this article, Lenin attacked pacifism and revisionism, arguing that revolutionary wars of liberation—from both imperialism and capitalism—are necessary to the eventual triumph of communism. Instead of disarming the workers, Lenin insists that they must be armed in preparation for the coming class war.

Many aspects of the Bolshevik revolution of 1917 are prefigured in the "Military Program." Lenin's recognition that a Communist revolution was likely to spark civil and international war, his internationalism and his support of colonized people's struggles against imperialism, and even his commitment to the emancipation of women, are all presented here in clear and forceful language.

FROM *The Military Programme of the Proletarian Revolution* by Lenin

Among the Dutch, Scandinavian, and Swiss revolutionary Social-Democrats . . . there have been voices in favor of replacing the old Social-Democratic minimum-programme demand for a "militia," or "the armed nation," by a new demand: "disarmament." . . .

Their principal argument is that the disarmament demand is the clearest, most decisive, most consistent expression of the struggle against all militarism and against all war.

But in this principal argument lies the disarmament advocates' principal error. Socialists cannot, without ceasing to be socialists, be opposed to all war.

Firstly, socialists have never been, nor can they ever be, opposed to revolutionary wars. The bourgeoisie of the imperialist "Great" Powers has become thoroughly reactionary, and the war *this* bourgeoisie is now waging we regard as a reactionary, slave-owners' and criminal war. But what about a war *against* this bourgeoisie? A war, for instance, waged by peoples oppressed by and dependent upon this bourgeoisie, or by colonial peoples, for liberation? . . .

The history of the 20th century, this century of "unbridled imperialism," is replete with colonial wars. But what we Europeans, the imperialist oppressors of the majority of the world's peoples, with our habitual, despicable European chauvinism, call "colonial wars" are often national wars, or national rebellions of these oppressed peoples. One of the main features of imperialism is that it accelerates capitalist development in the most backward countries, and thereby extends and intensifies the struggle against national oppression. . . .

To deny all possibility of national wars under imperialism is wrong in theory, obviously mistaken historically, and tantamount to European chauvinism in practice: we who belong to nations that oppress hundreds of millions in Europe, Africa, Asia, etc., are invited to tell the oppressed peoples that it is "impossible" for them to wage war against "our" nations!

Secondly, civil war is just as much a war as any other. He who accepts the class struggle cannot fail to accept civil wars, which in every class society are the natural, and under certain conditions inevitable, continuation, development and intensification of the class struggle. . . .

Thirdly, the victory of socialism in one country does not at one stroke eliminate all wars in general. On the contrary, it presupposes wars. The development of capitalism proceeds extremely unevenly in different countries. It cannot be otherwise under commodity production. From this it follows irrefutably that socialism cannot achieve victory simultaneously *in all* countries. It will achieve victory first in one or several countries, while the others will for some time remain bourgeois or pre-bourgeois. This is bound to create not only friction, but a direct attempt on the part of the bourgeoisie of other countries to crush the socialist state's victorious proletariat. In such cases, a war on our part would be a legitimate and just war. It would be a war for socialism, for the liberation of other nations from the bourgeoisie. . . .

Only after we have overthrown, finally vanquished and expropriated the bourgeoisie of the whole world, and not merely in one country, will wars become impossible. And from a scientific point of view it would be utterly wrong—and utterly unrevolutionary—for us to evade or gloss over the most important things: crushing the resistance of the bourgeoisie—the most difficult task, and one demanding the greatest amount of fighting, in the *transition* to socialism. . . .

An oppressed class which does not strive to learn to use arms, to acquire arms, only deserves to be treated like slaves. We cannot, unless we have become bourgeois pacifists or opportunists, forget that we are living in a class society from which there is no way out, nor can there be, save through the class struggle. In every class society, whether based on slavery, serfdom, or, as at present, wage-labor, the oppressor class is always armed. Not only the modern standing army, but even the modern militia . . . represent the bourgeoisie armed *against* the proletariat. That is such an elementary truth that it is hardly necessary to dwell upon it. Suffice it to point to the use of troops against strikers in all capitalist countries.

. . . Our slogan must be: arming of the proletariat to defeat, expropriate and disarm the bourgeoisie. These are the only tactics possible for a revolutionary class, tactics that follow logically from, and are dictated by, the whole *objective development* of capitalist militarism. Only *after* the proletariat has disarmed the bourgeoisie will it be able, without betraying its world-historic mission, to consign all armaments to the scrap-heap. . . .

If the present war rouses among the reactionary Christian socialists, among the whimpering petty bourgeoisie, *only* horror and fright, only aversion to all use of arms, to bloodshed, death, etc., then we must say: Capitalist society is and has always been *horror without end*. If this most reactionary of all wars is now preparing for that society an *end to horror*, we have no reason to fall into despair. But the disarmament "demand," or more correctly, the dream of disarmament, is, objectively, nothing but an expression of despair at a time when, as everyone can see, the bourgeoisie itself is paving the way for the only legitimate and revolutionary war—civil war against the imperialist bourgeoisie. . . .

The bourgeoisie makes it its business to promote trusts, drive women and children into the factories, subject them to corruption and suffering, condemn them to extreme poverty. We do not "demand" such development, we do not "support" it. We fight it. But *how* do we fight? We explain that trusts and the employment of women in industry are progressive. We do not want a return to the handicraft system, pre-monopoly capitalism, domestic drudgery for women. Forward through the trusts, etc., and beyond them to socialism!

With the necessary changes that argument is applicable also to the present militarization of the population. Today the imperialist bourgeoisie militarizes the youth as well as the adults; tomorrow, it may begin militarizing the women. Our attitude should be: All the better! Full speed ahead! For the faster we move, the nearer shall we be to the armed uprising against capitalism.

. . . Women and teenage children fought in the Paris Commune side by side with the men. It will be no different in the coming battles for the overthrow of the bourgeoisie. Proletarian women will not look on passively as poorly armed or unarmed workers are shot down by the well-armed forces of the bourgeoisie. They will take to arms, as they did in 1871, and from the cowed nations of today—or more correctly, from the present-day labor movement, disorganized more by the opportunists than by the governments—there will undoubtedly arise, sooner or later, but with absolute certainty, an international league of the "terrible nations" of the revolutionary proletariat.

Source: Lenin. "The Military Programme of the Proletarian Revolution." First published in *Jugend-Internationale*, Nos. 9 and 10, September and October 1917.

Questions
   Why does Lenin reject the "disarmament demand" of other Social De-
mocrats? When does he believe that war is necessary?
   Lenin denounces calls for disarmament as "European chauvinism."
What does he mean by this? What do his remarks tell you about his un-
derstanding of imperialism? Of nationalism and internationalism?
   Why does Lenin favor the "militarization" of women? What role does
he expect working women to play in the coming "class struggle"?

B. An American Communist Commemorates the Sacrifices of the Revolutionary Russian Workers

John Reed (1887–1920) was born in
Portland, Oregon, the son of an affluent
businessman. Reed attended Harvard
University, and then, after graduating in
1910, went to live in New York City's
Greenwich Village, where he pursued a
career in journalism. Drawn to the
socialist movements of the era, Reed wrote
for the leftist journal, *The Masses.* As a
reporter he traveled extensively, covering
a silk workers' strike in Paterson, New
Jersey, the Mexican Revolution (which
began in 1911), a miners' strike in
Colorado, and the western and eastern
fronts during World War I.
   After the February Revolution in
Russia, Reed set off for Petrograd, arriving
in time to personally witness the
Bolsheviks' October Revolution. On the
basis of his experiences, and using
documents collected during his stay in
Russia, Reed wrote one of the best-known
accounts of the Soviet Revolution, *Ten
Days That Shook the World*, which was first
published in 1919. Reed returned to the
United States in 1918 and became the head
of the American Communist Labor Party.

Indicted for treason as a result of his
political activities, he was forced to return
to the Soviet Union, where he died of
typhus in 1920, at the age of thirty-three.
   Much of Reed's writing was motivated
by a sincere sympathy for the laboring
poor and a deep commitment to the
international workers' movement. As a
political activist, Reed came to see all
workers—whether striking American
silkworkers or miners, Mexican peasants,
World War I soldiers, or Russian
revolutionaries—as united by their
subjection to the capitalist system.
   For all its historical value, *Ten Days That
Shook the World* is a highly personal
account of the revolutionary events of
1917—what Reed himself called a "slice of
intensified history—history as I saw it."
Caught up in the swirling drama of
unfolding events, Reed provides a day-by-
day account of the Bolshevik takeover. In
the days following the Bolshevik victory
in November, Reed left the "artificial city"
of Petrograd for Moscow, "real Russia," in
search of a glimpse at "the true feeling of
the Russian people about the Revolution."
While there, he witnessed the mass burial
of pro-Bolshevik workers killed during
the October Days.

FROM *Ten Days That Shook the World* by John Reed

Late in the night we went through the empty streets and under the Iberian Gate to the great Red Square in front of the Kremlin. . . .
   Mountains of dirt and rock were piled high near the base of the wall.
Climbing these we looked down into two massive pits, ten or fifteen feet
deep and fifty yards long, where hundreds of soldiers and workers were
digging in the light of huge fires.
   A young student spoke to us in German. "The Brotherhood Grave,"
he explained. "To-morrow we shall bury here five hundred proletarians
who died for the Revolution." . . .
   "Here in this holy place," said the student, "holiest of all Russia, we
shall bury our most holy. Here where are the tombs of the Tsars, our
Tsar—the People—shall sleep. . . ." His arm was in a sling, from a bullet-

wound gained in the fighting. He looked at it. "You foreigners look down on us Russians because so long we tolerated a medieval monarchy," said he. "But we saw that the Tsar was not the only tyrant in the world; capitalism was worse, and in all the countries of the world capitalism was Emperor. . . . Russian revolutionary tactics are best. . . ."

As we left, the workers in the pit, exhausted and running with sweat in spite of the cold, began to climb wearily out. Across the Red Square a dark knot of men came hurrying. They swarmed into the pits, picked up the tools and began digging, digging, without a word. . . .

So, all the long night volunteers of the People relieved each other, never halting in their driving speed, and the cold light of the dawn laid bare the great Square, white with snow, and the yawning brown pits of the Brotherhood Grave, quite finished.

We rose before sunrise, and hurried through the dark streets. . . .

We forced our way through the dense mass packed near the Kremlin wall, and stood upon one of the dirt-mountains. Already several men were there, among them Muranov, the soldier who had been elected Commandant of Moscow—a tall, simple-looking, bearded man with a gentle face.

Through all the streets to the Red Square the torrents of people poured, thousands upon thousands of them, all with the look of the poor and the toiling. A military band came marching up, playing the *Internationale,* and spontaneously the song caught and spread like wind-ripples on a sea, slow and solemn. From the top of the Kremlin wall gigantic banners unrolled to the ground; red, with great letters in gold and in white, saying, "Martyrs of the Beginning of World Social Revolution," and "Long Live the Brotherhood of Workers of the World."

A bitter wind swept the Square, lifting the banners. Now from the far quarters of the city the workers of the different factories were arriving, with their dead. They could be seen coming through the Gate, the blare of their banners, and the dull red—like blood—of the coffins they carried. These were rude boxes, made of unplaned wood and daubed with crimson, borne high on the shoulders of rough men who marched with tears streaming down their faces, and followed by women who sobbed and screamed, or walked stiffly, with white, dead faces. . . .

Between the factory-workers came companies of soldiers with their coffins, too, and squadrons of cavalry, riding at salute, and artillery batteries, the cannon wound with red and black—forever, it seemed. Their banners said, "Long live the Third International!" or "We Want an Honest, General, Democratic Peace!"

Slowly the marchers came with their coffins to the entrance of the grave, and the bearers clambered up with their burdens and went down into the pit. Many of them were women—squat, strong proletarian women. Behind the dead came other women—women young and broken, or old, wrinkled women making noises like hurt animals, who tried to follow their sons and husbands into the Brotherhood Grave, and shrieked when compassionate hands restrained them. The poor love each other so!

All the long day the funeral procession passed, coming in by the Iberian Gate and leaving the Square by way of the Nikolskaya, a river of red banners, bearing words of hope and brotherhood and stupendous prophecies, against a background of fifty thousand people,—under the eyes of the world's workers and their descendants forever. . . .

I suddenly realised that the devout Russian people no longer needed priests to pray them into heaven. On earth they were building a kingdom more bright than any heaven had to offer, and for which it was a glory to die. . . .

Source: John Reed. *Ten Days That Shook the World*, pp. 253–259. Boni & Liveright, 1919.

Questions
    How does Reed explain ordinary Russians' enthusiasm for the Bolshevik Revolution?
    In what ways is the ceremony described here "revolutionary"? According to Reed, what sort of political values does it demonstrate?
    On the basis of this account, who seems to have supported the Bolshevik Revolution in Moscow? Why?

9. IMPORTANT HISTORICAL FACTS: STUDY DRILLS

A. Multiple Choice

1. The Revolution of 1905 was in large part a result of
   A. the Russo-Japanese War.
   B. the Crimean War.
   C. Bolshevik agitation.
   D. the creation of a national Duma.

2. Tsarina Alexandra was widely disliked for all of the following reasons *except* that
   A. she was German by birth.
   B. she used her influence to control the weak-willed tsar.
   C. she unsuccessfully led Russia in the war against Germany.
   D. a debauched "holy man" was one of her closest friends and advisors.

3. After the February Revolution, Russia was governed by
   A. Tsar Nicholas II.
   B. the *zemstvos*.
   C. Vladimir Lenin.
   D. the provisional government and the Petrograd Soviet.

4. The military actions of the October Revolution were coordinated by
   A. Leon Trotsky.
   B. General Lavr Kornilov.
   C. Alexander Kerensky.
   D. army cadets loyal to the provisional government.

5. In 1918, the Bolsheviks ended Russia's participation in the Great War through their signing of
   A. the Treaty of London.
   B. the Treaty of Versailles.
   C. the Treaty of Brest-Litovsk.
   D. the April Theses.

6. During the Russian Civil War, "White" armies were led into battle by all of the following *except*
   A. General Anton Denikin.
   B. General Alexander Kolchak.
   C. General Lavr Kornilov.
   D. Tsar Nicholas II.

7. During the Russian Civil War, the Bolsheviks implemented the policy of "War Communism." This involved
   A. the redistribution of land to poor peasants.
   B. the forcible requisitioning of grain from the peasantry.
   C. the revival of small-scale private ownership of stores and factories.
   D. the forcible collectivization of agriculture.

8. In 1921, Lenin responded to widespread protest against "War Communism" with
   A. democratic centralism.
   B. the New Economic Policy.
   C. "socialism in one country."
   D. the First Five-Year Plan.

9. Peasants responded to the first Five-Year Plan by
   A. joining the Communist Party.
   B. becoming "kulaks."
   C. slaughtering their livestock.
   D. becoming "dizzy with success."

10. Stalin rejected the New Economic Policy because he feared it would lead to
    A. the restoration of capitalism.
    B. the collectivization of agriculture.
    C. industrialization.
    D. the abolition of private property.

B. Chronological Relationships

1. List the following events in chronological order and identify the dates at which they took place:

   The Bolsheviks overturn the provisional government and seize power.

   The first Five-Year Plan.

   The Kornilov Affair.

   The Ukrainian National Congress is founded.

   Nicholas II abdicates.

   The murder of Rasputin.

   The Russian Social Democratic Workers' Party splits into Bolshevik and Menshevik factions.

   The signing of the Treaty of Brest-Litovsk.

   Bloody Sunday.

   The Union of Soviet Socialist Republics is created.

2. What was the historical significance of each of the events listed above?

C. Matching Exercise: Historical Actors

_____ Bolshevik
_____ Kadet
_____ Alexander Kerensky
_____ General Lavr Kornilov
_____ Vladimir Lenin
_____ Menshevik
_____ Tsar Nicholas II
_____ Andrei Stakhanov
_____ Joseph Stalin
_____ Leon Trotsky

A. A key actor in the early stages of the Soviet Revolution, he provided crucial military leadership, but his espousal of "permanent revolution" later brought him into conflict with Stalin.

B. The last Romanov to rule Russia, he was executed by the Bolsheviks during the Russian Civil War.

C. Though in the "minority," he followed a strict Marxist line, arguing that a proletarian revolution could only come after a bourgeois revolution directed against the tsarist state.

D. In 1917 the Germans helped this radical revolutionary return to Russia from exile. He would go on to direct the Soviet Revolution until his early death in 1924.

E. A Socialist Revolutionary, he denounced the war in the Duma prior to the Revolution, and later served as the head of the short-lived provisional government.

F. Born in Georgia and educated in a religious seminary, this Bolshevik revolutionary eventually exercised dictatorial control over the Soviet Union, imposing harsh policies of collectivization on the Russian peasantry and "purging" his political opponents.

G. As a member of the majority Constitutional Democrat Party in the Duma, he joined the Progressive Bloc and favored a reduction in the tsar's powers.

H. This member of the "majority" believed that a proletarian revolution was possible in Russia if it was led by a secret organization of well-trained professional revolutionaries.

I. Commander in chief of the Russian army, this military leader failed to stage a conservative coup d'état in 1917, but later went on to lead a "White" army against the "Reds" during the Russian Civil War.

J. A "hero of labor," this coal miner became famous for his extraordinary productivity and dedication to the Soviet state in the 1930s.

D. Matching Exercise: Historical Organizations

_____ Cheka
_____ Communist International
_____ Communist Party
_____ Duma
_____ First All-Russian Muslim Congress
_____ Petrograd Soviet of Workers' and Soldiers' Deputies
_____ Provisional government
_____ Russian Social Democratic Workers' Party
_____ Union of Soviet Socialist Republics
_____ *Zemstvos*

A. Created by liberal members of the Duma, it provided temporary leadership to Russia after the February Revolution.

B. Founded in 1919, it was intended to assist revolutionary Communist parties in countries other than Russia.

C. A national representative body created in 1905 by Tsar Nicholas.

D. The name taken by the Bolsheviks in 1918.

E. A nationalist organization whose members included religious conservatives, Westernizers, and leftists.

F. A regional assembly.

G. Created in 1922, it united all of the Russian Empire as the new Bolshevik state.

H. A "council" that shared power with the provisional government after the February Revolution.

I. A centralized police authority created to root out the enemies of the Bolsheviks.

J. A Marxist political organization founded in 1898, it later split into Bolshevik and Menshevik factions.

IMPORTANT HISTORICAL FACTS: STUDY-DRILL ANSWERS

A. Multiple Choice

1. A. the Russo-Japanese War.
2. C. she unsuccessfully led Russia in the war against Germany.
3. D. the provisional government and the Petrograd Soviet.
4. A. Leon Trotsky.
5. C. the Treaty of Brest-Litovsk.
6. D. Tsar Nicholas II.
7. B. the forcible requisitioning of grain from the peasantry.
8. B. the New Economic Policy.
9. C. slaughtering their livestock.
10. A. the restoration of capitalism.

B. Chronological Relationships

1903	The Russian Social Democratic Workers' Party splits into Bolshevik and Menshevik factions.
January 1905	Bloody Sunday.
December 1916	The murder of Rasputin.
March 2, 1917	Nicholas II abdicates.
March 4, 1917	The Ukrainian National Congress is founded.
August 1917	The Kornilov Affair.
October 1917	The Bolsheviks seize power.
March 3, 1918	The signing of the Treaty of Brest-Litovsk.
1922	The Union of Soviet Socialist Republics is created.
1928–1933	The first Five-Year Plan.

C. Matching Exercise: Historical Actors

H. Bolshevik
G. Kadet
E. Alexander Kerensky
I. General Lavr Kornilov
D. Vladimir Lenin
C. Menshevik
B. Tsar Nicholas II
J. Andrei Stakhanov
F. Joseph Stalin
A. Leon Trotsky

D. Matching Exercise: Historical Organizations

I. Cheka
B. Communist International
D. Communist Party
C. Duma
E. First All-Russian Muslim Congress
H. Petrograd Soviet of Workers' and Soldiers' Deputies
A. Provisional government
J. Russian Social Democratic Workers' Party
G. Union of Soviet Socialist Republics
F. *Zemstvos*

26 *The Elusive Search for Stability in the 1920s*

1. CHAPTER OUTLINE

I. THE RESOLUTION OF THE WAR: The Great War left Europe in turmoil. The Allies attempted to negotiate a lasting settlement at the Paris Peace Conference, but their efforts left many peoples and nations dissatisfied.

   A. REVOLUTION IN GERMANY AND HUNGARY: The German and Austro-Hungarian Empires collapsed in 1918. In Germany, the weak Weimar Republic struggled against Communist revolts and right-wing militarism. In Hungary, a new republican government fell to the Communists, who were then quickly overthrown by a conservative military leader.

   B. THE TREATY OF VERSAILLES represented an uneasy compromise between Wilsonian idealism and the realism of British and French leaders. By the terms of this "victor's peace," Germany was forced to accept responsibility for the losses suffered by the Allies and was assessed substantial reparations payments. As a result of resurgent American isolationism the United States Senate refused to ratify the treaty.

   C. SETTLEMENTS IN EASTERN EUROPE: A series of subsequent treaties redrew the boundaries of Germany's Eastern European allies, usually to their disadvantage. Hungary, Bulgaria, Austria, and Turkey joined the ranks of "revisionist" states unhappy with the peace settlement.

II. NATIONAL AND ETHNIC CHALLENGES: The peace treaties made ethnicity a chief determinant of national boundaries, inspiring hopes for independent states among subject peoples around the world.

   A. THE NATIONAL QUESTION AND THE SUCCESSOR STATES: In Eastern Europe, small "successor" states emerged out of the pre-war empires. Despite attempts to satisfy the national aspirations of all Eastern Europeans, many exceptions were made to the rule of "self-determination," creating considerable conflict and instability in these new nations. In the 1920s, many fell under authoritarian rule.

   B. COLONIAL AND NATIONAL QUESTIONS: Eastern Europeans were granted independent states, but peoples colonized by the European Great Powers were denied their freedom. Former German colonies fell under the "mandate" of the Allies, and Arabs and Jews in Palestine, Irish, Indians on the subcontinent, and Chinese remained subject to foreign domination.

III. ECONOMIC AND SOCIAL INSTABILITY: During the "roaring

twenties" Europeans enjoyed a range of new leisure-time pursuits, but the period was also marked by considerable confusion and unrest. Many on the left felt that the state should provide expanded social services to its citizens.

A. SOCIAL TURMOIL: The economic dislocation caused by the war disrupted European political life. The business elite sought to retain its wartime gains, in some cases promoting "corporatist" cooperation between business, the state, and labor. Women were granted voting privileges in many countries, but radicalized workers were unable to democratize the economy due to concerted opposition from employers and national governments.

B. THE LEFT AND THE ORIGINS OF THE WELFARE STATE: After the war, the European left divided between revolutionary Communists and reformist socialists. In alliance with workers, socialists worked with liberal governments to lay the foundations of the welfare state.

IV. POLITICAL INSTABILITY posed a serious threat to the young German republic, but also to the established parliamentary governments of France and Britain.

A. GERMANY'S FRAGILE WEIMAR REPUBLIC: Confronted with challenges on the right and the left in the early 1920s, the German republic successfully weathered overthrow attempts, runaway inflation, and the French occupation of the Ruhr. After 1924, new reparations agreements and the Treaty of Locarno ushered in a period of relative peace and prosperity, although many Germans still opposed the liberal Weimar government.

B. THE ESTABLISHED DEMOCRACIES: BRITAIN AND FRANCE: British and French society continued to be marked by deep class divisions. In both countries, conservative governments suppressed workers' movements and ruled in the interest of economic elites.

V. ARTISTS AND INTELLECTUALS IN THE WASTELAND: The trauma of the Great War was also reflected in the culture of the 1920s. Rejecting traditional artistic conventions, the modernist "lost generation" championed strongly subjectivist styles such as dadaism and expressionism.

VI. THE RISE OF FASCISM: In Italy and Germany, right-wing anti-parliamentary movements gained strength and eventually won mass followings.

A. MUSSOLINI AND FASCISM IN ITALY: In the immediate post-war period, Italy's liberal government was destabilized by nationalist anger over the Versailles Settlement and the radicalism of unemployed workers and landless peasants. Right-wing activist Benito Mussolini, leader of the Italian National Fascist Party, convinced the king to make him prime minister in 1922, after which time Mussolini assumed dictatorial powers.

B. HITLER AND THE RISE OF THE NAZIS IN GERMANY: Like Mussolini, Adolf Hitler, the charismatic leader of the German Nazi Party, publicized his own right-wing nationalist critique of liberal parliamentarism. Despite the failure of a coup attempt in 1923, Hitler's anti-Communist and anti-Jewish rhetoric gained increasing numbers of followers in the late 1920s, especially among the hard-pressed lower middle class.

2. HISTORICAL GEOGRAPHY

MAP 26.1   POST-WAR EUROPE

Map Exercises

Familiarize yourself with the maps provided in your text, and then attempt to locate the following places on Blank Map 26.1.

POST-WAR EUROPE

Albania	Greece
Austria	Hungary
Belgium	Italy
Bulgaria	Latvia
Czechoslovakia	Lithuania
Denmark	Poland
East Prussia	Romania
Estonia	Turkey
Finland	U.S.S.R.
Germany	Yugoslavia

CONTESTED TERRITORIES

Alsace	Malmédy
Danzig	Northern Dalmatia
East Prussia	Polish Corridor
Eupen	Rhineland
Fiume (Rijeka)	Saar
Istria	Southern Tyrol
Lorraine	Upper Silesia

Map Questions

How were the national boundaries of Germany changed by the Versailles Settlement? To what extent did these changes represent a violation of the principle of "self-determination"?

Which territories in the Middle East came under British control after the war? Under French control?

How were Germany's colonial holdings redistributed at the end of the war?

3. PEOPLE AND TERMS TO IDENTIFY

Weimar Republic
Béla Kun
Woodrow Wilson
League of Nations
War Guilt Clause
Treaty of Versailles
Mustafa Kemal Pasha (Atatürk)
Successor states
Yugoslavia
Mandate system

Irish Free State
Roaring twenties
Corporatism
Léon Blum
Welfare state
Kapp Putsch
French occupation of the Ruhr
British miners' strike of 1926
Lost generation

Stream of consciousness
"Duce" Benito Mussolini
Italian National Fascist Party
Lateran Pacts of 1929
"Fuhrer" Adolf Hitler
National Socialist German Workers' Party (Nazi Party)
Beer Hall Putsch

4. STUDY QUESTIONS

1. *Historical Continuities:* How did the new Weimar Republic differ from previous German governments? Why was it so weak?

2. To what extent were French, British, Italian, and American demands and expectations incompatible at the outset of the Paris Peace Conference?

3. Why did Germany become a "revisionist" state in the inter-war years?

4. To what extent was the peace settlement a victory for the principle of "self-determination"?

5. Why did many new Eastern European states fall under authoritarian regimes in the 1920s?

6. Why were colonized peoples disappointed by the Versailles Settlement?

7. *Historical Continuities:* Was European society more or less democratic after the Great War than it had been in the second half of the nineteenth century?

8. What caused the rise of welfare state policies in the post-war period?

9. Compare and contrast Germany, France, and Britain in the 1920s. How did the experiences of these three nations differ during this period? What common concerns and problems did they share?

10. *Historical Continuities:* How does the art and literature of the early twentieth

century compare with that of the late nineteenth century?

11. Why were the Italian fascists able to seize power in 1922?

12. What attracted Germans to Hitler's Nazi Party?

13. What characteristics were shared by Italian fascism and German Nazism? How did the two movements differ from one another?

5. ANALYZING ART AND ARTIFACTS

How was the trauma of the wartime experience expressed in the dada poster reproduced in your text (p. 1173)? In Max Ernst's *Europe after the Rain* (p. 1175)?

How did the personal styles of Hitler and Mussolini—their clothing and their physical demeanor—help to convey the basic ideological premises of fascism?

(See additional illustrations in Chapter 27, pp. 1187, 1197, 1211, and 1218.)

6. TECHNOLOGY AND HISTORY

To what political uses were new forms of mass communication—the popular press, film, radio—put in the inter-war years?

7. HISTORICAL ANALYSIS: INTERPRETIVE ESSAYS

1. *Historical Continuities:* Were the problems that caused the Great War solved by the various treaties that brought the war to an end?

2. Write a critique of the Versailles Settlement from the perspective of a German nationalist.

3. *Historical Continuities:* Write a detailed analysis of the foreign policy implications for France of the

transformation of the political geography of Central and Eastern Europe between 1914 and 1919.

4. What factors contributed to the political instability of Europe during the inter-war years?

5. Explain why you, as an Italian, decided to join Mussolini's National Fascist Party.

8. HISTORICAL VOICES: THE AFTERMATH OF WAR—WARNINGS OF ECONOMIC DISORDER AND THE FASCIST PROMISE OF ORDER

A. An Economist Critiques the Versailles Settlement

The economic theories of British scholar John Maynard Keynes (1883–1946) have had a profound impact on the economic policies of Western governments in the twentieth century and on the lives of their citizens. Keynes' groundbreaking work in the 1930s (discussed in Chapter 27) forced a major revision of the laissez-faire thought that had dominated Western economics since the publication of Adam Smith's *Wealth of Nations* in 1776, and convinced many political leaders that governments could intervene to stimulate their nation's economies—through policies designed to lower unemployment rates, for example.

In 1919, when the formulation of his most important theories lay some years in the future, Keynes made his mark on world opinion with a scathing critique of the economic clauses of the Versailles Settlement. Having been involved in the treaty negotiations as an advisor to British Prime Minister David Lloyd George, Keynes abandoned his post in despair over the unreasonableness of the terms imposed on Germany, and quickly made public his concerns in *The Economic Consequences of the Peace* (1919). In the years since its appearance, this terse and intelligently written volume has been consistently praised as a prophetic warning about the economic and political instability that might—and, to a large extent, did—result from the economic stipulations of the treaty. However, the immediate appeal of Keynes' book lay not only in its economic arguments, but also in its readability. It offers a lively description of the treaty negotiations and perceptive, if not especially gentle, pencil portraits of the negotiators themselves.

Keynes' fundamental argument was that German reparations payments should be set at a reasonable rate and that inter-Allied debts (owed, for the most part, to the United States and, secondarily, to Britain) should be forgiven. France's insistence on substantial reparations payments from Germany was, at least in part, a product of France's own burden of debt. If the United States were willing to forgive its share of that debt, France and the other indebted Allies might feel less compelled to impose unrealistic demands on Germany. This would allow a stabilization and revitalization of the European economy—especially if a new infusion of loans was made available from U. S. investors—and the United States would benefit from increased international trade with healthy European economies. If these remedies were not applied, Keynes predicted growing political and economic instability throughout Europe, the nature of which he outlined in a chapter entitled "Europe After the Treaty."

FROM *The Economic Consequences of the Peace* by John Maynard Keynes

The significant features of the immediate situation can be grouped under three heads: first, the absolute falling off, for the time being, in Europe's internal productivity; second, the breakdown of transport and exchange by means of which its products could be conveyed where they were most wanted; and third, the inability of Europe to purchase its usual supplies from overseas.

The decrease of productivity cannot be easily estimated, and may be the subject of exaggeration. But the *prima facie* evidence of it is overwhelming . . . A variety of causes have produced it;—violent and prolonged internal disorder as in Russia and Hungary; the creation of new governments and their inexperience in the readjustment of economic relations, as in Poland and Czecho-Slovakia; the loss throughout the Continent of efficient labor, through the casualties of war or the continuance of mobilization; the falling-off in efficiency through continued underfeeding in the Central Empires; the exhaustion of the soil from lack of the usual applications of artificial manures throughout the course of the war; the unsettlement of the minds of the laboring classes on the fundamental economic issues of their lives. But above all (to quote Mr. Hoover), "there is a great relaxation of effort as the reflex of physical exhaustion of large sections of the population from privation and the mental and physical strain of the war." Many persons are for one reason or another out of employment altogether. . . . a summary of the unemployment bureaus in Europe in July, 1919, showed that 15,000,000 families were receiving unemployment allowances in one form or another, and were being paid in the main by a constant inflation of currency. In Germany there is the added deterrent to labor and to capital (in so far as the Reparation terms are taken literally), that anything, which they may produce beyond the barest level of subsistence, will for years to come be taken away from them.

Such definite data as we possess do not add much, perhaps, to the general picture of decay. But I will remind the reader of one or two of them. The coal production of Europe as a whole is estimated to have fallen off by 30 per cent; and upon coal the greater part of the industries of Europe and the whole of her transport system depend. Whereas before the war Germany produced 85 per cent of the total food consumed by her inhabitants, the productivity of the soil is now diminished by 40 per cent and the effective quality of the live-stock by 55 per cent. Of the European countries which formerly possessed a large exportable surplus, Russia, as much by reason of deficient transport as of diminished output, may herself starve. Hungary, apart from her other troubles, has been pillaged by the Roumanians immediately after harvest. Austria will have consumed the whole of her own harvest for 1919 before the end of the calendar year. The figures are almost too overwhelming to carry conviction to our minds; if they were not quite so bad, our effective belief in them might be stronger.

. . . in the final catastrophe the malady of the body passes over into malady of the mind. Economic privation proceeds by easy stages, and so long as men suffer it patiently the outside world cares little. Physical efficiency and resistance to disease slowly diminish, but life proceeds somehow, until the limit of human endurance is reached at last and counsels of despair and madness stir the sufferers from the lethargy which precedes the crisis. Then man shakes himself, and the bonds of custom are loosed. The power of ideas is sovereign, and he listens to whatever instruction of hope, illusion, or revenge is carried to him on the air. As I write, the flames of Russian Bolshevism seem, for the moment at least, to have burnt themselves out, and the peoples of Central and Eastern Europe are held in a dreadful torpor. The lately gathered harvest keeps off the worst privations, and Peace has been declared at Paris. But winter approaches. Men will have nothing to look forward to or to nourish hopes on. There will be little fuel to moderate the rigors of the season or to comfort the starved bodies of the town-dwellers.

But who can say how much is endurable, or in what direction men will seek at last to escape from their misfortunes?

Source: John Maynard Keynes. *The Economic Consequences of the Peace*, pp. 231–233, 250–251. New York: Harcourt, Brace and Howe, 1920.

Questions

According to Keynes, what economic problems did Europe confront in the immediate post-war period?

How might Allied demands that Germany pay reparations and that all war debts be repaid exacerbate these problems?

Keynes warns that Europeans' physical deprivation might result in "malady of the mind." What does he mean by that?

B. Between Communism and Capitalism: Italian Fascism and the Cult of the Leader

In hindsight, the brutality and authoritarianism of Italian fascism seem readily apparent. However, in the midst of the feverish ups and downs of the 1920s, many people were willing to forgive Mussolini his "excesses" and to congratulate him for the order and prosperity he had brought to the unruly Italian nation. When Margherita Sarfatti's *The Life of Benito Mussolini* appeared in 1925, it was greeted with surprisingly positive reviews in the American and British press.* Sarfatti herself was faulted for having written a "gossipy, excited and entirely uncritical essay in hero-worship" (*New Statesman*), but Mussolini, the subject of her study, was described as "the most interesting political personality of the age" (*New York Times*).

*Sarfatti's intention was to introduce Mussolini to the American and English public. The biography was published in English first, and only subsequently in Italian.

Sarfatti (1883–1961) was well qualified to write the Duce's biography. She had not only been his mistress for several years, but had also worked on the staff of his newspaper, *Il Popolo d'Italia* ("The People of Italy"). Like Mussolini, she had started out as a socialist, but had rejected that party's pacifism during World War I. After the creation of the Fascist Party in 1919, she became an active member and supported Mussolini when he was granted power in 1922. During the 1920s, she served as co-director of *Gerarchia* (Hierarchy), the official monthly journal of the Fascist Party. She was best known as an art critic, and her support for modernist art styles had a certain amount of influence on Mussolini. However, Sarfatti was of Jewish descent and was forced into exile in the late 1930s, when Italy's growing subservience to Nazi Germany resulted in the passage of anti-Semitic legislation in Italy and Sarfatti's expulsion from the Fascist Party.

Sarfatti's "authorized" biography is a skillful piece of propaganda, intended to present Mussolini as "a true leader of men." Although Mussolini himself always claimed to detest publicity, he cooperated with Sarfatti on the biography, in the interest of solidifying his claim to recognition as the legitimate Italian head of state and as a prominent world leader. Sarfatti describes Mussolini's fascism as an alternative to both communism and capitalism, a middle road that allowed Italians to avoid both the anarchy of liberal individualism and free-market economics and the rigidity of Soviet-style centralization. Similarly, she argues that Mussolini rejected the social leveling inherent in both socialism and democracy because inequality—the organization of society along the lines of a "natural" hierarchy of talent—was the best guarantee of political stability, economic security, and civic order. The Duce, at the apex of the hierarchy, was not a dictator, but a selfless defender of *true* liberty.

FROM *The Life of Benito Mussolini* by Margherita Sarfatti

Bolshevism arose in, and is confined to, Russia. Russia has adapted herself and her vital energies to its system, or perhaps the system has adapted itself to Russia. But can such a system be applied to Italy? Mussolini's reply was a definite "No."

. . . Mussolini gave himself to the task of showing up the Communist illusion, combating it foot by foot, pitting man against man, brain against brain, fighting both by action and by the spoken word, by propaganda, argument and "heavy artillery." . . .

And if a few "hard-heads" could be convinced by nothing else in the way of argument but by a tap on the head, the game was worth the candle. The game as played by the Fascisti only involved a few doses of castor oil and perhaps here and there a good cudgelling. The Russian tyranny had caused thousands and thousands of young men to lose even a life in which there no longer remained either joy or hope.

It must not be thought that "to fight Bolshevism" was the whole programme of Fascism. A general recognition existed of the fact that some sort of revolution was necessary for Italy. It was no longer possible for men to continue to breathe the old, stagnant, used-up air. But the crux of the problem lay in this: How and in what way should such a revolution be shaped—in accordance with the spirit of the past or in keeping with that of the future? The question was a serious one, for in all Italy the only man with the true temper of a revolutionary, the only man who could possibly be the leader of a revolution, was Mussolini! . . .

Mussolini laid down certain principles, which later were to become the basis of legislation under his rule.

"I do not intend to defend capitalism or capitalists," he wrote. "They, like everything human, have their defects. I only say that their possibilities of usefulness are not yet ended. Society has already assimilated some portion of Socialistic doctrines, which it has been able to adopt without evil results. . . . Capitalism has borne the monstrous burden of war and to-day still has the strength to shoulder the burdens of peace. . . . It is not simply and solely an accumulation of wealth, it is an elaboration, a selection, a co-ordination of values which is the work of centuries. . . .

If Communism has thus been shown to have failed as an ideal, the same bankruptcy has, owing to the war, overtaken the methods of democracy. Foresight and preparedness is an intellectual property which cannot be left to the mercy of mere numbers, but which necessitates a selection of individuals. This involves a contempt for parliamentarianism, for mere talking-machines, for electoral systems which give supremacy simply to numbers—and this contempt, though not new, has now become vastly stronger. Thus, for the first time, on the lips of all we find a growing use of the term "aristocracy." The first Fascists were an appeal to the aristocracy created by the war, one of fighters, of "men from the trenches," a reflection of the warlike superman of Nietzsche. . . .

Men feel the need of a leader, and it is so rare a thing to find one that, when this happens, there is an almost miraculous outburst of joy in the satisfaction of their desire. So Mussolini had not to think of any magic strokes of a wizard's wand when he imposed upon his people self-sacrifice, work, hardness of life and the curb that was needed to avert anarchy.

It is only the proud recognition that a Chief has been found once more, ready to work and to direct for all, that can explain the enthusiasm he evoked at gathering after gatherings, where his mere presence drew the people from all sides to greet him with frenzied acclamations. . . .

The women of the Abruzzi, and especially the widows and mothers of those who had fallen in the war, strove to touch his hand as they would crowd to touch a shrine or a relic. Some would hold up a fatherless child before him, others a war medal. There was not one of them who did not show with her sorrow the pride of sacrifice. . . .

Impulsive and meditative, a realist and an idealist, perfervid and yet wise, a romantic in his aspirations but a classic in his handling of practical affairs, Mussolini has a groundwork of consistency in him underlying all these seeming incompatibilities. This, above all, may be confidently said of him—he is a man of courage. He loves danger. The very idea of cowardice revolts him.

His physical courage has found amusing illustration of late in his treatment of the lioness which was presented to him some time ago and with which he is often to be seen playing in the Zoological Garden. *"Italia, Italia, bella!"* he calls out to it in tones of tender affection, and the splendid young animal comes bounding up to him. . . .

Nothing mean or petty can take root in him. And as he does not go through life haggling about things but pays the full price, he secures the big things, the important things, which are essential to his ambition—. . .

"I must get this people into some kind of order. Then I shall have fulfilled my task. I shall feel then that I am *someone.*"

Another silence. Then he went on:

"And yet—and yet! Yes, I am obsessed by this wild desire—it consumes my whole being. I want to make a mark on my era with my will, like a lion with its claw! A mark like this!"

And, as with a claw, he scratched the covering of a chair-back from end to end!

Source: Margherita G. Sarfatti. *The Life of Benito Mussolini*, pp. 261–264, 336–337, 342, 345. Trans. Frederic Whyte. New York: Frederick A. Stokes, 1926.

Questions

Why did Mussolini reject both Soviet-style communism and Western-style democracy? To what extent might Italian fascism be considered a response to the economic chaos of the post-war period predicted by J. M. Keynes?

In what sense is fascism an "aristocratic" movement?

How does Sarfatti portray Mussolini? What personal attributes does she emphasize in her portrait?

9. IMPORTANT HISTORICAL FACTS: STUDY DRILLS

A. Multiple Choice

1. In 1919, Béla Kun seized power and briefly attempted to establish a Soviet style regime in
   A. Albania.
   B. Bulgaria.
   C. Hungary.
   D. Poland.

2. Connect each of the "Big Four" leaders with the nations they represented at the Paris Peace Conference:
   A. Georges Clemenceau   A. America
   B. David Lloyd George   B. Britain
   C. Vittorio Orlando   C. France
   D. Woodrow Wilson   D. Italy

3. Connect each of the following territories with the empires to which they belonged prior to 1914:
   A. Alsace   A. Austro-Hungarian Empire
   B. Czechoslovakia   B. German Empire
   C. Finland   C. Ottoman Empire
   D. Turkey   D. Russian Empire

4. The new Yugoslavian nation was dominated by
   A. Bulgarians.
   B. Croatians.
   C. Hungarians.
   D. Serbians.

5. In the 1920s, the French Socialist Party was led by a Jewish intellectual who believed that socialism could be achieved through peaceful political action. His name was
   A. Léon Blum.
   B. André Breton.
   C. Georges Clemenceau.
   D. Gabriele D'Annunzio.

6. The Kapp Putsch was
   A. a Communist revolt in Hungary.
   B. a failed right-wing coup d'état in Germany.
   C. an assault on the Weimar Republic led by Adolf Hitler.
   D. one of the Italian "red leagues."

7. James Joyce's *Ulysses* was written in a style known as
   A. corporatism.
   B. dadaism.
   C. futurism.
   D. stream of consciousness.

8. The "Duce" of the Italian fascist movement was
   A. Gabriele D'Annunzio.
   B. Béla Kun.
   C. Benito Mussolini.
   D. Victor Emmanuel III.

9. Mussolini signed the Lateran Pacts of 1929 because
   A. he was a devout Catholic.
   B. he wished to seize the Vatican and remove the pope from Rome.
   C. he hoped to be granted a divorce from the wife he had married in a civil ceremony.

D. he wished to make peace with the Catholic Church in order to avoid any opposition to his political power in Italy.
10. The German National Socialist Workers' Party was led by
   A. Friedrich Ebert.
   B. Adolf Hitler.
   C. Walter Rathenau.
   D. Gustav Stresemann.

B. Chronological Relationships

1. Identify the date at which each of the following events occurred and arrange them in chronological order.

   German statesman Walter Rathenau signs the Rapallo Treaty, a mutual friendship pact, with the Soviet Union.

   Parliament establishes the Irish Free State, a Dominion within the British Commonwealth.

   Mussolini and the Catholic Church sign the Lateran Pacts, recognizing the territorial independence of the Vatican.

   French and Belgian troops occupy the Ruhr in retaliation for German failure to make reparations payments.

   The New York Stock Market crashes.

   A right-wing "putsch," led by Wolfgang Kapp, fails to overthrow the new Weimar Republic.

   King Zog establishes a dictatorial regime in Albania.

   The Locarno Treaty is signed, creating a mood of increasing international cooperation.

   In response to reduced wages and lengthened workdays, British miners go on strike.

   Hitler's attack on the Weimar Republic—the Beer Hall Putsch—fails, and he is sentenced to five years in prison.

2. What is the historical significance of each of the events listed above?

C. Fill in the Blanks

1. The German government established after the abdication of Emperor William II was known as the _____.

2. A pet project of Woodrow Wilson's, the _____ was intended to arbitrate international disputes and guarantee collective security.

3. Article 231 of the Versailles Treaty, also known as the _____, stated that Germany was responsible for the "loss and damage" caused to the Allies by the Great War.

4. In the _____, colonies formerly belonging to Germany were placed under League of Nations control, but were actually administered by Allied powers.

5. _____, known as _____, led Turkish nationalists to victory against foreign occupiers of the Anatolian peninsula.

6. After the war, some businessmen and state officials rejected laissez-faire economic principles in favor of _____, believing that social and political tensions might be reduced by close cooperation between state, business, and labor.

7. A national government that provided its citizens with unemployment insurance, old age pensions, subsidized housing, etc., is known as a _____.

8. Modernist writer Gertrude Stein called the survivors of the Great War a _____.

9. The political organization created by Benito Mussolini was known as the _____.

10. The German Nazi Party was led by _____, who was known as the _____ or "leader" of this organization.

IMPORTANT HISTORICAL FACTS: STUDY-DRILL ANSWERS

A. Multiple Choice
1. C. Hungary.
2. A. Georges Clemenceau—C. France
   B. David Lloyd George—B. Britain
   C. Vittorio Orlando—D. Italy
   D. Woodrow Wilson—A. America
3. A. Alsace—B. German Empire
   B. Czechoslovakia—A. Austro-Hungarian Empire
   C. Finland—D. Russian Empire
   D. Turkey—C. Ottoman Empire
4. D. Serbians.
5. A. Léon Blum.
6. B. a failed right-wing coup d'état in Germany.
7. D. stream of consciousness.
8. C. Benito Mussolini.
9. D. he wished to make peace with the Catholic Church in order to avoid any opposition to his political power in Italy.
10. B. Adolf Hitler.

B. Chronological Relationships
1919 A right-wing "putsch," led by Wolfgang Kapp, fails to overthrow the new Weimar Republic.

1922 Parliament establishes the Irish Free State, a Dominion within the British Commonwealth.

1922 German statesman Walter Rathenau signs the Rapallo Treaty, a mutual friendship pact, with the Soviet Union.

1923 French and Belgian troops occupy the Ruhr in retaliation for German failure to make reparations payments.

1923 Hitler's attack on the Weimar Republic—the Beer Hall Putsch—fails, and he is sentenced to five years in prison.

1925 The Locarno Treaty is signed, creating a mood of increasing international cooperation.

1926 In response to reduced wages and lengthened workdays, British miners go on strike.

1928 King Zog establishes a dictatorial regime in Albania.

1929 Mussolini and the Catholic Church sign the Lateran Pacts, recognizing the territorial independence of the Vatican.

1929 The New York Stock Market crashes.

C. Fill in the Blanks
1. Weimar Republic
2. League of Nations
3. War Guilt Clause
4. Mandate system
5. Mustafa Kemal Pasha; Atatürk
6. corporatism
7. welfare state
8. lost generation
9. Italian National Fascist Party
10. Adolf Hitler; Führer

27

The Europe of Depression and Dictatorship

1. CHAPTER OUTLINE

I. ECONOMIES IN CRISIS: In the 1930s, a global depression undermined political stability. Many Europeans sought scapegoats to blame for hard times.

  A. THE GREAT DEPRESSION: Industrial and agricultural overproduction, tariff barriers, financial speculation, and the economic interdependence created by wartime loans and post-war debts all worked to depress and destabilize the international economy.

  B. GRADUAL EUROPEAN ECONOMIC REVIVAL began in the early to mid-1930s as consumer spending slowly increased and governments experimented with non-traditional fiscal policies. However, the lingering hardships of the Depression era served as a crucial support for the rise of fascism during this decade.

II. FASCIST MOVEMENTS flourished in the 1930s, especially in Italy, Germany, and Eastern Europe. Distinct from right-wing authoritarianism, totalitarianism of the right and the left was typified by single-party dictatorship.

  A. THE DYNAMICS OF FASCISM: Economic frustration, fear of socialism, aggressive nationalism (and racism), anti-parliamentarianism, and a widespread desire for order—

combined with the trauma of the Great War experience—all contributed to the popularity of fascism throughout much of Europe.

  B. FASCISM IN MUSSOLINI'S ITALY: Mussolini strove to make Italy economically independent, to build the nation's military power, and to control the private lives of Italian citizens. Despite the weaknesses of Mussolini's "corporative state," most Italians continued to support (or at least acquiesce to) the Duce's fascist regime.

  C. FASCIST MOVEMENTS IN EASTERN EUROPE: In the agrarian east, right-wing demagogues came to power with the support of impoverished and often illiterate peasants. With the exception of Czechoslovakia, all of the Eastern European states fell under the control of right-wing dictators during the 1930s.

  D. FASCISM IN AUSTRIA: The German Nazi Party provided an attractive political model for conservative Austrians who feared the militancy of socialist workers.

  E. THE POPULAR FRONT IN FRANCE AGAINST THE FAR RIGHT: In the face of threats from right-wing and fascist organizations, French Radicals, Socialists, and Communists rallied to a "Popular Front" government in

315

1936. However, workers' strikes, economic difficulties, and continued opposition from conservatives and business caused the Popular Front to collapse in 1937.

F. FASCISM IN BELGIUM: The Rex movement attracted a small following, but most Belgians remained committed to parliamentary government.

III. NATIONAL SOCIALISM IN GERMANY: Taking power in 1933, Adolf Hitler moved to destroy all resistance to his regime and to rebuild Germany's military might.

A. THE COLLAPSE OF THE WEIMAR REPUBLIC: The Depression had eroded the centrist coalition governing Germany, increasing the power of extreme parties on the right and left. Members of the ruling elite convinced President Hindenburg to appoint Hitler chancellor, believing that the Nazi Party could be of use in their attempt to replace the Weimar government with a more traditionally authoritarian regime.

B. NAZI TOTALITARIANISM: Once in power, Hitler crushed all potential sources of opposition to his regime. He controlled the Nazi hierarchy by encouraging competition between the different branches of the party, enhancing his own personal power, but also hindering the realization of his economic goals. Nazi organizations soon infiltrated every sector of life, governing the economy, family relations, education, and culture.

C. HITLER'S NEW REICH AND THE JEWS: Hitler's virulent anti-Semitism found expression in the Nuremberg Laws, which deprived German Jews of their rights as citizens.

D. HITLER'S FOREIGN POLICY: Germany's military weakness forced Hitler to use caution in his dealings with the other European powers, but he made it clear that Germany had definitively rejected the terms of the Treaty of Versailles.

He began to rearm Germany in preparation for the conquest of "living space" in Eastern Europe.

E. HITLER AND MUSSOLINI recognized one another as natural allies, despite outstanding territorial conflicts between their nations. In the face of weak protest and ineffective action on the part of the British and the French, Hitler undermined Austrian independence and encouraged Mussolini in his assault on Ethiopia.

F. REMILITARIZATION AND REARMAMENT: In 1936 Hitler remilitarized the Rhineland and stepped up German preparations for war.

IV. THE SPANISH CIVIL WAR made Spain—still a backward, largely agricultural nation—the testing ground for new military weapons and modern techniques of warfare.

A. Spain was beset by SOCIAL AND POLITICAL INSTABILITY throughout the 1920s. The left-leaning Second Spanish Republic was established in 1931, but was weakened by divisions within its own ranks and by hostility from the right. In 1936, right-wing nationalist rebels led by General Francisco Franco began a military insurrection against the Republic's "Popular Front" government.

B. THE STRUGGLE BETWEEN LOYALISTS AND NATIONALISTS produced a savage civil war. Italy and Germany supplied the nationalists with weapons and troops, but the British and French failed to come to the aid of the loyalists. In early 1939 Barcelona fell and the nationalists established an authoritarian dictatorship under Franco.

V. THE COMING OF WORLD WAR II: In 1936 Hitler launched an aggressive diplomatic and military campaign of territorial conquest. France and Britain abandoned the policy of appeasement, and a new global war erupted.

A. THE AXIS: Having been drawn together by their participation in the Spanish Civil War, Hitler and

Mussolini signed a pact in 1936. Later that year, Japan—which had already seized Manchuria from China—also allied itself with Germany.

B. AGGRESSION AND APPEASEMENT: Hitler then moved rapidly to unite Austria to Germany, and to occupy western Czechoslovakia. Britain and France at first responded by appeasing Hitler, but when he began to move against Poland, they prepared for war.

C. THE UNHOLY ALLIANCE: To the shock of Britain and France, Hitler and Stalin announced the signing of a joint non-aggression pact in August 1939. One week later German troops invaded Poland and World War II began.

VI. CONCLUSION

2. HISTORICAL GEOGRAPHY

MAP 27.1   DEMOCRACIES AND DICTATORSHIPS

MAP 27.2   THE SPANISH CIVIL WAR

Map Exercises

Familiarize yourself with the maps provided in your text, and then attempt to locate the following places on Blank Maps 27.1 and 27.2.

DEMOCRACIES AND DICTATORSHIPS

Albania	Italy
Austria	Netherlands
Belgium	Poland
Bulgaria	Portugal
Czechoslovakia	Romania
France	Spain
Germany	Switzerland
Great Britain	Turkey
Greece	U.S.S.R.
Hungary	Yugoslavia

SPANISH CIVIL WAR

Barcelona	Madrid
Basque Country	Navarre
Catalonia	New Castile
Galicia	Old Castile
Gibraltar	Spanish Morocco
Guernica	

Map Questions

Which of the countries listed above remained democracies during the 1930s? Which fell under dictatorial regimes?

Summarize the movements of nationalist troops during the Spanish Civil War with reference to text Map 27.2 (p. 1225).

Which European territories had Germany captured (or reclaimed) by the end of 1939? (See text Map 27.3, p. 1233, for details.) How did Hitler justify these annexations?

3. PEOPLE AND TERMS TO IDENTIFY

Great Depression
American Stock Market
   Crash of 1929
British Union of Fascists
John Maynard Keynes
Fascism
National Community
Corporative State
Ustaša (Insurrection) Party
French Popular Front
Matignon Agreements
Rex

Franz von Papen
Stormtroopers
   (*Stürmabteilungen* or S.A.)
Hermann Göring
Night of the Long Knives
Hitler Youth/League of
   German Girls
Exhibition of Degenerate
   Art
Nuremberg Laws
Lebensraum ("Living
   Space")

Italian Invasion of Ethiopia
Stresa Front
Spanish Civil War
Second Spanish Republic
General Francisco Franco
Loyalists vs. Nationalists
The Axis
Manchukuo
Anschluss
Appeasement
Molotov-Ribbentrop Pact

4. STUDY QUESTIONS

1. *Historical Continuities:* What were the long-term causes of the Great Depression?

2. How did Western governments respond to the Depression? Why was this approach criticized by economist John Maynard Keynes?

3. What is fascism? How does it differ from traditional right-wing authoritarianism?

4. How did Mussolini use corporatism to increase the power of his fascist state?

5. *Historical Continuities:* Why were Eastern European nations so susceptible to fascism in the 1930s?

6. Why was there no fascist takeover in France?

7. How did Hitler come to power in Germany? *Historical Continuities:* What long-term factors in German political culture made dictatorship appear to be a desirable alternative to parliamentary democracy?

8. Once he was in power, how did Hitler consolidate Nazi control over the German people?

9. How were German Jews initially affected by Hitler's rise to power?

10. To what extent did Hitler's and Mussolini's plans for territorial expansion make them natural allies?

11. What caused the Spanish Civil War? What was its international significance?

12. Why did Hitler ally Germany with Italy, Japan, and the Soviet Union?

13. Why did Britain and France "appease" Hitler?

14. What caused World War II?

5. ANALYZING ART AND ARTIFACTS

What historical event is commemorated in Pablo Picasso's *Guernica* (p. 1226)? What message did Picasso intend to convey with this painting? Is the painting's non-traditional style effective in conveying this message?

6. TECHNOLOGY AND HISTORY

What new weapons and tactics were tested in Spain by Italy and Germany during the Spanish Civil War? On the basis of these military innovations, what sort of warfare might one expect to encounter in the case of a new outbreak of global conflict?

7. HISTORICAL ANALYSIS: INTERPRETIVE ESSAYS

1. *Historical Continuities:* Compare and contrast the origins of World War I with the origins of World War II.

2. What impact did the Depression have on Europe in the 1930s?

3. Imagine you are an Eastern European emulator of Hitler and Mussolini and you have just seized power from a weak parliamentary government.

Describe the regime you would create for your new fascist state.

4. Imagine you are an American veteran of the Spanish Civil War. Explain your reasons for having joined the Lincoln Brigade and describe your experience fighting anti-loyalist troops.

5. Write a defense of the appeasement policy.

8. HISTORICAL VOICES: THE TRAUMA OF THE DEPRESSION AND THE APPEAL OF FASCISM

A. Little Man, What Now?: The Crisis of Masculine Identity in the Inter-war Years

World War I was psychologically as well as physically devastating for the soldiers who fought in it, and especially for German combatants, who had made great sacrifices only to end up on the losing side. Their manhood battered by defeat in the military arena, German veterans returned to civilian society to find that men no longer enjoyed exclusive mastery in the political arena: After the establishment of the Weimar Republic in 1918, German women were granted the right to both vote and hold political office. Finally, with the economic hardship of the Depression years, many men found themselves incapable of living up to the expectation that a "real" man would be the sole breadwinner in his family. In response to economic disaster, established patterns of male and female behavior changed—often dramatically—but cultural stereotypes of masculinity and femininity did not always follow suit.

In 1932, the German author Hans Fallada (pseudonym of Rudolf Ditzen; 1893–1947) published *Little Man, What Now?*, a novel that deals forthrightly with the subject of male feelings of inadequacy in the face of unemployment. Based on Fallada's own very troubled life experiences, it consists of a sympathetic and realistic portrait of a "little man," an ordinary lower-middle-class German struggling to provide for his wife and infant son in the hard years of the late 1920s and early 1930s. Fallada describes the lives of Johannes and "Bunny" Pinneberg in a straightforward, sometimes comic manner. Yet, despite the deadpan simplicity of the narrative, the novel conveys the anxiety of a man desperately struggling to hold on to his job and to support his family, and the psychological trauma that results from his almost inevitable failure.

The political instability of the Weimar years provides the social and historical backdrop for the novel. While Pinneberg himself reacts to each new disaster with fatalistic resignation, other characters actively work to change their conditions. Lauterbach, Pinneberg's thuggish colleague, joins the Nazi Party; Karl, Bunny Pinneberg's brother, joins the Communist Party; while Heilbutt, Pinneberg's helpful friend, simply bucks the system, becoming a successful pornographer after losing his job at a men's clothing store.

By the end of the story, Pinneberg is out of work and on the dole. His wife supplements the family's meager unemployment benefits by going out to mend other people's clothes, and Pinneberg is reduced to playing the role of "Man as Woman": while Bunny works, Johannes cooks, cleans, and changes diapers. One day, as he walks through Berlin after having been to the Labor Exchange to pick up his unemployment check, he is brutally forced to acknowledge that he has become a social outcast.

FROM *Little Man, What Now?* **by Hans Fallada**

Pinneberg put the baby on the floor, gave him a paper to look at, and prepared to clear up the room. It was a very large newspaper for such a small child, and it lasted quite a while, until the baby had spread it all over the floor. The room was very small, only nine feet by nine. It contained a bed, two chairs, a table, and the dressing-table.

The baby had discovered the pictures on the inner pages of the paper and was chuckling with delight. "Yes," said Pinneberg encouragingly. "Those are pictures, baby." Whatever the baby took for a man, he called "Da-Da," and the women were all "Ma-Ma." He was delighted because there were so many people in the paper.

Pinneberg hung the mattresses out of the window to air, tidied the room and went into the kitchen. This was just a strip cut off the other room, nine feet long, and four and a half feet wide, the stove was about the smallest ever made, with only one oven. It was Bunny's greatest affliction. Here too Pinneberg tidied and washed up and swept the floor, all of which he was happy to do. But his next occupation he did not enjoy at all; he set himself to peel potatoes and scrape carrots for dinner.

. . . He just wanted to tell some human being what his life had once been, the smart suits he had had, and talk about—

He had entirely forgotten the boy's butter and bananas, it was now nine o'clock and all the shops would be shut! Pinneberg was furious with himself, and even more sorry than angry; he could not go home empty-handed, what would Bunny think of him? Perhaps he could get something at the side-door of a shop. There was a great grocer's shop, radiantly illuminated. Pinneberg flattened his nose against the window. Perhaps there was still someone about. He must get that butter and bananas!

A voice behind him said in a low tone: "Move on please!"

Pinneberg started—he was really quite frightened. A policeman stood beside him.

Was the man speaking to him?

"Move on there, do you hear?" said the policeman, loudly now.

There were other people standing at the shop-window, well-dressed people, but to them the policeman had undoubtedly not addressed himself. He meant Pinneberg.

"What? But why—? Can't I—?"

He stammered; he simply did not understand.

"Are you going?" asked the policeman. "Or shall I—?"

The loop of his rubber club was slipped round his wrist, and he raised the weapon slightly.

Everyone stared at Pinneberg. Some passers-by had stopped, a little crowd began to collect. The people looked on expectantly, they took no sides in the matter; on the previous day shop-windows had been broken on the Friedrich and the Leipziger.

The policeman had dark eyebrows, bright resolute eyes, a straight nose, red cheeks, and an energetic moustache.

"Well?" said the policeman calmly.

Pinneberg tried to speak; Pinneberg looked at the policeman; his lips quivered, and he looked at the bystanders. A little group was standing round the window, well-dressed people, respectable people, people who earned money.

But in the mirror of the window still stood a lone figure, a pale phantom, collarless, clad in a shabby ulster and tar-smeared trousers.

Suddenly Pinneberg understood everything; in the presence of this policeman, these respectable persons, this gleaming window, he understood that he was outside it all, that he no longer belonged here and that he was rightly chased away; he had slipped into the abyss, and was engulfed. Order and cleanliness; they were of the past. So too were work and safe subsistence. And past too were progress and hope. Poverty was not merely misery, poverty was an offence, poverty was evil, poverty meant that a man was suspect.

"Do you want one on the bean?" asked the policeman.

Pinneberg obeyed; he was aware of nothing but a longing to hurry to the Friedrichstrasse station and catch his train and get back to Bunny.

Source: Hans Fallada. *Little Man, What Now?*, pp. 345, 368–370. Trans. Eric Sutton. New York: Simon & Schuster, 1933.

Questions

How do you think contemporary readers would have responded to Fallada's description of Johannes Pinneberg's housekeeping and child-care activities?

Based on this reading, what sort of psychological impact do you think unemployment had on ordinary European men? On their female counterparts?

Imagine that, after having picked up his unemployment check, Pinneberg leaves the Labor Exchange and is handed two political pamphlets. One is entitled: "Out of Work? Join the Communist Party!"; the other: "Out of Work? Join the Nazi Party!" What do these pamphlets say?

B. "Hard as Steel": The Reaffirmation of Masculine Identity in Nazi Theory

To men who felt humiliated by Germany's military defeat and by their own inability to earn a living wage for themselves and their families, Adolf Hitler's National Socialist German Worker's Party offered a new source of optimism and self-confidence. Under his leadership, Hitler proclaimed, the former-soldier and the unemployed worker—so long as they were of "pure" Aryan descent—would be able to join forces and reassert German superiority, triumphing over the threatening forces of Bolshevism and international Jewish finance. A revitalized economy and new military triumphs—especially the conquest of "living space" in the east—would provide jobs for German men and restore their honor.

Hitler, a veteran himself, absolved the World War I soldier of any responsibility for the "collapse" of Germany at the end of the war. The military defeat, Hitler argued, was merely a symptom of the diseased condition of German society in general. This "softening up" of the German people was the result of a wide range of factors, including the decline of the German peasantry, the rise of monopoly capitalism and the "internationalization" of the German economy, the flabby parliamentarianism of the despised Weimar regime, the corrupting influence of the mass media and degenerate modern art, the spread of syphilis and tuberculosis, and the "desecration of the race" through Germans' interbreeding with non-Aryans. And at the root of all of these problems, as Hitler saw it, lay the diabolical machinations of an international Jewish conspiracy designed to destroy the "national principle" binding the German people together as a "master race."

Hitler presented his solution to the Depression-era crisis of masculinity in his discussion of the education of Aryan youth included in *Mein Kampf* (1925). In opposition to effeminacy and racial degeneration, Hitler promoted the militarization of society and racial "hygiene." The leadership of Germany, he insisted, must be in the hands of those men "in whom spirit and body had acquired those military virtues which can perhaps best be described as follows: swift as greyhounds, tough as leather, and hard as Krupp steel" (*Mein Kampf*, p. 356). In addition, eugenics programs must be put in place to ensure that racial purity would be preserved and that only physically and morally healthy Germans would reproduce. Attacking feeble "Jewish" intellectualism, Hitler called on young German men to harden their bodies as well as their minds. Young women, who receive far less attention in Hitler's plans for the "Third Reich," were called upon to resist the seductions of "bow-legged repulsive Jewish bastards" and marry only purebred Aryans, in the interest of producing a racially pure generation of soldiers for the fatherland.

FROM *Mein Kampf* by Adolf Hitler

. . . If today, even in the curriculum of the secondary schools, gymnastics gets barely two hours a week and participation in it is not even obligatory, but is left open to the individual, that is a gross incongruity compared to the purely mental training. Not a day should go by in which the young man does not receive one hour's physical training in the morning and one in the afternoon, covering every type of sport and gymnastics. And here one sport in particular must not be forgotten, which in the eyes of many "folkish" minded people is considered vulgar and undignified: boxing. It is incredible what false opinions are widespread in "educated" circles. It is regarded as natural and honorable that a young man should learn to fence and proceed to fight duels right and left, but if he boxes, it is supposed to be vulgar! Why? There is no sport that so much as this one promotes the spirit of attack, demands lightning decisions, and trains the body in steel dexterity. It is no more vulgar for two young men to fight out a difference of opinion with their fists than with a piece of whetted iron. It is not less noble if a man who has been attacked defends himself against his assailant with his fists, instead of running away and yelling for a policeman. But above all, the young, healthy body must also learn to suffer blows. Of course this may seem wild to the eyes of our present spiritual fighters. But it is not the function of the folkish state to breed a colony of peaceful aesthetes and physical degenerates. Not in the respectable shopkeeper or virtuous old maid does it see its ideal of humanity, but in the defiant embodiment of manly strength and in women who are able to bring men into the world.

And so sport does not exist only to make the individual strong, agile and bold; it should also toughen him and teach him to bear hardships.

If our entire intellectual upper crust had not been brought up so exclusively on upper-class etiquette; if instead they had learned boxing thoroughly, a German revolution of pimps, deserters, and such-like rabble would never have been possible; for what gave this revolution success was not the bold, courageous energy of the revolutionaries, but the cowardly, wretched indecision of those who led the state and were responsible for it. The fact is that our whole intellectual leadership had received only "intellectual" education and hence could not help but be defenseless the moment not intellectual weapons but the crowbar went into action on the opposing side. All this was possible only because as a matter of principle especially our higher educational system did not train men, but officials, engineers, technicians, chemists, jurists, journalists, and to keep these intellectuals from dying out, professors. . . .

Particularly our German people which today lies broken and defenseless, exposed to the kicks of all the world, needs that suggestive force that lies in self-confidence. This self-confidence must be inculcated in the young national comrade from childhood on. His whole education and training must be so ordered as to give him the conviction that he is absolutely superior to others. Through his physical strength and dexterity, he must recover his faith in the invincibility of his whole people. For what formerly led the German army to victory was the sum of the confidence which each individual had in himself and all together in their leadership. What will raise the German people up again is confidence in the possibility of regaining its freedom. And this conviction can only be the final product of the same feeling in millions of individuals. . . .

Analogous to the education of the boy, the folkish state can conduct the education of the girl from the same viewpoint. There, too, the chief emphasis must be laid on physical training, and only subsequently on the promotion of spiritual and finally intellectual values. The goal of female education must invariably be the future mother.

Source: Adolf Hitler. *Mein Kampf*, pp. 409–412, 414. Trans. Ralph Mannheim. Boston: Houghton Mifflin, 1971.

Questions

Mussolini once described boxing as "an essentially fascist method of self-expression." Why do you think that both he and Hitler championed this sport?

What sort of men and women is Nazi education designed to produce?

Why might a man like Johannes Pinneberg have been attracted to Nazism?

9. IMPORTANT HISTORICAL FACTS: STUDY DRILLS

A. Multiple Choice

1. This maverick economist argued that Europe would recover from the Depression more rapidly if governments *increased* their expenditures:
   A. Herbert Hoover
   B. John Maynard Keynes
   C. Ramsey MacDonald
   D. Oswald Mosley

2. The *Ustaša* (Insurrection) Party agitated for
   A. a right-wing dictatorship in Belgium.
   B. Austrian unification with Germany.
   C. a Soviet-style revolution in Hungary.
   D. an independent Croatian state.

3. The Matignon Agreements of 1936 guaranteed
   A. the western border of Poland.
   B. the territorial integrity of Austria.
   C. a forty-hour workweek, pay raises, and paid vacations for French workers.

   D. German payment of reparations to France and Britain.

4. As vice-chancellor of Germany in 1933, he convinced President Hindenburg to appoint Hitler chancellor:
   A. Martin Heidegger
   B. Franz von Papen
   C. Arnold Schoenberg
   D. Fritz Thyssen

5. In their campaign against "degenerate" art, the Nazis condemned all of the following *except*
   A. Walter Gropius' Bauhaus style of architecture.
   B. expressionist and dadaist painting.
   C. the music of Gustav Mahler.
   D. the music of Richard Wagner.

6. When Hitler called for *Lebensraum* ("Living Space") for Germany, he was demanding
   A. agricultural land in Eastern Europe.
   B. colonies in Asia and Africa.

C. better housing for German workers.

D. industrial resources in Western Europe.

7. In 1935, Haile Selassie appealed to the League of Nations to do something about the fact that
   A. the Japanese army had invaded Manchuria.
   B. Hitler had remilitarized the Rhineland.
   C. a military insurrection had erupted in Spanish Morocco.
   D. Mussolini had invaded Ethiopia.

8. During the Spanish Civil War, the nationalist troops were led by
   A. General Miguel Primo de Rivera.
   B. General Francisco Franco.
   C. King Alfonso XIII.
   D. "La Pasionaria" Dolores Ibarruri.

9. The statesman most often identified with the policy of appeasement is
   A. Eduard Beneš.
   B. Kurt von Schuschnigg.
   C. Neville Chamberlain.
   D. Winston Churchill.

10. The startling non-aggression agreement signed by Germany and the Soviet Union in August of 1939 was known as
    A. the Molotov-Ribbentrop Pact.
    B. the Stresa Front.
    C. the Axis.
    D. the Anti-Comintern Pact.

B. Chronological Relationships

1. Identify the date at which each of the following events occurred and arrange them in chronological order.
   Italian armies invade Ethiopia.
   Ernst Röhm and the Stormtroopers are "purged" on the Night of the Long Knives.
   Russia and Germany sign the Molotov-Ribbentrop Pact.
   Barcelona falls to nationalist troops led by Franco.
   Hitler and Mussolini sign a pact and the "Axis" is formed.
   The New York Stock Market crashes.
   Manchuria—now known as Manchukuo—becomes a client state of Japan.
   The Second Spanish Republic is founded.

Anschluss: Austria is united with Germany by Hitler.
Jewish homes and businesses are attacked throughout Germany on *Kristallnacht.*

2. What is the historical significance of each of the events listed above?

C. Fill in the Blanks

1. Founded by the vehemently anti-Semitic Oswald Mosley in 1932, the _____ was the focus of considerable international attention but never attracted more than 20,000 members.

2. In their attempt to downplay class divisions within German and Italian society, fascist leaders such as Hitler and Mussolini argued that their compatriots were all members of a _____ with a shared identity that transcended differences in income.

3. In the _____ conceived by Mussolini, workers and employers would meet together to settle their differences, avoiding the extremes of both unchecked capitalism and contentious socialism and communism.

4. Confronted with the possibility of a right-wing overthrow of the Third Republic in 1936, French Radicals, Socialists and Communists united to form the _____.

5. Led by Ernst Röhm, the _____ were known for their brutal support of the Nazi movement in its early years, but were crushed after Hitler took power because he feared that they were alienating Germany's professional army from his regime.

6. A long-time follower of Hitler and minister of the interior in Prussia, _____ organized an auxiliary police force that seconded Hitler in his bid for power in 1933.

7. Enthusiasm for the Nazi regime was instilled in young people through organizations such as the _____, for boys, and the _____.

8. In 1935, German Jews were deprived of their citizenship rights by the _____.

9. During the Spanish Civil War, the Second Spanish Republic was

defended by the _____, whereas the _____ fought to establish an authoritarian dictatorship.
10. Hitler's military takeover of Austria, known as the _____, was accepted by many Europeans as a justifiable revision of the Versailles Settlement.

IMPORTANT HISTORICAL FACTS: STUDY-DRILL ANSWERS

A. Multiple Choice
1. B. John Maynard Keynes
2. D. an independent Croatian state.
3. C. a forty-hour workweek, pay raises, and paid vacations for French workers.
4. B. Franz von Papen
5. D. the music of Richard Wagner.
6. A. agricultural land in Eastern Europe.
7. D. Mussolini had invaded Ethiopia.
8. B. General Francisco Franco.
9. C. Neville Chamberlain.
10. A. The Molotov-Ribbentrop Pact.

B. Chronological Relationships

October 1929	The New York Stock Market crashes.
April 1931	The Second Spanish Republic is founded.
1932	Manchuria—now known as Manchukuo— becomes a client state of Japan.
30 June 1934	Ernst Röhm and the Stormtroopers are "purged" on the Night of the Long Knives.
3 October 1935	Italian armies invade Ethiopia.
October 1936	Hitler and Mussolini sign a pact and the "Axis" is formed.
12 March 1938	*Anschluss:* Austria is united with Germany by Hitler.
9 November 1938	Jewish homes and businesses are attacked throughout Germany on *Kristallnacht.*
January 1939	Barcelona falls to nationalist troops led by Franco.
23 August 1939	Russia and Germany sign the Molotov-Ribbentrop Pact.

C. Fill in the Blanks
1. British Union of Fascists
2. national community
3. corporative state
4. French Popular Front
5. Stormtroopers (*Stürmabteilungen* or S.A.)
6. Hermann Göring
7. Hitler Youth; League of German Girls
8. Nuremberg Laws
9. Loyalists; Nationalists
10. *Anschluss*

28 *World War II*

1. CHAPTER OUTLINE

I. THE WAR IN EUROPE BEGINS: Hitler's attack on Poland was only the first in a series of German assaults on other neighboring European states.
    A. THE GERMAN INVASION OF POLAND: Poland fell to the lightning German onslaught in less than one month. Acting on a secret agreement with Hitler, Stalin sent troops into eastern Poland.
    B. THE "PHONY WAR": Hitler postponed his attack on France until the spring of 1940, but the French and British failed to take advantage of this temporary reprieve.
    C. THE WAR IN THE FROZEN NORTH: In the meantime, Soviet troops defeated Finland, while Germany defeated Denmark and Norway. In Britain, Churchill replaced Chamberlain as prime minister.
    D. THE FALL OF FRANCE: In May 1940, the "phony war" ended when Germany attacked France. The French and British Allied defense quickly collapsed, and France surrendered to Germany in June.
    E. THE BATTLE OF BRITAIN: Under Churchill's leadership, Britain fought on alone, fending off Hitler's Operation Sea Lion with a determined air defense.
II. World War II quickly became A GLOBAL WAR involving all of the world's major powers. At the same time, it also became a "total" war involving civilians as well as military personnel.
    A. TOTAL WAR: The British war effort involved a total mobilization of the nation's resources. With "Lend-Lease" aid from the United States, the British government moved to coordinate all aspects of the military resistance to Germany.
    B. HITLER'S ALLIES included Italy and Japan, as well as Bulgaria, Hungary, and a conquered Romania. Despite Hitler's urgings, Spain refused to enter the war on the German side. Mussolini's independent initiatives brought humiliating defeats for Italy and diverted German troops to Africa.
    C. THE GERMAN INVASION OF RUSSIA, long planned by Hitler, began in June 1941. Having enjoyed some initial successes, "Operation Barbarossa" ultimately failed to break the resistance of the Soviet Union, and Germany suffered devastating military losses.
    D. JAPAN'S ATTACK ON THE UNITED STATES: After a surprise Japanese attack on Pearl Harbor, the United States entered the war on the side of Britain. U. S. military leaders agreed to postpone their assault on Japan, instead giving highest priority to the defeat of Germany in the European theater.
III. HITLER'S EUROPE: German troops occupied much of Europe, extracting raw materials and murdering Jews

and other members of "inferior races."
Some of those living in occupied
territories collaborated with their
conquerors, while others resisted Nazi
rule.

A. THE NAZI "NEW EUROPEAN
ORDER": Sufficiently "Aryan"
states—and allies who followed
Hitler's orders—were allowed
considerable autonomy, but Poles
and Russians were subjected to a
brutal regime of slave labor and
selective extermination. The
resources of all countries subject to
German domination were
systematically plundered.

B. THE "FINAL SOLUTION":
Having conquered much of
Europe, Hitler and his followers
now implemented their racial
theories, slaughtering or working
to death millions of people deemed
unfit to live, including Slavs,
Gypsies, and—especially—Jews.
Extermination camps such as
Auschwitz were built as a "final
solution" to the Jewish "problem."
In some places, governments or
individuals refused to cooperate
with this genocide, but many
Europeans acquiesced in the
Holocaust.

C. Despite fierce repression,
RESISTANCE TO THE NAZIS
developed in some conquered
territories, especially where
geography and low concentrations
of German troops combined to
make armed resistance possible.
Tito led a highly successful
Yugoslav resistance movement,
while the collaborationist Vichy
regime in France was opposed by
de Gaulle's Free French forces.

D. AGAINST HITLER IN GERMANY:
Resistance to Nazism within
Germany was extremely
dangerous, but some highly
motivated activists opposed
Hitler's regime.

IV. THE TIDE TURNS: With the American
entry into the war, and the Red
Army's victory in Russia, German
defeat was all but inevitable. The Big
Three looked ahead to the post-war
settlement, generating tensions
between the Western allies and Stalin.

A. GERMANY ON THE DEFENSIVE:
German women and foreign
laborers were conscripted into
armaments production, but the
German war effort continued to be
hampered by chaotic
administration. German military
commanders banked on starving
the British military by closing
Allied shipping lanes, but the U-
boat campaign failed.

B. THE WAR IN NORTH AFRICA:
Having beaten back Rommel in
North Africa, the Allies decided—
at Churchill's urging and to the
chagrin of Stalin—to launch an
assault on Italy rather than attempt
a massive invasion of France.

C. HITLER'S RUSSIAN DISASTER:
Hard-pressed Leningrad
withstood a long German siege,
and the Red Army defeated
German troops in the crucial battle
of Stalingrad. Allied bombers
devastated German cities, and
Germany was deserted by its allies
in the Balkans (many of whom
then fell under Soviet control).

D. THE ALLIED INVASION OF
ITALY: Having secured North
Africa, the Allies began their attack
on the Italian mainland. Mussolini
was soon removed from power by
King Victor Emmanuel III, but
German troops in central and
northern Italy resisted the Allied
advance, making the Italian
campaign both long and costly.

E. THE BIG THREE: In 1943,
Churchill, Roosevelt, and Stalin
began negotiations on the sensitive
topic of post-war territorial
settlements, but they reached no
firm agreements.

F. THE D-DAY INVASION OF
FRANCE: On June 6, 1944, the
Allies launched Operation
Overlord, establishing a beachhead
on the coast of Normandy. Forced
to retreat, the Germans attempted
a last stand in the Ardennes Forest
but were decisively defeated in the
Battle of the Bulge. Eastward

moving American and British troops eventually met the westward moving Red Army south of Berlin.

V. ALLIED VICTORY: As the war wound down, territorial settlements took priority in Big Three negotiations.

A. VICTORY IN EUROPE: Meeting at Yalta, the Big Three decided the fates of Germany and Poland, and organized the United Nations, a new peace-keeping body intended to replace the League of Nations. After Hitler's suicide, Germany surrendered to the Allies on May 8, 1945.

B. THE DEFEAT OF JAPAN: The American offensive in the Pacific proceeded from island to island in brutal and deadly combat. Having established bases within range of the Japanese mainland by mid-1945, American planes first firebombed Japanese cities and then dropped atomic bombs on Hiroshima and Nagasaki, provoking a Japanese surrender.

VI. CONCLUSION

2. HISTORICAL GEOGRAPHY

Map Exercises

Familiarize yourself with the maps provided in your text, and then attempt to locate the following places on Blank Map 28.1.

HITLER'S EUROPE

Albania	Libya
Algeria	Morocco
Belgium	Netherlands
Bulgaria	Norway
Denmark	Romania
Finland	Serbia
France	Slovakia
Germany	Tunisia
Greece	Ukraine
Italy	Vichy France

BATTLE SITES

Antwerp	Königsberg
Anzio	Kursk
Ardennes Forest	Leningrad
Battle of the Bulge	Minsk
Berlin	Montmédy
Caen	Moscow
Cassino	Normandy
Dieppe	Stalingrad
El Alamein	Vienna
Kiev	Warsaw

Map Questions

Be able to locate countries occupied by or allied with Germany, neutral countries, and Allied powers.

Where were most of the Nazi concentration camps? Why were they concentrated in this part of Europe?

Compare the boundaries of Germany before, during, and after the war.

MAP 28.1 WORLD WAR II IN EUROPE

3. PEOPLE AND TERMS TO IDENTIFY

Blitzkrieg	Operation Barbarossa	Operation Torch
Maginot Line	Japanese attack on Pearl	Battle of Stalingrad
Phony War	Harbor	Anzio
Winston Churchill	Final Solution	Big Three
Operation Sea Lion	Holocaust	Operation Overlord
Total War	Anne Frank	Battle of the Bulge
Lend-Lease Act	Tito (Josip Broz)	Yalta Conference
Tripartite Pact	"Country, Family, Work"	United Nations
General Erwin Rommel	General Charles de Gaulle	Hiroshima

4. STUDY QUESTIONS

1. *Historical Continuities:* How innovative was the German strategy of *Blitzkrieg*? To what extent was it an outgrowth of military problems first encountered during World War I?

2. Why did France lose its battle with Germany? Why did the British survive the German assault?

3. What is "total war"?

4. Why did "Operation Barbarossa" fail?

5. Why did the United States enter World War II in 1941? What impact was this event likely to have on the outcome of the war?

6. *Historical Continuities:* To what extent was the Holocaust a logical outcome of the racialist thinking of the late nineteenth and early twentieth centuries?

7. What made resistance to fascism possible? Why were resistance leaders like Tito and de Gaulle successful?

8. Why did so many Europeans continue to support fascist movements, even during the war?

9. How did Stalin's and Churchill's approaches to Allied strategy in Europe differ? Why?

10. Why were relations between the "Big Three" strained? What specific concerns separated the leaders of the three major Allied powers?

11. How was the Allied "Victory in Europe" achieved?

12. What arrangements were made at the Yalta conference? *Historical Continuities:* On the basis of this agreement, how would the political geography of post-war Europe differ from that of pre-war Europe?

13. How was Japan defeated?

5. ANALYZING ART AND ARTIFACTS

In *On Photography,* the American cultural critic Susan Sontag described her response to photographs of the concentration camps released after World War II. She said:

Nothing I have seen—in photographs or real life—ever cut me as sharply, deeply, instantaneously. . . . When I looked at those photographs, something broke. Some limit had been reached, and not only that of horror; I felt irrevocably grieved, wounded, but a part of my feelings started to tighten; something went dead; something is still crying.

How do you expect Europeans responded to these photographs? What impact do they have on you today?

6. TECHNOLOGY AND HISTORY

Historical Continuities: Compare the trench warfare of World War I with the *Blitzkrieg* of World War II. To what extent were the differences between these two styles of warfare based on technological change? On military strategy?

Two major new technologies—jet airplanes and the atom bomb—came into use at the end of World War II. What impact did they have on the war? What impact do you expect they would have on post-war society? How have they affected your own life?

7. HISTORICAL ANALYSIS: INTERPRETIVE ESSAYS

1. *Historical Continuities:* Write an essay arguing one of the following points:
   - A. World War I was significantly different from World War II.
   - B. World War I and World War II were very similar events.

2. It has often been argued that the Battle of Britain was the crucial battle of World War II. If the outcome had been different—if Britain had been defeated by Germany—how might the subsequent course of the war have differed?

3. What impact did Hitler's racial theories have on the war?

4. Imagine that you are a Yugoslavian fighting with Tito's partisans. Explain what made you decide to join this armed resistance movement.

5. Why did Hitler lose the war?

8. HISTORICAL VOICES: CHILDREN OF WAR

The destruction visited upon the world by World War II was unprecedented in its scale. Not since the Thirty Years' War of the seventeenth century had civilian populations in Europe been so devastated by warfare, and even children were drawn into the maelstrom of "total war." The youngest victims of the war had little understanding of why it was being fought, and were certainly not responsible for its horrors. Nevertheless, they would be marked, both physically and mentally, for the rest of their lives by the experiences they underwent during this period of tremendous upheaval.

For some children, especially those too young to understand the seriousness of the situation, and fortunate enough to be living in regions not overly affected by actual military engagements or severe food shortages, the war sometimes seemed like an entertaining diversion. War interfered with normal school attendance and often slackened family discipline, and it could be excitingly disruptive, a great adventure—just as it is represented in John Boorman's film *Hope and Glory* (1987), a loving reconstruction of the director's childhood experiences during the London blitz. Like Boorman, many English children who lived through the blitz enjoyed "camping out" underground in subway tunnels during air raids, collecting spent cartridges and other military paraphernalia, and watching exploding bombs lighting up the evening sky like fireworks. One woman who had been six in 1940, remembered, years later, her responses to an air raid in which one of her neighbors had died.

FROM *Children of the Blitz* by Robert Westall

There was a tremendous bang, and the shelter lights went out. I expected the shelter to collapse, but nothing hit me. We heard bricks falling, people shouting.

"My God, we're hit," screamed Mother, and immediately got out of the shelter. Then she leant back in, outlined by searchlights.

"Come out," she said. "I don't believe it."

We climbed up the ladder. All the hens were cackling wildly and flapping. Fires in the distance, but everything looked the same as usual. We ran up the back-garden path and through the house. Just then my uncle came in the front door.

"Keep those children in," he shouted. But we all ran past him.

There was a huge hole opposite—two houses down, looking like teeth that needed filling in the semi-dark. Bricks were still falling and a ring of wardens shouting "Keep back, keep back!" to the people who were pouring in, from up and down the street. . . .

After a long time, bombs falling all around, whistles blowing, planes roaring, searchlights picking out planes and barrage balloons overhead, the ambulance came. A stretcher was carried out, the body covered over completely. Then another, but the face showing, covered with blood.

"It's Margaret," everyone whispered. "Then Mrs. Leggatt is dead." . . .

A warden yelled at my mother "Get those kids indoors—there's a bloody raid going on!" . . .

All our downstairs windows were broken, but for some reason, the upstairs ones weren't. The broken glass had got into the yellow chrysanthemums. My mother immediately picked it all out, and they lived for three more weeks. The house was thick with fallen soot. Precious, my doll, had a white Victorian frilled nightie that had to be destroyed, it was so filthy. I *hated* Hitler.

After the bomb site had been tidied up, our gang used to play there and have secret fires. Until one day a woman saw us and said "That's where Mrs Leggatt died. You kids ought to be ashamed." We never went there again to play, but set up a little stone and put flowers on it in summer, and leaves in winter, and holly at Christmas. . . .

On Christmas Eve we all went to the bomb site and sang "Away in a Manger," then

> Whistle while you work
> Hitler is a twerp
> Goering's barmy
> So's his army
> Whistle while you work.

Then we didn't know what to do, so we all went home, and got into trouble for being so dirty.

For Jewish children on the continent, the war was never an adventure. Although some relief organizations made special efforts to smuggle Jewish children out of Europe, the vast majority of young Jews did not escape. And those who were captured and deported to the concentration camps were more likely to be exterminated than able-bodied adults—being too young to work, they were of no use to the Third Reich.

Rachella Velt Meekoms turned twelve on the day the Germans invaded her homeland, the Netherlands. Because she was a Jew, the bicycle she had received as a birthday present was immediately confiscated by the occupying forces. Rachella and her older sister went into hiding when the Germans began to deport Dutch Jews, and the two girls were not apprehended until late in the war. Because they were then old enough—and still healthy enough—to work in a factory when they arrived at Auschwitz, they managed to survive until the end of the war. In 1952, Rachella emigrated to the United States, joining her sister in Portland, Oregon. Rachella insisted that her own children be given a strong grounding in the Jewish tradition and that they learn about their parents' wartime experiences. In the mid-1970s, she agreed to make a tape recording of her story for inclusion in the William E. Wiener Oral History Library. In the following excerpt from this tape, she describes her arrival at Auschwitz.

FROM *Voices from the Holocaust* by Sylvia Rothchild

Just after my sixteenth birthday we were sent off on another transport. We went through the mountains and came to places with Polish names. It was very dark when we came out of the train and when I looked up I saw a red sky with flames shooting up and the air was smoky. I heard the Germans say, "This is the Phillips group," and they marched us five by five through a huge gate. I was the youngest. They brought us into a sauna and then we stood naked for hours and waited for our names to be called. "Your name is now Sarah," they said, and tattooed a number on my arm. It stung but I was so full of anxiety and pain on the inside that I didn't feel pain on the outside. They kept us standing all through the night. They shaved us and gave us a gray prison dress to wear.

We were in barracks with a lot of nationalities, Gypsies and many vicious criminals. There were three levels of bunk beds and the Dutch girls huddled together and tried to give each other strength. The sleeping situation was awful. There were five people in each bunk and when one turned everybody had to turn. The bathroom was very far away and the path was muddy so we slipped and fell and there was no water to wash. When it rained we would catch the drippings from the gutter and wash our hands and face.

Every day was terrifying. I lost about twenty pounds the first two weeks. We were all sick but afraid to go to the hospital barrack because they made selections there. My number was 81793 and my sister's was 81792. We tried always to be called up together because we held each other up. When we were working together on the bricks I would get so weak from carrying the heavy bricks that I would just cry, "Dear God, where the hell are you?" And when I was ready to drop Flora would come and carry the bricks for me. She was always stronger and she would take four and I would take two. One day the overseer beat her for helping me. She kept telling her I was her sister and I was sick but there was no pity there, no pity at all. . . .

Then one day a man came and asked for the Phillips group. He was the manager of the Telefunken factory, and he interviewed us and marched us out of the gate of Auschwitz. . . . I said, "God, if you are there please listen, and keep us safe and save all these people in hell." I prayed very hard. I had cursed God a week before. I couldn't believe there was a God. I was really sick in my mind.

They put us on a train and gave us some food. And we went to work in the factory. A lot of people there came from Berlin. It was the same kind of work we did for Phillips and we were treated as workers during the day. We worked eight hours at a shift but there were breaks for meals and then they would march us back to the camp. I remember the little children on the side of the road spitting at us when we went by. Five-year-olds were already taught to hate Jews.

Like the Jewish children of Europe, the Japanese children of Hiroshima and Nagasaki suffered severe physical and psychological trauma as a result of the war. In recent years, medical studies of Japanese children exposed to atomic radiation have appeared in print, documenting the long-term health consequences of the first deployment of atomic weapons.

James N. Yamazaki, an American citizen of Japanese descent, was in medical school when World War II was declared. Having enlisted in the army, he was called up one week before the Japanese bombing of Pearl Harbor. While he served as a surgeon on the western front, his parents and siblings were interned at Camp Jerome in Arkansas, along with thousands of other Japanese-Americans. Having specialized in pediatric medicine, Yamazaki was asked to work as a researcher for the American Bomb Casualty Commission after the war. In 1949 he traveled to Japan (for the first time in his life) to study the "flash babies" of Nagasaki—children who had been exposed to radiation while still in their mother's womb. Yamazaki's interest in the "children of the atomic bomb" has continued to the present, as demonstrated in his recently published memoirs. On a trip to Hiroshima in 1989, Yamazaki was told the following story by Hiroshima resident Akihiro Takahashi, who was fourteen when the bomb was dropped on his city.

FROM *Children of the Atomic Bomb,* by **James N. Yamazaki**

"The all clear had sounded," he recalled. "But I saw a lone plane in the sky. Suddenly, there was an explosive wind, so powerful that it tore off my clothes. And then I felt intense burning."

When he turned his head, I could see only the nub of one ear. That side of his face, and a third of his body, had been literally seared, for he was scarcely a mile from the hypocenter.

"Skin was draped from my arms and body. The exposed flesh was bleeding. I wondered what had happened. Bewildered, I remembered only the drills we had had. Run for the river."

For ten minutes he could do nothing, see nothing. Clouds of debris, smoke, and ash blinded him, darkened the city. When he could see a few yards, he began to run. But he stopped when he heard, "Help me, help me," from a friend. The other boy was in excruciating pain, his legs and the bottoms of his feet burned by the blast.

"So I helped him and we made our way to the Fukushima Bridge. It was shattered but we managed to crawl across remaining beams. We had to pass many bodies, many crying for help. Everything was on fire. We had to keep moving."

He lived, recovering slowly over the next two years, one of eleven survivors in a classroom of sixty. His friend died two weeks later.

To the friend who died, and the others like him in the schoolyards of the city, each Hiroshima school had erected its own stone memorial along this lovely parkway. . . .

The names of the dead children are etched in the stone. Four thousand, five hundred names. I had to repeat the number to begin to grasp its dimension. Four thousand, five hundred. . . .

Unimaginable figures. A pediatrician inevitably deals with death, but it is the death of a single child, and even then one can see the terrible toll it takes on the family. But here we were speaking of sudden deaths on a scale previously unknown, a disruption of families beyond calculation. Death touched every family in Hiroshima that day.

World War II was indeed a different kind of war. It was different in terms of the immense increase in the power of the weapons used, culminating in the atomic bombs. And it was different in the indiscriminate way these increasingly lethal weapons were used against entire populations, women and children among them.

While the horrific wartime experiences of Jewish and Japanese children are now more or less familiar, the hardships endured by many German children are not as well known. Nazism brought untold suffering to those peoples conquered by the armies of the Third Reich, but it also brought misfortune to Germans themselves.

At the end of World War II, the German army was struggling to stave off the advances of Allied armies in the east and west. In a desperate last-ditch effort to save the Nazi regime from defeat, Hitler called for young boys to "volunteer" for military service. When the German army at last surrendered in May 1945, many thousands of very young soldiers—some no more than fourteen or fifteen years old—were being trained for action, or were already on the battlefield. In a collection of short essays titled "Remaking Germany," published by a British Socialist press at the end of the war, Minna Specht addressed the problem of re-educating these child-soldiers, whom she labelled "Little Fuehrers."

FROM "German Education To-Day and To-Morrow" by Minna Specht

We now come to the problem of the sixteen-year-olds who "volunteered" for combatant service, many of them in the infantry, one of the most dangerous sections of the army. . . . Why did they go? The answer is obvious. They were moved by fanaticism, by an exaggerated sense of their own importance, by the feeling that the Fuehrer depended on them, by the conviction that their entry into the war might turn the tide and destroy the enemy's illusion that Germany was defeated. All this was helped by their lack of experience and of reliable reports on life at the front with all its hardships. And they were sick of gathering firewood and helping with the harvest, of learning nothing and getting no training for their future work. And where this did not work upon them there was always the fear that the whole family would have to pay the penalty if they refused, or that, as Hitler hinted, they would be called up in any case, even if they did not volunteer. . . .

. . . A whole generation of Nazi trainees! Truly, the heaviest burden which the Nazi educational system has bequeathed to us. Yet they have to be brought back into normal life. They have to be made to understand what has happened and, if this can be done, their cooperation in the reconstruction of Germany must be gained. . . .

Even when all these precautions have been taken, when we have made arrangements to keep them occupied, to give them the society of mature people and supervision, there will be some who will slip through the meshes of our system and who will plan and work evil. . . . Juvenile crimes cannot be absolutely prevented, but their scope can be limited. . . . Those who disagree may sacrifice to the fetish of "security" the great opportunity of bringing about a change in these children themselves, a change which would be a better guarantee of peace than any preventive measures. Where the spirit of oppression is nurtured it will flourish and expand. Germany provides sad evidence of the truth of this old saying. Can we then do other than try the new way. . . . Within a framework of ordered and just relations to show our willingness to help and our trust in many of the German youth, and to strive to get their cooperation in this work.

Sources: Robert Westall, ed. *Children of the Blitz: Memories of Wartime Childhood*, pp. 110–112. Harmondsworth, Eng.: Viking, 1985.

Sylvia Rothchild, ed. *Voices from the Holocaust.* pp. 179–180. New York: New American Library, 1981.

Yamazaki, James N., with Louis B. Fleming. *Children of the Atomic Bomb: An American Physician's Memoir of Nagasaki, Hiroshima, and the Marshall Islands,* pp. 140–141. Durham, NC: Duke University Press, 1995.

Specht, Minna. "German Education To-Day and To-Morrow." In *Re-making Germany,* pp. 37–39. London: International Publishing Co., 1945.

Questions

What do these children's experiences tell you about World War II? What impact did the war have on civilian populations? Why were children so exposed to the hardships of this particular war?

How did Rachella Velt Meekoms survive her internment at Auschwitz? What does her testimony tell you about the concentration camp experience?

Is James Yamazaki right when he says that World War II was "a different kind of war"? What does he mean by this?

Why would the re-education of the "Little Fuehrers" described by Minna Specht have been considered a serious issue in the post-war period?

9. IMPORTANT HISTORICAL FACTS: STUDY DRILLS

A. Multiple Choice

1. Hitler's *Blitzkrieg* strategy relied on
   A. unrestricted submarine warfare.
   B. V1 and V2 rocket attacks.
   C. unrelenting broadcasts of radio propaganda in occupied territories.
   D. a rapid, coordinated assault by tanks supported by aircraft.

2. After World War I, the French built a network of fortifications from Switzerland to the Belgian border. This supposedly impregnable defensive system was known as
   A. the Maginot Line.
   B. the Siegfried Line.
   C. the Ardennes.
   D. the French Sphere of Influence.

3. By the terms of the Lend-Lease Act of 1941, the U. S. Congress agreed to
   A. enter the war on the side of Britain in exchange for that nation's payment of its World War I debts.
   B. lend materiel and food to all European nations in exchange for the promise of repayment after the war.
   C. lend materiel and food to Britain in exchange for naval bases.
   D. forbid the lending or leasing of any American assets to European powers that had defaulted on their World War I loans.

4. Signed in September 1940, this agreement created a formal alliance between Germany, Italy, and Japan and was known as
   A. the Pact of Steel.
   B. the Atlantic Charter.
   C. the Big Three.
   D. the Tripartite Pact.

5. Known as the "Desert Fox," this German general directed a highly successful campaign in North Africa until his defeat by General Bernard Montgomery:
   A. Heinrich Himmler
   B. Erwin Rommel
   C. Albert Speer
   D. Klaus von Stauffenberg

6. In Yugoslavia, the highly successful armed resistance movement was led by a Communist "partisan" who went by the code name of
   A. Anzio.
   B. Barbarossa.
   C. Maquis.
   D. Tito.

7. The motto of France's collaborationist Vichy regime was
   A. "liberty, equality, fraternity."
   B. "remember Pearl Harbor."
   C. "country, family, work."
   D. "wage war, by sea, land, and air."

8. The "Big Three" consisted of
   A. Himmler, Ribbentrop, and Göring.
   B. Churchill, Roosevelt, and Stalin.
   C. De Gaulle, Montgomery, and Eisenhower.
   D. Churchill, Pétain, and Stalin.

9. At Yalta, the Big Three agreed to
   A. invade Italy.
   B. divide Germany into four zones of military occupation.
   C. drop an atomic bomb on Hiroshima.
   D. initiate the D-Day invasion of Normandy.
10. The United Nations was created as a replacement for
   A. the League of Nations.
   B. the Tripartite Pact.
   C. the Communist International.
   D. the New European Order.

B. Chronological Relationships
1. Identify the date at which each of the following events occurred and arrange them in chronological order.
   The "Big Three" meet at Yalta.
   The Battle of Stalingrad ends with the surrender of German troops.
   Japan attacks Pearl Harbor and the United States enters the war.
   The Battle of Britain begins.
   Winston Churchill becomes prime minister of Britain.
   The U. S. drops an atom bomb on Hiroshima.
   Germany invades Poland, starting World War II.
   The U. S. Congress passes the Lend-Lease Act.
   The D-Day invasion of Normandy.
   Germany attacks France and the "phony war" ends.
2. List the military engagements in Exercise C in chronological order.

C. Matching Exercise: Important Military Engagements
_____ Anzio
_____ Battle of the Bulge
_____ Battle of the Coral Sea
_____ Battle of Stalingrad
_____ Operation Barbarossa
_____ Operation Overlord
_____ Operation Sea Lion
_____ Operation Torch
_____ Pearl Harbor
_____ Phony War

A. On D-Day (June 6, 1944), British and American troops established beachheads along the coast of Normandy as the successful first step of the Allied invasion of France.
B. Expecting little opposition from the Russians, Hitler began his invasion of the Soviet Union on June 22, 1941, greatly surprising Stalin.
C. American victory in this 1942 naval encounter with Japan protected Australia from possible invasion.
D. Having decided to clear all German and Italian troops from North Africa prior to an invasion of France from Britain, the Allies began by landing troops in French Algeria and Morocco in November 1942.
E. In the winter of 1942–1943, the Red Army made a successful stand against the Germans at an important industrial city on the Volga River. This Soviet victory proved to be a crucial turning point of the war—and allowed the Russian military to end the long siege of Leningrad.
F. Following Hitler's attack on Poland in September 1939, the French and British sat out the winter, anxiously awaiting the German invasion of Western Europe.
G. On December 7, 1941—"a day that will live in infamy"—Japanese aircraft launched a surprise attack on an American base in Hawaii, provoking the United States to declare war on Japan.
H. As the first stage of a planned invasion of Britain, the German Luftwaffe attempted to establish control of the skies over the British Isles between July and October 1940, but it failed to overcome determined resistance from the Royal Air Force.
I. During the long Allied campaign against German troops in Italy, two Allied divisions were landed in German-controlled territory near Rome in January 1944. Unable to break out of their position, they remained trapped—and suffered terrible losses—until later that spring.
J. Having retreated into northeastern France in late 1944, the German military launched a massive counterattack against the Allies from the Ardennes but was soon forced back.

IMPORTANT HISTORICAL FACTS: STUDY-DRILL ANSWERS

A. Multiple Choice
1. D. a rapid, coordinated assault by tanks supported by aircraft.
2. A. the Maginot Line.
3. C. lend materiel and food to Britain in exchange for naval bases.
4. D. the Tripartite Pact.
5. B. Erwin Rommel
6. D. Tito.
7. C. "country, family, work."
8. B. Churchill, Roosevelt, and Stalin.
9. B. divide Germany into four zones of military occupation.
10. A. the League of Nations.

B. Chronological Relationships

1.
September 1, 1939	Germany invades Poland, starting World War II.
May 10, 1940	Winston Churchill becomes prime minister of Britain.
May 10, 1940	Germany attacks France and the "phony war" ends.
July 31, 1940	The Battle of Britain begins.
March 1941	The U. S. Congress passes the Lend-Lease Act.
December 7, 1941	Japan attacks Pearl Harbor and the U. S. enters the war.
February 2, 1943	The Battle of Stalingrad ends with the surrender of German troops.
June 6, 1944	The D-Day invasion of Normandy.
February 1945	The "Big Three" meet at Yalta.
August 6, 1945	The U. S. drops an atom bomb on Hiroshima.

2.
Winter 1939/1940	Phony War
July/October 1940	Operation Sea Lion
June 22, 1941	Operation Barbarossa
December 7, 1941	Pearl Harbor
May 1942	Battle of the Coral Sea
November 1942	Operation Torch
Winter 1942/1943	Battle of Stalingrad
January 1944	Anzio
June 6, 1944	Operation Overlord
December 1944	Battle of the Bulge

C. Matching Exercise: Important Military Engagements
I. Anzio
J. Battle of the Bulge
C. Battle of the Coral Sea
E. Battle of Stalingrad
B. Operation Barbarossa
A. Operation Overlord
H. Operation Sea Lion
D. Operation Torch
G. Pearl Harbor
F. Phony War

29 *Rebuilding Divided Europe*

1. CHAPTER OUTLINE

I. EUROPE AT THE END OF THE WAR: World War II had devastated Europe, killing tens of millions and destroying or damaging vast amounts of property.
   A. THE POTSDAM SETTLEMENT created a divided Europe. An "iron curtain" fell between Western European and Soviet-dominated Eastern Europe. As the Cold War took shape, atomic weapons added a new element of danger to superpower rivalries.
   B. THE UNITED NATIONS AND COLD WAR ALLIANCES: Limited in its powers, the United Nations nevertheless provided an arena for the peaceable mediation of Cold War disputes. However, the European states also formed defensive military alliances—NATO in the West and the Warsaw Pact in the East—as additional guarantees of security.
   C. ECONOMIC AND SOCIAL TURMOIL: European economies lay in ruins in 1944. Tens of millions of "displaced persons" were forced to relocate, and all Europeans confronted the problem of punishing those who had led or collaborated with fascist regimes.
   D. INTELLECTUAL CURRENTS IN THE POST-WAR ERA: European culture reflected the trauma of World War II. Philosophers and playwrights were preoccupied

with the absurdity of modern life, while anthropologists and historians deemphasized individual experience in favor of larger social and economic structures and trends. In the Soviet Union, state censorship put strict limits on artistic expression and scientific research.

II. POLITICAL REALIGNMENTS: Much of Eastern Europe fell under Communist rule and Communist parties gained power in the West. The United States responded to Communist successes with the Truman Doctrine and the Marshall Plan.
   A. DIVIDED GERMANY became a focus for Cold War tensions. The Western Allies oversaw the establishment of a stable democracy in the German Federal Republic; to the east, the German Democratic Republic was governed by the Communist Party, which took its orders from the Soviet Union.
   B. EASTERN EUROPE UNDER THE SOVIET SHADOW: Most of Eastern Europe fell under Soviet control after World War II, although Yugoslavia and Greece maintained their independence.
   C. POLITICS IN THE WEST: In Britain, the Labour Party won the first post-war election, but Conservatives returned to power

in 1951. In France, the Fourth Republic was plagued by instability, but the economy prospered under the guidance of government technocrats. In Italy, north-south divisions lingered, but the Christian Democratic Party provided political and economic stability.

D. POLITICS IN THE SOVIET UNION: After Stalin's death in 1953, a struggle for power within the Soviet leadership ended in victory for Khrushchev. The Communist Party maintained its absolute authority, but censorship was eased and the quality of ordinary people's lives gradually improved.

III. DECOLONIZATION: With the decline of European global supremacy after World War II, nationalist movements became more active in the Third World and most European colonies eventually won their independence.

A. DECOLONIZATION IN INDIA AND SOUTHEAST ASIA: A persistent nationalist movement convinced the British to grant largely Hindu India and largely Muslim Pakistan independence in 1947. Indonesia gained independence from Dutch rule in 1949.

B. BRITAIN AND THE MIDDLE EAST: British withdrawal from Palestine resulted in its division into the Jewish state of Israel and the Arab state of Jordan.

C. THE SUEZ CANAL CRISIS: Led by Arab nationalist leader Nasser, Egypt claimed control of the Suez Canal. An Israeli army, supported by France and Britain, invaded Egypt in 1956, but U.S. and Soviet pressure put an end to this military venture.

D. FRENCH DECOLONIZATION: France lost its colonial empire after World War II. Defeated at Dien Bien Phu in 1956, France withdrew from Southeast Asia. After a long and divisive conflict over the future of France's North African holdings, de Gaulle took power and granted Algeria independence. He sought to maintain France's influence in the Third World by providing an alternative to American or Soviet domination.

E. DECOLONIZATION IN AFRICA proceeded apace after World War II, but it did not always go smoothly. Following independence, former British colonies South Africa and Rhodesia remained subject to rule by white minorities; former Belgian colony Zaire suffered internal conflict and military dictatorship; and former Portuguese colonies Angola and Mozambique were torn by warfare between right- and left-wing factions.

IV. ECONOMIC AND SOCIAL CHANGES: Europe became more urbanized and Europeans enjoyed an increase in state-provided social services.

A. ECONOMIC RECOVERY AND THE WELFARE STATE: The European Economic Community helped to sustain the post-war economic growth that made possible expanded social welfare benefits. Both Eastern and Western European states provided their citizens with unemployment insurance, health care, education, etc.

B. ECONOMIC GROWTH IN THE WEST: Western Europe experienced an economic boom between 1950 and 1973. With the aid of state planning, nationalized industries and private conglomerates generated substantial improvements in the standard of living and helped to create a mass consumer culture.

C. COMMUNIST ECONOMIES were less successful, but even in Eastern Europe, economic cooperation— under the auspices of COMECON— increased productivity.

D. AN URBAN WORLD: After 1944, cities like Moscow and Paris attracted large numbers of residents—many of whom were accommodated in suburban high-rise apartments. Cars and factories, key factors in the urban boom, increased pollution levels.

E. THE GREEN REVOLUTION greatly increased agricultural productivity and the spread of commercial farming allowed many Western Europeans to leave agriculture. In the East, collectivization continued and efficiency increased, further stimulating industry and urbanization.

F. DEMOGRAPHIC CHANGES: A "baby boom" replenished the depleted European population, and educational opportunities increased to provide for this postwar generation. Nevertheless, class divisions and economic inequality remained substantial.

V. Tensions between the United States and the Soviet Union led to a series of COLD WAR CRISES, which took on an unprecedented seriousness due to the availability of nuclear weapons.

A. THE KOREAN WAR pitted Communist China against the United States, heightening Cold War tensions in Europe.

B. Stalin's death in 1953 produced STIRRINGS IN EASTERN EUROPE. East Germans, Poles, and Hungarians protested in favor of economic, political, and cultural liberalization, but government crackdowns—and Soviet tanks—put an end to these initiatives.

C. Despite a thaw in East-West relations as a result of Khrushchev's advent to power, SOVIET-U. S. TENSIONS were aggravated by the space race and the building of the Berlin Wall. The Cuban Missile Crisis brought the world to the verge of nuclear war and reinforced the ongoing arms race. In 1964, the United States became involved in the Vietnamese civil war, in hopes of limiting the expansion of communism in Southeast Asia.

D. SINO-SOVIET RIVALRY: Mao Zedong's anger over Khrushchev's rejection of Stalinism helped to produce a falling-out between Communist China and the Soviet Union. China and Russia competed for support in the Third World, and China won Albania as an ally.

E. THE BREZHNEV ERA: In 1964, Khrushchev was ousted from power and replaced by Brezhnev, ending post-Stalin liberalization in the Soviet Union.

VI. CONCLUSION

2. HISTORICAL GEOGRAPHY

Map Exercises

Familiarize yourself with the maps provided in your text, and then attempt to locate the following places on Blank Map 29.1.

DIVIDED EUROPE IN 1955

Albania	Greece
Austria	Hungary
Belgium	Ireland
Bulgaria	Italy
Czechoslovakia	Luxembourg
Denmark	Netherlands
East Germany	Norway
Finland	Poland
France	Portugal
Great Britain	Romania
Spain	U. S. S. R.
Sweden	West Germany
Switzerland	Yugoslavia
Turkey	

Map Questions

Historical Continuities: Describe the major territorial changes that occurred in Europe as a result of World War II.

Which of the nations listed above belonged to the Western bloc? The Eastern bloc? Which participated in NATO? In the Warsaw Pact? Which remained neutral or unaligned?

Identify the former European owners of the new African and Asian nations shown in text Map 29.3 (p. 1325).

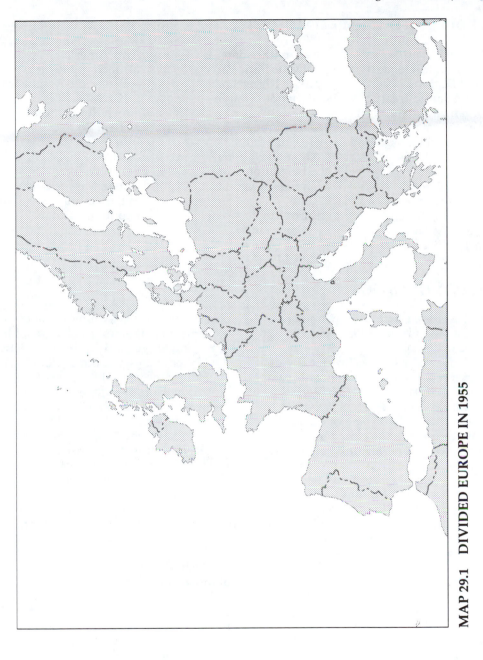

MAP 29.1   DIVIDED EUROPE IN 1955

3. PEOPLE AND TERMS TO IDENTIFY

Cold War
Potsdam Conference
United Nations
North Atlantic Treaty
   Organization (NATO) /
   Warsaw Pact
Displaced persons
Nuremberg trials
Existentialism
Waiting for Godot
Marshall Plan
Konrad Adenauer
Clement Attlee
French Office of Planning

Italian Christian
   Democratic Party
Nikita Khrushchev
Mohandas Gandhi
Israel
Gamal Abdel Nasser
Ho Chi Minh
Algerian National
   Liberation Front
Charles de Gaulle
Zaire
European Economic
   Community (EEC)
Welfare State

Anti-Americanism
Council of Mutual
   Economic Assistance
   (COMECON)
Green Revolution
Korean War
Imre Nagy
Sputnik
Berlin Wall
Cuban Missile Crisis
Mao Zedong
Leonid Brezhnev

4. STUDY QUESTIONS

1. *Historical Continuities:* Compare and contrast the Europe of 1939 with the Europe of 1944.

2. How and why was Europe divided into two separate and often hostile camps at the end of World War II? *Historical Continuities:* To what extent was this division a logical outcome of earlier twentieth-century developments?

3. *Historical Continuities:* Between 1914 and 1944, Europeans had suffered through an almost unbroken string of devastating crises. How was the trauma of this period expressed in the culture of the post-World War II period?

4. Compare and contrast the governments of West Germany (the German Federal Republic) and East Germany (the German Democratic Republic).

5. What common difficulties confronted the governments of Britain, France, and Italy after 1944? How successful were these governments in their responses to post-war problems?

6. What impact did the death of Stalin have on the Soviet Union?

7. What caused decolonization? What factors shaped the different European

powers' responses to independence movements in their own colonial holdings?

8. How did Cold War tensions between the United States and the Soviet Union affect the process of decolonization?

9. What sort of regimes replaced European colonial administrations in Asia and Africa after World War II?

10. What is the "welfare state"? What kinds of benefits did it provide for Western Europeans after 1944?

11. What caused the "economic miracle" in post-war Western Europe?

12. How did the post-war economic development of Eastern Europe compare with that of the West?

13. Why did Europe become increasingly urbanized in the second half of the twentieth century?

14. What characterized the mass consumer culture of post-war Europe? In what ways was European culture "Americanized" after World War II?

15. How was Western Europe affected by the Cold War tensions between the United States and the Soviet Union?

16. Why did attempts to liberalize the Communist regimes of Eastern Europe fail after the death of Stalin?

5. ANALYZING ART AND ARTIFACTS

What political purpose did graphic art (for example, pp. 1304 and 1307) serve in the Eastern bloc after World War II?

What was the symbolic meaning of the Berlin Wall in the Cold War era? What did a bottle of Coca Cola represent during this same period?

6. TECHNOLOGY AND HISTORY

What impact did new agricultural techniques and technologies have on European societies after World War II?

To what extent have communications, transportation, and military technologies internationalized human experience in the second half of the twentieth century?

7. HISTORICAL ANALYSIS: INTERPRETIVE ESSAYS

1. Describe the differences in the lives of two Germans, one living in East Berlin and one in West Berlin during the Cold War.

2. *Historical Continuities:* It can be argued that Western Europeans lived better, happier lives in the 1960s than they ever had before. To what extent was this true?

3. It is 1964 and you are a world-renowned Western European intellectual. Write an article entitled: "Rebuilding Europe: An Evaluation of Twenty Years of Post-war Reconstruction."

4. *Historical Continuities:* It is 1964 and you are a world-renowned Third World intellectual. Give a speech to the United Nations entitled: "The Rise and Fall of European Imperialism."

5. It is 1957 and you are a Hungarian intellectual. In an unpublished essay (later smuggled out of Hungary and published in the West), explain why you and other Eastern Europeans joined reform movements after 1953 and why you think these movements failed.

8. HISTORICAL VOICES: THE RECOVERY OF EUROPE, THE END OF EMPIRE

A. The United States Rejects Isolationism: The Marshall Plan and the Rebuilding of the European Economy

Following World War II, the political and economic leadership of the United States made a decisive break with pre-1945 foreign policy, rejecting the isolationism that had typified American international relations throughout the first half of the twentieth century. The European Recovery Program, more commonly known as the Marshall Plan, originated as an explicit repudiation of the U. S. government's course of action after World War I and won the support of a large number of American politicians, economic analysts, foreign affairs specialists, business people, and ordinary citizens. Allen W. Dulles, a lawyer who later served as director of the Central Intelligence Agency between 1953 and 1961, lobbied actively for the passage of Marshall Plan legislation. In a book written late in 1947, Dulles argued that it was now incumbent on the United States to accept a larger role in world affairs than it had after 1919:

At that time, emerging from a great war and following a great victory, we were faced with a decision whether or not to build on that victory and make common cause with our Allies in organizing the peace. We turned aside from that course and decided to go our own way.

Twenty years later we had good cause to regret our action.*

---

* Allen W. Dulles, *The Marshall Plan* (Providence, RI: Berg Publishers, 1993), p. 1.

In 1948, the National Planning Association, a private, Washington-based think tank, published a pamphlet on the Marshall Plan by Harvard professor Sidney S. Alexander. Alexander's forceful yet concise presentation was intended to convince Americans that providing financial aid to Europe was not only humane, but would also result in significant long-term economic and political benefits for the United States. As is demonstrated by the following passages from this pamphlet, supporters of the Marshall Plan were influenced by multiple considerations, whether political, economic, or humanitarian, when they called upon the government of the United States to invest billions of dollars in the post-war recovery of Western Europe.

After enabling legislation was passed by the U. S. Congress in 1948, Marshall Plan grants and loans were disbursed to Western European nations through the Economic Cooperation Administration, which distributed almost $13 billion during its existence. The program was highly successful, inspiring U.S. president Harry S. Truman to propose the creation of a similar aid plan targeted at less-developed nations, an idea which was implemented as the Point IV Program.

FROM *The Marshall Plan* by Sidney S. Alexander

OUR INTEREST IN EUROPEAN PROSPERITY

The advantages to Europe of the recovery program are obvious. But why should the United States support such a plan?

The answer that many Americans would give is that if the people of Europe are hungry, we should do what we can to help feed them.

Not only charity but faith impels us to go to the aid of Europe. Faith in democracy requires us to do what we can. In those lands of Europe from which America has drawn its cultural heritage, as well as its peoples, present economic and political conditions threaten the end not only of democracy but of most of the values that we cherish. We in the United States have the power to alter those economic conditions and to provide a basis for Europe to build an economic and political environment in which democracy and the values we respect can survive and develop. If the people of Europe cannot democratically achieve a decent livelihood, then they will certainly try another way, and the loss to the world—and to the United States—will be great.

The motives of charity and of faith are buttressed by the motive of self-interest. The self-interest of the United States is well served by an investment in the recovery of Europe. Preservation of our own security must be the primary aim of the United States in international affairs. A peaceful, prosperous Europe is an important requirement for that security.

The United States today is the most productive country of the world. But we have long refused to recognize that productivity means power; and power means responsibility. We have cherished the illusion that we were a country set apart from the political affairs of the rest of the world. The simple fact is that when trouble arises anywhere in the world it is bound to bother us. That's what it means to be a world power.

In particular, when trouble arises in Europe, it will mean trouble for the United States. If, for example, Western Europe should go Communist, the threat to the United States is obvious. Suppose, however, that the countries of Western Europe should go Fascist—anti-Communist but also anti-democratic. To hope that the two totalitarian groups of Eastern and Western Europe would just balance each other and leave us secure would be to make once again the tragic mistake that Britain made in

1938. Munich and Pearl Harbor were not unrelated events. We have an interest in preventing Western Europe from going Fascist because, one way or another, Fascism has led to aggression. Even clearer is the threat to the United States of Western Europe going Communist. Then the unification of Europe under the red banner would give Stalin in fact the power of which Hitler dreamt.

In plain language, the United States has an interest in keeping Western Europe from the extremes of right or left because either extreme is likely to lead to aggressive action. It will be much less expensive in human lives if we recognize where our interests lie well before it is necessary to wage war to defend those interests. . . .

THE MARSHALL PLAN AND OUR RELATIONS WITH RUSSIA

Our relations with Russia pose the fundamental problem of our foreign policy. Upon our solution of that problem hangs not only the question of war or peace, but also the continued survival of democracy in Europe and perhaps in America. Our attempts at solving the problem have, to date, been singularly unsuccessful. We have tried again and again to settle our differences with Russia by negotiation, only to find that Russia took a stand so extreme as to make any agreement by negotiation impossible.

In the matters of the treatment of Germany and of the control of atomic energy, the two most pressing international issues of our time, our repeated attempts at finding a ground of common discussion with Russia have failed. When two parties to a negotiation fail to find common ground for discussion, at least one of them must have the wrong appraisal of the other's situation.

Russia's appraisal of the situation of the United States may be inferred easily—both from Marxist doctrine and from statements emanating from the Kremlin. Russia expects a depression in the United States. She also expects an intensification of the economic difficulties of Europe leading to the spread of Communism beyond the area now under Russian influence. A depression in the United States will, in Russia's view, divert our attention from the affairs of Europe, leaving Russia in undisputed control of a Europe rapidly going Communist. With such anticipation of an easy and painless victory, Moscow probably reasons that it would be foolish to compromise.

The only way for us to create a better basis for negotiating with the Russians is to prove them wrong in their fundamental assumptions. The past history of Soviet foreign and domestic policy shows that the Communist leaders are able to adjust to the facts of the situation once those facts become evident. If we demonstrate our ability to maintain prosperity in the United States and to help develop conditions in Europe in which democracy and freedom of the individual can survive, we can expect a change in the policy of the Soviet Union. . . .

CONCLUSIONS

The hard-headed argument for the Marshall Plan over and above the dictates of simple charity and faith in democracy is that economic deterioration of Europe will create a political situation which will threaten the peace and security of the United States. Our peace will be endangered by the triumph of totalitarianism in Europe. Will the Marshall Plan protect us? No honest man can give a certain answer to that question.

The Marshall Plan will not solve the political problems of Europe once and for all. It won't even completely settle some of the most pressing economic problems. The Plan will create an economic environment in Europe favorable for the growth and development of democratic processes and economic prosperity. It will not end Europe's problems, but it can prevent a breakdown of the political and economic structure of Europe. The Plan can offer the hope of success, but no certainty. Without the Plan the failure of democracy in Europe seems a certainty.

Source: Sidney S. Alexander. *The Marshall Plan*, pp. 8–9, 12–14. Washington, DC: National Planning Association, Planning Pamphlet Nos. 60–61, February 1948.

Questions

Why, according to Sidney Alexander, was isolationism no longer a possibility for the United States after 1945? To what extent are his concerns about American foreign policy a product of the emerging Cold War?

What lessons has Alexander learned from John Maynard Keynes (see Chapter 26, pp. 308–309, for the reading excerpt from Keynes' *The Economic Consequences of the Peace*)?

What specific benefits might the United States derive from helping to rebuild Europe, according to Alexander?

B. "A Locust Fighting an Elephant": Ho Chi Minh and the Vietnamese National Liberation Struggle

If the Marshall Plan was a success, other American foreign policy initiatives did not fare so well in the years following 1945. Determined to forestall the spread of communism, the U.S. government pumped $2.5 billion into the French government's unsuccessful effort to reestablish colonial control over Indochina after World War II—and then became embroiled itself in the conflict between North and South Vietnam in the 1960s. Both France and the United States discovered that "Third World" peoples were increasingly unwilling to accept Western domination after World War II.

In Indochina, the Vietnamese independence movement was led by Nguyen Tat Thanh (1890–1969), better known by his revolutionary pseudonym, Ho Chi Minh ("He Who Enlightens"). Of humble origins, Ho left Vietnam in 1911, having taken a menial job on board a French ship, and did not return to his homeland for the next thirty years. He settled in Paris during the Great War, where he became involved in left-wing political organizations and eventually joined the Communist Party.

When Ho Chi Minh returned to Vietnam in 1941, he brought years of experience as a political activist to bear on the struggle for independence from France. Sensing an opportunity for Vietnamese independence in the Japanese occupation of Southeast Asia during World War II, Ho returned to Vietnam in 1941 and began to organize the Vietminh, a nationalist organization dominated by Communists. When the Japanese were defeated in 1945, the Vietminh seized power, and Ho became president of the newly independent Vietnamese nation. The French refused to accept the loss of Indochina, and declared war on Vietnam in 1946. After a long and bitter struggle, culminating in the Vietnamese victory at Dien Bien Phu in 1954, the French accepted defeat and withdrew from Southeast Asia.

Ho Chi Minh's leadership of the Vietnamese independence movement earned him international attention. Although condemned by Western leaders as a Communist, he was in reality an ardent nationalist whose chief concern was the independence of the Vietnamese people. One of Ho's most important contributions to anti-imperialist movements in general was his insistence that small nations with few resources could triumph over powerful Western regimes through persistence and whole-hearted dedication to the struggle, an argument that served as an inspiration to nationalist leaders throughout the world. In the following excerpt from a 1951 speech, Ho describes his strategy against the French.

FROM "Political Report Read at the Second National Congress of the Viet-Nam Workers' Party, Held in February, 1951" by Ho Chi Minh

The enemy schemed a lightning war. As they wanted to attack swiftly and win swiftly, our Party and Government put forth the slogan "Long-term Resistance War." The enemy plotted to sow dissension among us, so our slogan was "Unity of the Entire People." Therefore, right from the start, our strategy prevailed over the enemy's.

To wage a long-term resistance war, there must be an adequate supply of arms and munitions to the army, of food and clothing to the troops and the people. Our country is poor and our technique low. The cities and towns which have some industry are occupied by the enemy. We tried to offset our material deficiencies by the enthusiasm of the entire people. So the Party and the Government promoted the patriotic emulation. Emulation covers all fields, but it is aimed at three main points: doing away with famine, wiping out illiteracy, and annihilating the foreign invaders.

Our workers emulated in manufacturing weapons for our troops, who enthusiastically trained themselves and magnificently scored feats of arms. The recent victories were proof of this. Our people ardently emulated and got satisfactory results. Our country is economically backward, we have been waging the Resistance War for almost five years and still can withstand it without suffering too many privations. This is a fact. The majority of our population are freed from illiteracy. This is a glorious achievement lauded by the world. I suggest that our Congress should send affectionate thanks and congratulations to our troops and compatriots.

But our organization, supervision, exchange, and summing up of experiences are still weak. This is our shortcoming. From now on, we strive to overcome them and the emulation movement will certainly bring about many more and better results.

The military aspect is the key one in the Resistance War.

At the beginning of the Resistance War our army was young. Though full of heroism, it lacked weapons, experience, officers, everything.

The enemy army was well known in the world. They had navy, infantry, and air forces. Moreover, they were supported by the British and American imperialists, especially by the latter.

The difference between our forces and the enemy's was so great that there were at the time people who likened our Resistance War to a "locust fighting an elephant."

It was so if things were seen from the material side, in their actual conditions and with a narrow mind. We had then to oppose airplanes and cannons with bamboo sticks. But guided by Marxism-Leninism, our Party did not look only at the present but also at the future and had firm confidence in the spirit and forces of the masses, of the nation. Therefore we resolutely told the wavering and pessimistic people that "Today the locust fights the elephant, but tomorrow the elephant will be disemboweled."

Practical life has shown that the colonialist "elephant" is being disemboweled while our army has grown up into a powerful tiger.

At the beginning, the enemy was the stronger and we the weaker. However, we doggedly waged the Resistance War, scored many successes, and firmly believed in our final victory because our cause is just and our troops courageous, our people united and undaunted, and because we are supported by the French people and the world democratic camp, and also because our strategy is correct.

Source: Ho Chi Minh. "Political Report Read at the Second National Congress of the Viet-Nam Workers' Party, Held in February, 1951." In *Ho Chi Minh on Revolution: Selected Writings, 1920–1966,* pp. 214–216. Ed. Bernard B. Fall. New York: Frederick A. Praeger, 1967.

Questions

What is a "Long-term Resistance War"? Why is this an especially appropriate strategy for the Vietnamese independence movement?

What are Ho Chi Minh's long-term goals for the Vietnamese people? What sort of nation does he wish to build after the French have been defeated?

Why do you think Ho's strategy might appeal to other leaders of independence movements?

9. IMPORTANT HISTORICAL FACTS: STUDY DRILLS

A. Multiple Choice

1. In 1945, the charter for this international body was drawn up in San Francisco:
   A. The League of Nations
   B. The North Atlantic Treaty Organization
   C. The United Nations
   D. The Warsaw Pact

2. In 1945, an international tribunal met at Nuremberg to
   A. determine the fate of Palestine.
   B. distribute Marshall Plan money.
   C. establish the post-war boundaries of Germany.
   D. try Nazi war criminals.

3. Two of the best known existentialist writers of the post-war period were
   A. Albert Camus and Jean-Paul Sartre.
   B. Albert Einstein and Trofim Lysenko.
   C. Alfred Hitchcock and Gilles Pontecorvo.
   D. Jean Monnet and Boris Pasternak.

4. Bureaucracies like the French Office of Planning relied on these individuals to help governments coordinate the modernization of post-war industry:
   A. Christian Democrats
   B. Members of the Presidium of the Communist Party
   C. Social Realists
   D. Technocrats

5. After World War II, Italian political life was dominated by
   A. the Christian Democratic Party.
   B. the Communist Party.
   C. Federico Fellini.
   D. Pope John XXIII.

6. Algeria's anti-imperialist independence movement was led by
   A. the French Officer Corps.
   B. Guy Mollet.
   C. the National Liberation Front.
   D. the *Pieds Noirs.*

7. Which of the following African nations were once a part of the British Empire?
   A. Algeria, Morocco, and Tunisia
   B. Angola and Mozambique
   C. Eritrea, Libya, and Somaliland
   D. Ghana, Kenya, and Nigeria

8. As a result of the creation of "welfare states" after World War II, most Western Europeans could expect to enjoy
   A. equal incomes.
   B. health care and unemployment benefits.
   C. freedom from taxation.
   D. the end of class differences.

9. In the post-war period, some European intellectuals reacted against what they saw as the vulgar materialism of American culture, rejecting all of the following *except:*

A. Coca Cola.
B. the Marshall Plan.
C. *Reader's Digest.*
D. TV westerns and soap operas.
10. The Berlin Wall was built in 1961 in order to
   A. commemorate John F. Kennedy's visit to Berlin.
   B. keep doctors and other specialists in East Germany.
   C. prevent Hungarian dissidents from escaping to Western Europe.
   D. unify the Eastern and Western halves of Berlin.

B. Chronological Relationships

1. The Cold War: Identify the date at which each of the following events occurred and arrange them in chronological order.

   The Western Allies airlift supplies into blockaded West Berlin.

   The Cuban Missile Crisis.

   Imre Nagy leads an insurrection against Soviet domination of Hungary.

   Communist North Korea invades South Korea.

   The Potsdam Conference.

   The Soviet Union launches Sputnik.

   The Death of Stalin.

   The United States officially enters the Vietnam War.

   East Germany builds a wall between East and West Berlin.

   Declaration of the (Communist) People's Republic of China.

2. Decolonization: Identify the date at which each of the following European colonies won their independence and list the new states' names.

COLONY	DATE OF INDEPENDENCE	NEW NAME
Belgian Congo		
British Ghana		
British Indian Empire		
British Palestine		
Dutch East Indies		
French Algeria		
French Indochina		
Italian Libya		
Portuguese Angola		
Portuguese Mozambique		

C. Matching Exercise: Historical Actors

_____ Konrad Adenauer
_____ Clement Attlee
_____ Leonid Brezhnev
_____ Mohandas Gandhi
_____ Charles de Gaulle
_____ Ho Chi Minh
_____ Nikita Khrushchev
_____ Imre Nagy
_____ Gamal Abdel Nasser
_____ Mao Zedong

A. A leader of the Indian independence movement, he advocated peaceful, nonviolent resistance to British rule.
B. He became general secretary of the Communist Party in 1964, reestablishing a repressive orthodox Communist regime after the short-lived post-Stalinist "thaw."
C. Leader of the French resistance movement, he later served as first president of the Fifth Republic and surprised his fellow French citizens with his decision to grant Algeria its independence.
D. A leader of the Vietnamese independence movement, he became president of the Communist Democratic Republic of Vietnam.
E. This sheepish but effective member of the British Labour Party became prime minister immediately after World War II.
F. Leader of the Chinese Communist Party, he broke with the Soviet Union

over (among other things) Khrushchev's retreat from Stalinism.

G. After the death of Stalin, this coarse but pragmatic Communist Party member rose to power in the Soviet Union. He repudiated the Stalinist "cult of personality" and encouraged greater production of consumer goods.

H. This liberal prime minister of Hungary led the 1956 insurrection against Soviet domination, but was executed after Soviet troops put down the revolt.

I. Having actively opposed Nazism, this Christian Democrat became chancellor of the German Federal Republic after World War II.

J. Head of Egypt after 1952 and a leader of the post-colonial Pan-Arab movement, he nationalized the Suez Canal in 1956.

D. Fill in the Blanks

1. At the _____ in 1945, the "Big Three" decided to reunify Germany after that defeated nation had been disarmed and de-Nazified, but the emerging Cold War prevented this from happening and Germany remained divided.

2. After World War II, the division of Europe was formalized through the creation of two opposed military alliances, the _____ and the _____.

3. In the years following World War II, tens of millions of _____, including refugees and prisoners of war, were resettled in new locations.

4. The collapse of moral absolutes after World War II was evident in the "theater of the absurd," an example of which is Samuel Beckett's play, _____.

5. In the hopes of diminishing the appeal of communism, and of revitalizing European trade relations with the United States, the American government sponsored the _____, which infused over $9 billion into the economies of Western Europe in the late 1940s.

6. After the horrors of World War II, many European Jews emigrated to Palestine, where they eventually established an independent state known as _____.

7. In 1949, the Soviet Union created the _____, which was designed to coordinate economic planning between the U.S.S.R. and its Eastern European allies. In 1957, six Western European nations established a somewhat similar organization, the _____, which gradually eliminated trade barriers between member states and greatly stimulated the Western European economy.

8. A dramatic increase in agricultural productivity, known as the _____, was the result of the introduction of large-scale, commercialized agriculture in post-war Europe.

9. In 1957, East-West tensions were exacerbated by the Soviet Union's launching of a space rocket known as _____.

10. During the _____ of 1962, a nuclear war between the United States and the Soviet Union was only narrowly averted through successful negotiations between Khrushchev and Kennedy.

IMPORTANT HISTORICAL FACTS: STUDY-DRILL ANSWERS

A. Multiple Choice

1. C. The United Nations
2. D. try Nazi war criminals.
3. A. Albert Camus and Jean-Paul Sartre.
4. D. Technocrats
5. A. the Christian Democratic Party.
6. C. the National Liberation Front.
7. D. Ghana, Kenya, and Nigeria
8. B. health care and unemployment benefits.
9. B. the Marshall Plan.
10. B. keep doctors and other specialists in East Germany.

B. Chronological Relationships

1. The Cold War
   1945 The Potsdam Conference.
   1948 The Western Allies airlift supplies into blockaded West Berlin.
   1949 Declaration of the (Communist) People's Republic of China.

1950 Communist North Korea invades South Korea.
1953 The Death of Stalin.
1956 Imre Nagy leads an insurrection against Soviet domination of Hungary.
1957 The Soviet Union launches Sputnik.

1961 East Germany builds a wall between East and West Berlin.
1962 The Cuban Missile Crisis.
1964 The United States officially enters the Vietnam War.

2. Decolonization

COLONY	DATE OF INDEPENDENCE	NEW NAME
British Palestine	1946, 1948	Jordan, Israel
British Indian Empire	1947	India, Pakistan
Dutch East Indies	1949	Indonesia
Italian Libya	1951	Libya
French Indochina	1954	Cambodia, Laos, North and South Vietnam
British Ghana	1957	Ghana
Belgian Congo	1960	Zaire (renamed in 1971)
French Algeria	1962	Algeria
Portuguese Angola	1975	Angola
Portuguese Mozambique	1975	Mozambique

C. Matching Exercise: Historical Actors

I. Konrad Adenauer
E. Clement Attlee
B. Leonid Brezhnev
A. Mohandas Gandhi
C. Charles de Gaulle
D. Ho Chi Minh
G. Nikita Khrushchev
H. Imre Nagy
J. Gamal Abdel Nasser
F. Mao Zedong

D. Fill in the Blanks

1. Potsdam Conference
2. North Atlantic Treaty Organization (NATO); Warsaw Pact
3. displaced persons
4. *Waiting for Godot*
5. Marshall Plan
6. Israel
7. Council of Mutual Economic Assistance (COMECON); European Economic Community (EEC)
8. Green Revolution
9. Sputnik
10. Cuban Missile Crisis

30 The Emergence of Contemporary Europe and the Collapse of Communism

1. CHAPTER OUTLINE

I. POLITICS IN A CHANGING WESTERN WORLD: In the late 1960s, a student protest movement swept the Western world, provoking a leftward trend in politics. However, in the late 1970s many European governments returned to more conservative policies, while at the same time rejecting U.S. foreign policy domination.

   A. STUDENT PROTESTS CHALLENGE GAULLIST FRANCE: French students and workers united to demand improvements in education and work conditions. Workers won some concessions, but forceful action on President de Gaulle's part brought an end to the student protests.

   B. SHIFTS IN WESTERN EUROPEAN POLITICS AFTER 1968: Centrist parties tended to dominate politics in the 1970s, but late in that decade a rightward trend became apparent. Social Democrats took power in Germany in 1968 but were replaced by Christian Democrats in 1982; Britain's Labour Party controlled the government until the advent of Conservative Thatcher in 1979; bucking this trend, France replaced a centrist with Socialist Mitterrand in 1981; Italian politics continued to be plagued by instability and corruption. Environmental issues became a major concern in most Western European states, and economic difficulties sparked calls for decreases in government spending.

   C. THE TRANSITION TO DEMOCRACY IN SOUTHERN EUROPE: Greece became a democratic republic after the collapse of a right-wing military coup in 1967; both Portugal and Spain became democracies in the 1970s after the deaths of their long-time dictators.

   D. CATHOLICISM IN MODERN EUROPE: Despite the continuing secularization of much of European society, the Catholic Church was revitalized after World War II by the initiatives of liberal Pope John XXIII and the more conservative Pope John Paul II.

   E. THE EUROPEAN COMMUNITY AND THE EUROPEAN UNION: Since World War II, efforts have been made to unify the national economies of Western Europe. While largely successful, this movement has also met with substantial resistance, especially from nationalists.

II. ECONOMIC GROWTH AND LIMITS: In the post-war world, national cultures and economies became increasingly internationalized as a result of advances in global communications and transportation.

    A. PROSPERITY AND MASS CULTURE: Television has created international cultural links—and "Americanized" world culture in the process—while increased affluence and leisure time have generated a rapid rise in international tourism.

    B. OIL AND THE GLOBAL ECONOMY: The Arab oil embargo of 1973 has had a profound (and continuing) impact on Western economies, contributing to high rates of inflation and unemployment.

    C. CHANGING CONTOURS OF ECONOMIC LIFE: The Western European workforce has been transformed since World War II: far fewer people now work in agriculture, many more work in the service sector, more women are paid employees, and foreign workers now constitute a substantial percentage of European workers.

III. THREATS TO PEACE in Europe include the nuclear arsenals of the Cold War, international terrorism, and ethnic and religious conflicts.

    A. NUCLEAR WEAPONS AND TENSIONS BETWEEN THE SUPERPOWERS: In the 1970s, the U.S. and the U.S.S.R. negotiated limits on the development of nuclear weapons systems, bringing a period of détente in East-West relations, but this ended in 1979 when the Soviet Union invaded Afghanistan.

    B. Dissatisfied by their inability to effect change through legitimate means, militant nationalists, right- and left-wing extremists, and Islamic fundamentalists engaged in acts of TERRORISM in the 1970s and 1980s.

    C. RELIGIOUS AND ETHNIC DIVISIONS continue to generate outbreaks of violence in Europe. From the Basques of Spain to the Catholics of Northern Ireland, ethnic and religious minorities agitate, and sometimes fight, for recognition of their grievances.

IV. THE FALL OF COMMUNISM came abruptly to Eastern Europe in the late 1980s. On the heels of Gorbachev's reforms in the Soviet Union, the communist regimes of Europe collapsed, bringing euphoria—and new political and economic problems.

    A. EASTERN EUROPE AND THE SOVIET SHADOW: After crushing a reform movement in Czechoslovakia in 1968, the Soviet Union asserted its right to intervene in all Eastern European satellite states. Opposition to communism continued, especially in Poland, but pro-Soviet Eastern European leaders refused to liberalize their regimes.

    B. THE GORBACHEV ERA: In 1985, Soviet leader Gorbachev called for an increased openness in Soviet government and a restructuring of the economy. His reform efforts encouraged ethnic minorities and democrats within the Soviet Union to voice their opposition to the Communist state. An economic crisis in the late 1980s convinced many in the U.S.S.R. that communism must be abolished, not reformed. In Eastern Europe, a reform movement emerged when it became apparent that Gorbachev had abandoned the "Brezhnev Doctrine." Some Eastern European leaders were willing to enter negotiations with opposition movements, but others clung to power.

    C. The peaceful TRANSITION TO PARLIAMENTARY GOVERNMENT IN POLAND AND HUNGARY was the result of a combination of determined action on the part of the democratic opposition and of a willingness to step aside more or less gracefully on the part of the Communist leaderships, which recognized that they had lost their legitimacy in the eyes of the people.

D. THE COLLAPSE OF THE BERLIN WALL AND EAST GERMAN COMMUNISM: In the face of Honecker's adamant rejection of reform, East Germans fled their country in droves. In late 1989 the Communist leadership accepted the inevitable, and ordered the Berlin Wall to be torn down. Open elections returned a Christian Democrat majority, which then oversaw the reunification of the two Germanies.

E. THE "VELVET REVOLUTION" IN CZECHOSLOVAKIA: After the fall of the Berlin Wall, Czechoslovakians—led by the Civic Forum—overturned the Communist government in just ten days. Growing ethnic tensions resulted in the creation of independent Czech and Slovak states at the beginning of 1993.

F. REVOLUTIONS IN BULGARIA, ROMANIA, AND ALBANIA: Despite the initial absence of indigenous reform movements, change came even in the most backward Communist states of Eastern Europe. Zhivkov was ousted in Bulgaria, but a renamed Communist Party won a majority of seats in the new government; Romanian leader Ceausescu resorted to force in his efforts to stay in power, but he too was ousted—and killed; in isolated Albania, Communist rule also came to an end, and Alia was forced to resign as president.

G. THE COLLAPSE OF THE SOVIET UNION: As its former satellites one by one rejected Communist rule, the Soviet Union itself moved toward democracy, eventually disintegrating into its component republics. Boris Yeltsin, president of the Russian Republic, took a key role in the process. Acknowledging the dissolution of the U.S.S.R., Gorbachev resigned his post in December 1991.

H. THE DISINTEGRATION OF YUGOSLAVIA was largely the result of longstanding ethnic rivalries in the Balkans. Serbian leader Milošević's determination to build a "Greater Serbia" produced a bitter civil war, pitting Serbs against Croats and Muslim Bosnians.

I. CHALLENGES IN THE POST-COMMUNIST WORLD: The transition to democratic political structures and free market economies has not been easy in Eastern Europe. Lacking in democratic traditions, and plagued by weak economies and persistent ethnic hostilities, many former Communist states risk falling under the authoritarian rule of right-wing nationalists or "reformed" former Communists, while the risk of warfare between newly independent nations remains high.

V. CONCLUSION

2. HISTORICAL GEOGRAPHY

MAP 30.1   WESTERN EUROPE IN 1995

Map Exercises

Familiarize yourself with the maps provided in your text, and then attempt to locate the following places on Blank Maps 30.1 and 30.2.

WESTERN EUROPE IN 1995

Austria	Italy
Belgium	Luxembourg
Denmark	Netherlands
Finland	Norway
France	Portugal
Germany	Spain
Great Britain	Sweden
Iceland	Switzerland
Ireland	

MAP 30.2 EASTERN EUROPE IN 1995

EASTERN EUROPE IN 1995

Albania	Latvia
Armenia	Lithuania
Azerbaijan	Macedonia
Belarus	Moldova
Bosnia-	Poland
Herzegovina	Romania
Bulgaria	Russia
Croatia	Slovakia
Czech Republic	Slovenia
Estonia	Tajikistan
Georgia	Turkey
Greece	Turkmenistan
Hungary	Ukraine
Kazakhstan	Uzbekistan
Kyrgyzstan	Yugoslavia

Map Questions

What territorial changes have taken place in Eastern Europe since 1989? What are the reasons for these changes?

What has happened to Yugoslavia since the collapse of communism?

Where are the affluent European countries? The poor European countries?

Identify: a) the members of the European Union; b) the former satellite states of the Soviet Union; c) the former "socialist republics" of the Soviet Union.

3. PEOPLE AND TERMS TO IDENTIFY

French student protests of 1968

Willy Brandt

Margaret Thatcher

François Mitterrand

Bettino Craxi

Green Parties

Juan Carlos

Pope John Paul II

European Community

Treaty of Maastricht

Euro-Disney

Organization of Petroleum Exporting Countries (OPEC)

"Guest workers"

Détente

Red Brigades

Irish Republican Army

Brezhnev Doctrine

Solidarity

Lech Walesa

Mikhail Gorbachev

Glasnost and *Perestroika*

Andrei Sakharov

Hungarian Democratic Forum

German reunification

Václav Havel

Todor Zhivkov

Nicolae Ceausescu

Boris Yeltsin

Commonwealth of Independent States

Slobodan Milošević

Ethnic cleansing

Chechnya

4. STUDY QUESTIONS

1. What caused the student protests of the late 1960s? How successful were they?

2. Describe the general tendencies of Western European politics in the years between 1968 and 1989. To what extent were national politics shaped by international trends and concerns during this period?

3. What brought Margaret Thatcher to power in 1979 in Great Britain?

4. What benefits would Europeans derive from the European Economic Area projected by the Treaty of Maastricht? Why do some Europeans oppose the economic unification of Europe?

5. How did the Arab oil embargo of 1973 affect the world economy? What specific impact did it have on Western European nations?

6. *Historical Continuities:* How does the Western European workforce of the second half of the twentieth century differ from its pre-World War II antecedent?

7. What threats to post-war peace and prosperity have appeared in Western Europe in the last twenty-five years?

8. What characteristics did the political regimes of the Eastern European Communist states share in the 1970s and 1980s? Why did many Eastern Europeans oppose these regimes?

9. What did Mikhail Gorbachev do to reform the Soviet government? *Historical Continuities:* How would Lenin have responded to these reforms? Stalin?

10. Why was the transition to democracy so peaceful in Poland, Hungary, and Czechoslovakia?

11. *Historical Continuities:* Review the history of Germany in the nineteenth and twentieth centuries. To what extent can this nation be considered "central" to the historical development of modern Europe? What role do you expect Germany to play in the future?

12. Why was the Czechoslovakian revolt against Communist rule a "velvet revolution"?

13. How did the revolutions in Bulgaria, Romania, and Albania differ from those in other Eastern European satellite states?

14. Why did the Soviet Union disintegrate into its component parts in 1991? What problems must be solved by the newly independent former Soviet republics?

15. What caused the civil war in the former Yugoslavia? *Historical Continuities:* To what extent might this war be considered a continuation of the ethnic and nationalist conflicts of the first half of the twentieth century?

16. What "challenges" are now faced by the post-Communist states of Eastern Europe in their attempts to build democratic governments and free market economies?

5. ANALYZING ART AND ARTIFACTS

Compare the dress of Parisian student protesters with that of counter-demonstrators (p. 1354). To what extent can differences in political allegiances be read in these activists' clothing? Does the clothing of the Eastern European political leaders and activists pictured in your text tell you anything about *their* political tendencies?

How was Margaret Thatcher's administration caricatured in the press (p. 1357)?

What do you think the destruction of the Berlin Wall meant to the border guards shown in the photograph on p. 1387 of your text? To the protesters breaking down the wall?

6. TECHNOLOGY AND HISTORY

How have changes in communications and transportation technology affected the leisure activities of Europeans?

Why have nuclear power plants become an important source of energy in Europe?

What was the political impact of the Chernobyl nuclear power plant disaster of 1986?

7. HISTORICAL ANALYSIS: INTERPRETIVE ESSAYS

1. *Historical Continuities:* Write a narrative description of the political history of either Great Britain or France between 1914 and 1995. To what extent is the history of this nation representative of the general Western European political experience during this same period?

2. Write an essay arguing that an economic union of Western European nations is necessary to the future economic viability of each individual state. Introduce your arguments with a brief history of the movement toward economic union.

3. Was the fall of communism inevitable? Why or why not?

4. If you were called in as a political and economic consultant to a struggling, newly democratic Eastern European state, what sort of advice would you give to the country's leaders?

5. *Historical Continuities:* Write an essay arguing that nationalism has been *the* determining factor in twentieth-century European history.

8. HISTORICAL VOICES: YOUTH AND THE FUTURE OF THE POST-SOVIET WORLD

In 1989, the Cold War ended as the Soviet bloc crumbled, prompting some scholars to claim that humanity had arrived at "the end of history." The British pop group Jesus Jones joined in the chorus, commemorating the tearing down of the Berlin Wall with a much-played song that celebrated "watching the world wake up from history." However, the demise of history (as Mark Twain once wryly remarked about premature reports of his own death), may have been greatly exaggerated. Rather, argues historian Paul Hockenos: "In 1989, history did not perish—it was reborn." The exact form that rebirth will take has yet to be decided, but it will be determined largely by the actions of those young people coming of age today and in the next several decades.

A. "Free to Hate": Youth Violence in Eastern Europe

Between 1989 and 1993, historian Paul Hockenos traveled throughout Eastern Europe, studying the various right-wing movements that have emerged in the wake of the collapse of that region's Communist regimes. As Hockenos notes in *Free to Hate: The Rise of the Right in Post-Communist Eastern Europe,* the book that resulted from his years of research, Eastern Europe's "new right" differs significantly from the mainstream conservative political parties of Western Europe and the United States. In Eastern Europe, the right wing is often characterized by a rejection of both democracy and capitalism, combined with an extreme nationalism. Its supporters feel threatened by the dismantling of state-controlled Communist economies and often reject free-market economic principles as a dangerous Western imposition. They fear that open, democratic elections will result in anarchy, and they look to authoritarian regimes to provide stability and to protect nationalist traditions, usually at the expense of ethnic and religious minorities.

In many former Communist states, right-wing parties have attracted large followings. Although the leaders and the followers of these parties come from all walks of life, it is young men who often serve as the "shock troops" for these movements and who are largely responsible for the many incidents of ethnic and religious violence that have plagued the region since 1989.* Often mirroring trends in Western youth culture, these young right-wing activists adopt distinctive styles of dress—most often the Skinhead's shaved head, jackboots, and bomber jacket—and specific popular musical styles, especially "ska" and "oi." Like the British Skinheads of the 1980s, whose racial and ethnic hostilities were expressed in "Paki [i.e., Pakistani] bashing" rampages, Eastern European right-wing youth lash out against minority populations, whose specific identity differs from region to region (although gypsies—"Roma"—are scapegoated almost everywhere).

In the following excerpts from *Free to Hate,* Hockenos describes a 1989 visit to an East Berlin "youth club" and discusses the increase in Skinhead violence in Hungary in the early 1990s.

FROM *Free to Hate* by Paul Hockenos

Nearly an hour's trip away on the *S-Bahn,* the commuter railroad, the Malibu lay at the base of a labyrinth of tall, cement-gray high rises, the kind of Stalinist housing projects that dominate East Berlin beyond its refurbished tourist center. Inside the disco, a sparse, box-like room that served as a cafeteria by day, a strobe light flashed wearily to some 1970s

---

*In Eastern Europe, right-wing women often associate taking an active role in politics with the excesses of the Communist era, and they prefer to retreat to the private sphere entirely, leaving public expressions of political activism to men.

pop hits. A rotund man in his mid-thirties, perhaps a communist youth functionary a month ago, presided over the turntables as a handful of teenage girls danced with one another. There were no Skinheads to be seen, but outside on the terrace, a group of young guys in collarless "baseball jackets," with short haircuts and thin moustaches, stood about smoking cigarettes. Some sat on the dirty steps, while others paced anxiously back and forth, disappearing inside for a few minutes and then reappearing. The boys shared a similar nervousness in their movements and blank, cruel gazes. They had about them an aura of adolescent meanness, anger, and restlessness.

The boys recognized me at once as a stranger. Though wary, they seemed curious enough about my presence in Hellersdorf on Christmas Eve to agree to chat. No, they said, they hadn't been following the events in Romania. Yes, they agreed, the opening of the Berlin Wall was a fine thing, even if it was only the first step to ousting the communists once and for all. As for politics, they didn't have much use for them, and none of them identified with any of the political parties, East or West. At the same time, they all considered themselves "right wing," which translated first into being anti-communist and second into wanting the reunification of Germany. Finally, they said, they could be "proud to be Germans again."

They knew the Skinheads who frequented the Malibu, who would usually show up later in the evening and start fights or shout "Sieg Heil!", "Foreigners Out!", and other such slogans. The adolescents in the baseball jackets weren't fascists, but they didn't have anything against the Skinheads either. "On some things, like the niggers and the *Fidschis* (Asians), the Skins say it like it is," said one of the guys, a pimple-faced teenager a bit more talkative than the others. "They come here from the third world and get everything that they want, just because they're communists. But now that's come to an end." When I asked, they said that they knew about the murdered Mozambican. The worker, one said, had been "harassing all of the local girls." . . .

The latent racism that erupted in 1990 [in Hungary] encompassed the breadth of society—from the person on the street to the government. Yet, a growing, organized Skinhead movement stands behind the lion's share of the violent attacks against people of color. . . .

In and out of prison, the young, largely working-class male Skinheads and their followers maintained the movement mostly through the underground music scene, which enjoyed significantly more leeway than in other East bloc countries. . . . One of the original Budapest oi bands, the 1982-formed Mos-oi, flouted some of the strongest lyrics. In their "Immigrants' Share," for example, they sang:

> We'll get rid of everyone we don't need,
> Including the garbage immigrants.
> The immigrants' fate can only be death,
> We'll have to drive out all of the Blacks,
> For the Arabs—to be sure—machine guns are waiting,
> Over Palestine atomic clouds are gathering.

In another song, the Roma are their target:

> The flamethrower is the only weapon I need to win,
> All Gypsy adults and children we'll exterminate,
> We can kill all of them at once in unison,
> When it's done we can advertise: Gypsy-free zone. . . .

With the capitulation of the single-party state, the Skinhead movement suddenly found itself not only with new space within which to operate, but also with an ever larger mass of disillusioned, socially alienated youth to draw upon. Throughout 1990 and 1991, the presence of Skins on the streets of Budapest and at soccer matches, particularly those of their favorite team, Ferencváros, skyrocketed. At the Ferencváros games, fans shouted insults such as "dirty Jews!" and "stinking Gypsies!" at their rivals. Spraypainted swastikas appeared—and remained for months at a time—on building walls and monuments. The outbursts of violence against Roma and foreigners of color in late 1990 and 1991 brought the Skinhead phenomenon into the public spotlight for the first time. In early 1992, Budapest police sources estimated the total number of Skinheads in Hungary at between 1500 and 2500, with about one-fifth of that constituting a hard neo-fascist core. As in the former GDR and elsewhere, the youth are mostly industrial working-class boys in their late teens and early twenties, concentrated heavily in the communist-constructed social housing projects.

Source: Paul Hockenos. *Free to Hate: The Rise of the Right in Post-Communist Eastern Europe,* pp. 2–3, 155–157. New York & London: Routledge, 1993.

Questions

According to Hockenos, what motivates young Eastern Europeans to accept right-wing ideology and even participate in politically motivated hate crimes?

Historical Continuities: What do these young people share with the young Europeans who joined fascist movements in the 1920s and 1930s?

To what extent does the activism of Hungarian Skinheads, for example, reflect deeper trends in post-Communist Eastern European society in general?

B. Educating the Global Citizen: Mikhail Gorbachev Calls on Young People to Help Build a Better World in the Post-Communist Era

In the 1992 Romanian film, *The Oak,* director Lucian Pintilie condemned the fallen Ceausescu regime both for its brutality and for its wanton destruction of the environment. Looking out across a landscape of belching smokestacks, one of the main characters, a doctor, remarks: "If [Romania] respected the European pollution standards . . . we'd have to evacuate [this] city, and fence it off like a mine field."

When Mikhail Gorbachev stepped down as leader of the Soviet Union in 1991, many people expected him to pursue a career in Russian politics, but he instead decided to dedicate himself to research—as president of the International Foundation for Socio-Economic and Political Studies (The Gorbachev Foundation)—and to increasing international awareness about environmental issues—as president of Green Cross International. During his tenure as Soviet president, Gorbachev had been forced to focus his attention on urgent political reforms, but he had nevertheless been deeply affected by the Chernobyl nuclear power plant disaster of 1986. In 1993, he explained that his decision not to pursue elected office (for the time being) was the result of his growing concern about the possibility of ecological cataclysm: "I believe that now, since we have ended the Cold War, the environment is the number one priority in the world."

Having rejected the Marxist-Leninist tradition of violent revolution, Gorbachev has now become an advocate for a gradual and peaceful transformation of the global economic and political balance of power. In a speech entitled, "Entering the 21st Century," given at the Second World Peace Conference in Seoul, South Korea, on

March 2, 1994, he remarked: "I am . . . convinced that the path to the future can not and must not be a revolutionary one. It must be an evolutionary transition by way of reforms, gradual stages, and consistent changes . . ."

In 1992, Gorbachev accepted an honorary degree from Emory University in Atlanta, Georgia, and he delivered a speech to that year's graduating class entitled "The Laws of Life and Political Responsibility." In this address to American college students, he expressed his hope that they would play an active role in promoting the development of global democracy while at the same time working to safeguard the environment for future generations. Having himself helped to bring about the end the Cold War—and the "rebirth" of history—Gorbachev called on the younger generation to accept responsibility for directing the future unfolding of our planet's life story.

FROM "The Laws of Life and Political Responsibility" by Mikhail Gorbachev

Never before has the thrust of education, its ethical aspect, been more significant than today, as we confront the global challenges facing humanity on the threshold of a new century.

The ancients said: *primum vivere, deinde philosophari*—meaning, first live and then philosophize. The coming era will prompt us to turn this maxim upside down and state: First philosophize! . . .

Not everyone, of course, can be and should be a philosopher. But every thinking person should reflect on the future, and meditate about the destiny of mankind here on earth.

The place of the individual has changed. The totality of the results of human activity is provoking global processes which threaten the very existence of civilization, even of life on Earth. The individual can become, indeed, is becoming, hostage to his own technological prowess, the uncontrolled consequences of his activities. . . .

There is broad acceptance of fatalism about the future. Many people feel it to be unpredictable: that people as such are impotent to alter the implacable course of events, or even to affect it in any substantial way.

Here they refer to history. But in a new epoch such as ours, arguments "from the past" are hardly justified. The world has changed and continues to change with amazing rapidity. Technical progress compresses space and accelerates the march of time. If negative processes were allowed to develop exponentially, catastrophe would be inevitable. This suggests that we must adopt a different approach to the future than we had before.

Fortunately, the present generation of leaders of the Great Powers had the wisdom to overcome the logic of fatalism. Consequently, they succeeded in preventing a slide into nuclear catastrophe; they managed to end the "Cold War" and halt the arms race.

But we are still far from stability in the world. We have evaded a major war, but, as it appears, are sinking into a chaos of conflicts of a different order.

The immediate causes of conflicts may seem varied, at least from the outside, but they always involve giving full vent to extremism and separatism, furious armed clashes and terror, many deaths, and streams of refugees.

. . . As President of the USSR I warned against giving in to the thoughtless and emotional urge to declare sovereignty. Where peoples and countries are so interdependent, making sovereignty an absolute value leads to tragedy. . . .

It is especially dangerous that this should be occurring at a time when the world community is confronted with mortal threats on a global scale. What is happening with us? Are people capable of rising above their private, group, and local interests? Today, the fate of humanity depends on it.

. . . What seems to be happening is the socio-political externalization of such global problems as ecological deterioration, the congestion of populations in large cities, tension over energy resources, inadequate food supplies, insufficient fresh water, undernourishment and hunger, increased crime and violence. These "local" protuberances, taken together, signify deterioration of the overall situation and undermine international stability.

This definitely leads to one conclusion: the roots of the crisis of civilization are found in the individual, in the failure of his intellectual and moral growth to keep pace with the altering circumstances of existence, in difficulties of psychological adaptation to the increased pace of change.

Centuries of cultural evolution have led to the emergence of an ego-based morality. Personal interest, personal initiative and enterprise have become powerful driving forces of material progress. But healthy egoism has also degenerated into greed, hard-heartedness, and an exploitative attitude to nature.

Is this not one of the principal causes of the present spiritual crisis? and of such phenomena as the loss of moral bearings, the weakening of the family and of religion, the feeling that everything is allowed, licentiousness, violence, and cruelty.

If these dangerous tendencies are to be altered, we must in many respects change ourselves. We must become aware of our own unique role in this world and our own unique responsibility. We must develop an awareness which enables us to evaluate any deeds, actions, or purposes from the viewpoint of their global consequences. We must assimilate the ethic of common responsibility and self-limitation, the ethic of solidarity and cooperation for the sake of survival and progress for all.

It is not a question of ideology. I am speaking about what is human in the individual, about people's attitudes to one another and to Nature, about establishing conscious control over those spontaneous processes which threaten the existence of humanity.

Here, however, voices of warning can be heard: one should not meddle with the natural order of things; leave everything to the "invisible hand," to evolutionary mechanisms, and all will be for the best.

Should we really refrain from trying to exert intelligent control over objective processes? That would be a fatal mistake. . . .

Spontaneous development is full of inertia, reproducing the long-past negative consequences of day-to-day human activity, but on an expanded scale. What are needed are coordinated decisions which would adjust for these consequences, and such decisions cannot be postponed. . . .

Many processes such as environmental contamination, the greenhouse effect, and destruction of the ozone layer can become irreversible. Indeed, some of them are already heading that way. Alas, the people of my generation came very late to thinking about all these issues. Our energies were absorbed by the purely political problems we inherited from the past. International politics in the 20th century has been governed by irrationality, and much time was lost.

But how is the "global citizen" to emerge? Whence do we arrive at an ethic of the common good? Like many others, I put my hope in the educated younger generation. You are freer of stereotypes and more receptive to new ideas. From your ranks will emerge the formulators of policy in the 21st century. I feel that you will be leaders of a new type, thinking on a broad scale and without prejudices, leaders who are not thinking just about the next elections but about mankind's long-term goals and common interests. . . .

You are entering professional, business, and political life at the beginning of an era. The confrontational atmosphere of the "Cold War" made it impossible for peoples and states to act in solidarity to achieve common goals. The opportunities opening up before you are completely new and unprecedented.

Of course, this all depends on avoiding a new and fateful division of the world—whether economic, racial, religious, or ideological. This cannot be permitted to happen, and your generation must not allow it.

Yes, everyone in the world is different. The historical process has generated an enormous diversity of national and ethnic features, cultural traditions, psychologies, customs, and religious beliefs. No two peoples or nations have had an identical history. God has endowed each with different natural and climatic conditions, a different geographical location, and different levels of natural resources.

But we all live on the same Earth. It is our common home. And we must all give thought to its preservation. As it is, while we fight and quarrel with one another, cracks are appearing in its walls, and maybe even in its foundations. . . .

Devotion to democracy is the necessary condition of a peaceful world order. Democracy is not only a political principle but also a moral standard. "Democracy without values," to use the words of Pope John Paul II, "is easily converted into open or disguised totalitarianism."

Freedom of conscience, respect for each individual, tolerance, sympathy, the ability to put oneself in another's place, preference for that which unites over that which separates, readiness for compromise—are the qualities we need as we enter the new era. . . .

The future is a challenge. But mankind can find a worthy response. This response will be forthcoming if we recognize the unity of the world, that we have a common fate, that each bears personal responsibility for preserving life on Earth.

Education, especially university education, will play a special role. It must be expanded. We must train a new generation to comprehend an increasingly complex world. We must develop more advanced education. . . .

. . . I hope your knowledge and enthusiasm will be put to work serving the noble cause of perfecting mankind in the spirit of those exalted intellectual and moral qualities which will be decisive for the realization of our common hopes for a brighter future.

Source: Mikhail Gorbachev. "The Laws of Life and Political Responsibility." Emory University, May 11, 1992. Downloaded from the Gorbachev Home Page, Green Cross International, http://greencross.unige.ch/greencross/gorby/gorby.html.

Questions

What does Gorbachev mean when he says: "First philosophize!"?

To what extent is Gorbachev still a socialist? To what extent are his arguments influenced by the economic and political theory and practice of Western Europe and the United States?

Gorbachev quotes Pope John Paul II in the course of his speech. Is this surprising to you? How important a factor is religion in Gorbachev's philosophy?

9. IMPORTANT HISTORICAL FACTS: STUDY DRILLS

A. Multiple Choice

1. The French student protests of 1968 were set off by
   A. Charles de Gaulle's speech about national *grandeur.*
   B. the expulsion of a student radical from the University of Paris.
   C. overcrowding at the University of Rome.
   D. worker support for the United States' participation in the Vietnam War.

2. During the 1980s, single issue "green" parties agitated in favor of
   A. building more nuclear power plants.
   B. encouraging Americans to invest their "greenbacks" in Europe.
   C. increasing tourism, especially along the Mediterranean coast.
   D. saving Europe's forests from industrial pollution.

3. If ratified, the Treaty of Maastricht would be likely to produce all of the following results *except*
   A. the abolition of tariff barriers between member nations.
   B. a common currency for all member nations.
   C. a coordinated foreign policy among all member nations.
   D. a single government for all member nations.

4. The Organization of Petroleum Exporting Countries imposed an embargo on oil shipments to Europe and the United States because of
   A. British and Norwegian offshore oil extraction.
   B. overproduction of oil among the member states.
   C. Soviet support for the stateless Palestinian people.
   D. Western support for Israel.

5. Match the following Western European nations with the nations from which they have been most likely to recruit "guest workers."
   A. Britain   Algeria
   B. France   Italy
   C. Germany   Pakistan
   D. Switzerland   Turkey

6. In the 1970s, negotiations between Soviet leader Leonid Brezhnev and American presidents Richard Nixon and Jimmy Carter resulted in
   A. the Brezhnev Doctrine.
   B. the Helsinki Accords.
   C. the Strategic Arms Limitations Talks.
   D. the Treaty of Maastricht.

7. The Red Brigades were
   A. Albanian militias that received their training in Communist China.
   B. Basque nationalists who engaged in acts of terrorism against Spain.
   C. Italian left-wing guerrilla groups.
   D. Soviet youth organizations.

8. The goal of the Irish Republican Army has been to
   A. drive the Catholics out of Northern Ireland.
   B. unite Ulster with the Republic of Ireland.
   C. return the Republic of Ireland to the British Commonwealth.
   D. protect British troops stationed in Northern Ireland.

9. Under the "Brezhnev Doctrine," the Soviet leadership reserved the right to
   A. complete the collectivization of agriculture in Eastern Europe.
   B. intervene militarily in Eastern European satellite states.
   C. lend support to Western European Eurocommunists.
   D. supply weapons to Communist movements in the Third World.

10. When Mikhail Gorbachev spoke of *glasnost* ("openness") and *perestroika* ("restructuring"), he was understood to mean that he supported
    A. relaxing censorship and encouraging economic privatization.
    B. opening the "iron curtain" and reorganizing the Communist Party.
    C. honesty in personal relations and a rethinking of family organization.
    D. unrestricted travel and urban renewal.

11. In Hungary, the opposition to communism was led by
    A. the Civic Forum.
    B. the Democratic Forum.

C. the National Salvation Front.

D. Solidarity.

12. In 1990, the first elections in the newly unified Germany resulted in a victory for
    A. Erich Honecker and the Communist Party.
    B. Helmut Kohl and the Christian Democrats.
    C. Egon Krenz and the renamed Communist Party.
    D. Helmut Schmidt and the Social Democrats.

13. The Commonwealth of Independent States created by Boris Yeltsin included
    A. Belarus, Russia, and Ukraine.
    B. Bosnia-Herzegovina, Croatia, and Serbia.
    C. Estonia, Latvia, and Lithuania.
    D. the fifteen "socialist republics" of the former Soviet Union.

14. The policy of removing non-Serbs from Serb-controlled regions of Bosnia was known as
    A. ethnic cleansing.
    B. Islamization.
    C. humanitarian relief.
    D. national salvation.

15. Beginning in 1991, Russian troops began a continuing battle with nationalist insurgents in
    A. Azerbaijan.
    B. the Caucasus.
    C. Chechnya.
    D. Tajikistan.

B. Chronological Relationships

1. Politics in Western Europe: Identify the date at which each of the following events occurred and arrange them in chronological order.

   Portuguese dictator Antonio Salazar dies, and Portugal begins a bumpy but bloodless transition to democracy.

   Bettino Craxi, former prime minister of Italy, flees to Tunisia after being convicted of corruption.

   Charles de Gaulle resigns as president of France, after his government has survived a major student and worker revolt.

   Spanish dictator Francisco Franco dies, and his successor, King Juan Carlos, allows the creation of a constitutional monarchy.

   François Mitterrand, a Socialist, is elected to his first term as president of France.

   Military officers take power in Greece, planning to seize the island of Cyprus.

   Christian Democrat Helmut Kohl replaces Social Democrat Helmut Schmidt as chancellor of Germany.

   John Major becomes prime minister of Great Britain.

   Margaret Thatcher becomes prime minister of Great Britain.

   Social Democrat Willy Brandt becomes chancellor of the German Federal Republic.

2. Politics in Eastern Europe: Identify the date at which each of the following events occurred and arrange them in chronological order.

   Soviet leader Leonid Brezhnev dies and is replaced by the slightly more liberal Yuri Andropov.

   Romanian leader Nicolae Ceausescu and his wife are executed after being hastily convicted of embezzlement and murder.

   Czechoslovakia is separated into two independent states, the Czech Republic and Slovakia.

   Hungarian cultural leaders protest their government's human rights violations by signing "Charter 77."

   Czechoslovakian leader Alexander Dubček attempts to put a "human face" on socialism during the "Prague Spring."

   East German Communist leader Egon Krenz orders that the Berlin Wall be torn down.

   Labor organizer Lech Walesa is elected president of Poland.

   Mikhail Gorbachev becomes general secretary of the Soviet Union's Communist Party.

   The German Federal Republic and the German Democratic Republic are reunited as Germany.

   The trade union organization Solidarity is granted official recognition by the Communist Central Committee of Poland.

C. Matching Exercise: Historical Actors

_____ Willy Brandt
_____ Nicolae Ceausescu
_____ Bettino Craxi
_____ Mikhail Gorbachev
_____ Václav Havel
_____ John Paul II
_____ Juan Carlos
_____ Mickey Mouse
_____ Slobodan Milošević
_____ François Mitterrand
_____ Andrei Sakharov
_____ Margaret Thatcher
_____ Lech Walesa
_____ Boris Yeltsin
_____ Todor Zhivkov

A. This Socialist president of France was forced to "co-habit" with a right-dominated Chamber of Deputies after the 1986 elections and was replaced by right-leaning Jacques Chirac in 1995.

B. In 1979, this leader of the British Conservative Party became prime minister, serving in this post until 1990.

C. Having served in the Norwegian resistance movement, he returned to Germany after World War II, became a leader of the Social Democrats, and served as chancellor of the German Federal Republic between 1968 and 1974.

D. Having succeeded Francisco Franco in 1975, this Spanish head of state surprised everyone by rejecting authoritarianism in favor of a democratic political structure.

E. A well-known playwright, this Czech intellectual was imprisoned for opposing the Communist regime, but later became the president of Czechoslovakia as a result of the "velvet revolution."

F. You are likely to find him at Euro-Disney, drinking Coca Cola and eating a Big Mac.

G. This Polish electrician was the leader of the trade union organization Solidarity. Imprisoned for his activism by General Jaruzelski early in the 1980s, he was elected president of post-Communist Poland in 1990.

H. This Socialist politician provided Italians with more governmental stability than they were used to, serving as president for an unusually long term—three years (1983 to 1986).

I. Named general secretary of the Communist Party in 1985, this Soviet leader sought to revitalize communism through openness and restructuring.

J. This former Communist has led the Serbian nationalist movement in its efforts to build a "Greater Serbia" and is largely responsible for the ongoing war in the former Yugoslavia.

K. A Nobel Prize winning physicist, this Russian dissident campaigned for human rights in the Soviet Union, fueling the democratic opposition to the Communist regime.

L. Corrupt and widely disliked, this Bulgarian Communist leader attempted to redirect Bulgarians' anger against the minority Turkish population, but he was ousted from power by his own party in 1989.

M. Conservative on matters of faith, this religious leader has nonetheless championed social justice, becoming a symbol of hope for millions of oppressed people.

N. This hard-drinking liberal reformer supported democracy against hard-line Communists during the collapse of the Soviet state, and now serves as president of the independent Russian state.

O. This "Genius of the Carpathians" ruled Romania with an iron—and bloody—fist, but was overthrown and summarily executed on Christmas Day of 1989.

IMPORTANT HISTORICAL FACTS: STUDY-DRILL ANSWERS

A. Multiple Choice

1. B. the expulsion of a student radical from the University of Paris.
2. D. saving Europe's forests from industrial pollution.
3. D. a single government for all member nations.
4. D. Western support for Israel.
5. A. Britain—Pakistan
   B. France—Algeria
   C. Germany—Turkey
   D. Switzerland—Italy
6. C. the Strategic Arms Limitations Talks.
7. C. Italian left-wing guerrilla groups.
8. B. unite Ulster with the Republic of Ireland.
9. B. intervene militarily in Eastern European satellite states.
10. A. relaxing censorship and encouraging economic privatization.
11. B. the Democratic Forum.
12. B. Helmut Kohl and the Christian Democrats.
13. A. Belarus, Russia, and Ukraine.
14. A. ethnic cleansing.
15. C. Chechnya.

B. Chronological Relationships

1. Politics in Western Europe

   1967   Military officers take power in Greece, planning to capture the island of Cyprus.

   1968   Social Democrat Willy Brandt becomes chancellor of the German Federal Republic.

   1969   Charles de Gaulle resigns as president of France, after his government had survived a major student and worker revolt.

   1970   Portuguese dictator Antonio Salazar dies, and Portugal begins a bumpy but bloodless transition to democracy.

   1975   Spanish dictator Francisco Franco dies, and his successor, King Juan Carlos, allows the creation of a constitutional monarchy.

   1979   Margaret Thatcher becomes prime minister of Great Britain.

   1981   François Mitterrand, a Socialist, is elected to his first term as president of France.

   1982   Christian Democrat Helmut Kohl replaces Social Democrat Helmut Schmidt as chancellor of Germany.

   1990   John Major becomes prime minister of Great Britain.

   1993   Bettino Craxi, former prime minister of Italy, flees to Tunisia after being convicted of corruption.

2. Politics in Eastern Europe

   1968   Czechoslovakian leader Alexander Dubček attempts to put a "human face" on socialism during the "Prague Spring."

   1977   Hungarian activists protest their government's human rights violations by signing "Charter 77."

   1980   The trade union organization Solidarity is granted official recognition by the Communist Central Committee of Poland.

   1982   Soviet leader Leonid Brezhnev dies and is replaced by the slightly more liberal Yuri Andropov.

   1985   Mikhail Gorbachev becomes general secretary of the Soviet Union's Communist Party.

   Nov. 1989   East German Communist leader Egon Krenz orders that the Berlin Wall be torn down.

   Dec. 1989   Romanian leader Nicolae Ceausescu and his wife are executed after being hastily convicted of embezzlement and murder.

   Oct. 1990   The German Federal Republic and the German Democratic Republic are reunited as Germany.

   Dec. 1990   Labor organizer Lech Walesa is elected president of Poland.

   1993   Czechoslovakia is separated into two independent states, the Czech Republic and Slovakia.

C. Matching Exercise: Historical Actors

C. Willy Brandt

O. Nicolae Ceausescu

H. Bettino Craxi

I. Mikhail Gorbachev

E. Václav Havel

M. John Paul II

D. Juan Carlos

F. Mickey Mouse

J. Slobodan Milošević

A. François Mitterrand

K. Andrei Sakharov

B. Margaret Thatcher

G. Lech Walesa

N. Boris Yeltsin

L. Todor Zhivkov

EUROPE

THE WORLD

Credits

Chapter 12
pp. 132–133   Hardman, John, ed. and trans. "The Declaration of the Rights of Man and Citizen." In *The French Revolution: The Fall of the Ancien Regime to the Thermidorian Reaction, 1785–1795*, pp. 114–117. New York: St. Martin's Press, 1982. Reprinted by permission of St. Martin's Press.
pp. 132–133   de Gouges, Olympe. "Declaration of the Rights of Woman and Citizen." In *European Women: A Documentary History, 1789–1945*, pp. 63–66. Eds. Eleanor S. Reimer and John C. Fout. New York: Schocken Books, 1980. Reprinted by permission of Schocken Books, a division of Random House, Inc.
pp. 135–136   Wollstonecraft, Mary. *A Vindication of the Rights of Men*, pp. 7–10. Delmar, NY: Scholars' Facsimiles and Reprints, 1975. Reprinted by permission.

Chapter 20
pp. 230–231   From *On Dreams*, pp. 93–95, 105–106, 108–109, by Sigmund Freud, translated by James Strachey. Translation copyright 1952 by W. W. Norton & Company, Inc., renewed © 1980 by Alix S. Strachey. Reprinted by permission of W. W. Norton Company, Inc., and Hogarth Press.
pp. 232–233   Nietzsche, Frederick. *Twilight of the Idols, or, How One Philosophizes with a Hammer*, and *First Book: The Antichrist*. In *The Portable Nietzsche*, pp. 522–523, 570–571. Ed. Walter Kaufman. New York: Viking Press, 1954. Reprinted by permission of Viking Penguin, a division of Penguin Books USA Inc.

Chapter 24
p. 282   Edmonds, Charles. [Charles Edmund Carrington]. *A Subaltern's War*. New York: Arno Press, 1972.
pp. 282–284   Ölçen, Mehmet Arif. *Vetluga Memoir: A Turkish Prisoner of War in Russia, 1916–1918*. Trans. Gary Leiser. Gainesville, Fla: University Press of Florida, 1995. Reprinted by permission.

Chapter 26
pp. 310–312   Sarfatti, Margherita G. *The Life of Benito Mussolini*, pp. 261–264, 336–337, 342, 345. Trans. Frederic Whyte. New York: Frederick A. Stokes, 1926. Reprinted by permission.

Chapter 27
pp. 321–322   Fallada, Hans. *Little Man, What Now?* Trans. Eric Sutton. New York: Simon & Schuster, 1933. Reprinted by permission of Simon & Schuster, a division of Viacom, Inc.

Chapter 28

Chapter 29

Chapter 30